Lecture Notes in Artificial Intelligence   3369

Edited by J. G. Carbonell and J. Siekmann

Subseries of Lecture Notes in Computer Science

T0223564

V. Richard Benjamins   Pompeu Casanovas
Joost Breuker   Aldo Gangemi (Eds.)

Law and the
Semantic Web

Legal Ontologies, Methodologies,
Legal Information Retrieval, and Applications

 Springer

Series Editors

Jaime G. Carbonell, Carnegie Mellon University, Pittsburgh, PA, USA
Jörg Siekmann, University of Saarland, Saarbrücken, Germany

Volume Editors

V. Richard Benjamins
Intelligent Software Components (iSOCO)
Pedro de Valdivia 10, 28006 Madrid, Spain
E-mail: rbenjamins@isoco.com

Pompeu Casanovas
Autonomous University of Barcelona, Institute of Law and Technology
UAB Sociolegal Studies Group, 08193 Cerdanyola, Barcelona, Spain
E-mail: pompeu.casanovas@uab.es

Joost Breuker
University of Amsterdam, Leibniz Center for Law
1000 BA Amsterdam, The Netherlands
E-mail: breuker@lri.jur.uva.nl

Aldo Gangemi
Laboratory for Applied Ontology
Viale Marx 15, 00137 Rome, Italy
E-mail: gangemi@ip.rm.cnr.it

Library of Congress Control Number: 2005921097

CR Subject Classification (1998): I.2, H.4, H.3, H.5, J.1, K.4.1-2

ISSN 0302-9743
ISBN 3-540-25063-8 Springer Berlin Heidelberg New York

Springer is a part of Springer Science+Business Media

springeronline.com

© Springer-Verlag Berlin Heidelberg 2005
Printed in Germany

Typesetting: Camera-ready by author, data conversion by Scientific Publishing Services, Chennai, India
Printed on acid-free paper   SPIN: 11398134   06/3142   5 4 3 2 1 0

Foreword
by Roberto Cencioni

At the Lisbon Summit in March 2000, European heads of state and government set a new goal for the European Union — to become the most competitive knowledge-based society in the world by 2010. As part of this objective, ICT (information and communication technologies) services should become available for every citizen, and for all schools, homes and businesses.

The book you have in front of you is about Semantic Web technology and law. Law is something omnipresent; all citizens — at some points in their lives — have to deal with it. In addition, law involves a large group of professionals, and is a multi-billion business world wide. Information technology is important because it that can improve citizens' interaction with law, as well as improve legal professionals' work environment. Legal professionals dedicate a significant amount of their time to finding, reading, analyzing and synthesizing information in order to take decisions, and prepare advice and trials, among other tasks. As part of the "Semantic-Based Knowledge and Content Systems" Strategic Objective, the European Commission is funding projects to construct technology to make the Semantic Web vision come true. The articles in this book are related to two current foci of the Strategic Objective[1]:

- Knowledge acquisition and modelling, capturing knowledge from raw information and multimedia content in webs and other distributed repositories to turn poorly structured information into machine-processable knowledge.
- Knowledge sharing and use, combining semantically enriched information with context to provide actionable meaning, applying inferencing and reasoning for decision support and collaborative use of trusted knowledge between organizations.

This book is a good example of bringing together two communities: the IST research and development community and the legal community. In other words, it brings together technology *providers* and technology *users*, an essential requirement for building scalable and usable Information Society technology.

Luxembourg
November 2004

Roberto Cencioni
European Commission
Head of Division, INFSO/E.2
Knowledge Management and Content Creation

---

[1] http://www.cordis.lu/ist/workprogramme/wp0506_en/2_4_7.htm

Foreword
by Joaquín Bayo Delgado

In recent years, many initiatives have been taken to update the working methods of the administration of justice to the continuously changing environment of ICT services. The judiciary, in the larger sense of the word, has particular needs of its own, but it also shares common problems, and possible solutions, with other knowledge-based activities.

As in any other field, the Web has become the crucial reference for any work tool to be designed. The computer is no longer the tool as such, or it is better to say that the Web is the global computer that everyone uses. The approach, then, is how to take the most from this global instrument without being overflowed with information, a situation almost as bad as if no information was available.

Many reasons explain the reluctance of the judiciary to taking up ICT services: legal changes may be needed before we can introduce these technologies (videoconferencing may be an example), there is a tendency to tradition and secrecy amongst jurists in general and judges in particular, etc. But there are two main reasons shared by jurists with other professionals, namely the information overload and the lack of a cyberculture. The Semantic Web overcomes these two barriers by helping in finding the relevant information and by doing so through a friendly interface.

But some other considerations are relevant when judicial work is analyzed in the context of the Web. Three areas are to be distinguished: the internal workflow in the court, the final decision making, and the openness towards citizens. At first glance it may seem that the Semantic Web is irrelevant in some of those areas, but a closer view shows that that is not the case. The internal workflow is not an automatic process. The stakeholders (judges, but also registrars and staff personnel) do make decisions that need information and present complexity. Interim decisions are, in many cases, fundamental. The example of a judge on duty can illustrate the idea. Therefore, in this area workflow applications and knowledge ontologies have to be developed. In practice the latter are missing: knowledge is being transmitted through personal contacts among experienced and in experienced judges, registrars, public prosecutors, etc., and little information is available, not only in the Web but also in local databases. Interim decisions are frequently disregarded but they are the basic know-how for legal professionals.

The final decision making process is the main area where information is needed. Legal systems, namely continental law and common law, are increasingly merging. The European Union legal system is an example. But because of the Anglo-Saxon cultural predominance in the Web, and in informatics in general, ontologies pay attention basically to case law. This is very useful even in continental law systems, but there are some areas where knowledge of applicable statute law is crucial and not so easy to reach. Administrative law may be the clear example. There, the constant legislative production, both at the European and the national levels, makes it necessary to have a knowledge tool for the judiciary. This is becoming also true in other legal areas, such as civil and criminal, where European and international law has to be increasingly taken into account; and frequently it is not, due to the lack of easy and friendly access. The Semantic Web is the means to achieving this access.

As the Web is a universal environment, other legal professionals and many citizens are also present in it. So the e-court (electronic-supported court) will develop into a cybercourt, as the next step, i.e., the court will go out to cyberspace. And new challenges and problems will appear. It will not only be the judiciary using the Web but also the legal professionals and citizens using it to interact with the courts and, therefore, retrieving information. It is a wholly new concept of the old "public hearing," limited until now to the final phase of most proceedings and to the physical environment of the courtroom. The information flow becomes bidirectional. Semantic techniques will also be applied.

Several potentially conflicting aspects have to be borne in mind, though. The level of cyberculture knowledge is anything but homogeneous among citizens, and these differences are even greater between citizens and corporations. Equal opportunities of defence must be guaranteed. Other fundamental rights are also at stake, among them privacy and data protection. Here again the cultural differences play an important role. The tension between privacy and transparency (access to documents) is not understood in the same way worldwide, and does not play the same role in political and judicial decisions. Nor can data protection be seen just as the right to privacy in the European Union and its members and other countries. E-courts now, and future cybercourts, have to be designed in full compliance with the legal requirements that protect those fundamental rights, and privacy-enhancing technologies must be implemented.

Many of these ideas and problems are analyzed in this book, entitled "Law and the Semantic Web." Its editors have gathered 15 papers most relevant to the analysis and to finding proper solutions for these questions. Efforts like this bring us closer to these future of legal and judicial practice.

Brussels   Joaquín Bayo Delgado
November 2004   Judge
                        Deputy European Data Protection Supervisor

Preface

The book you have in front of you is based on the celebration of two international events related to the Semantic Web and the legal domain held in Edinburgh, UK and Barcelona, Spain. The first event was the Workshop on Legal Ontologies and Web-Based Legal Information Management held on June 28, 2003, Edinburgh, UK, which was part of the 9th International Conference on Artificial Intelligence and Law, ICAIL 2003. The second event was the International Seminar on Law and the Semantic Web held on November 20–21, 2003, Barcelona, Spain. Papers have been revised since then according to the specific topic of this book.

For legal professionals, dealing with information and knowledge is an essential part of their daily work. They are "knowledge workers" and vulnerable to suffering from phenomena like information overload. Technologies that can help in overcoming this problem could result in a significant improvement in productivity. In this book, we hope to show to legal professionals the potential value of Semantic Web-related technology for their profession.

The Web has profoundly changed the way we communicate, do business, and perform our jobs. We can communicate at very low cost with almost anyone at anytime. We can initiate and (to some extent) conclude online business transactions. We have access to millions of resources, irrespective of their physical location and language. All these factors have contributed to the success story of the Web. However, at the same time, those success factors also cause one of the Web's main problems: information overload. This is where the Semantic Web comes in. "The Semantic Web is an extension of the current Web in which information is given well-defined meaning, better enabling computers and people to work in cooperation" [Tim Berners-Lee, James Hendler, Ora Lassila, Scientific American, May 2001]. Semantic Web technology aims at the automatic processing of content, thereby enabling people to delegate tasks to software. With this book, for researchers and practitioners of the Semantic Web, we hope to show that the legal domain is a challenging and interesting area for performing research and for developing applications.

This volume contains 15 papers on topics relevant for law and the Semantic Web. The papers are structured in three parts. Part I sets the context; it introduces the relevant concepts, describes some of the final users (legal professionals), and puts into historical context how legal professionals think about the use and application of the law. Part II presents theoretical papers concerned with the construction of legal ontologies, both from a legal and a methodological point of view. Part III collects several papers describing applications of Semantic Web-related technology to the legal domain.

We would like to thank the organizers of both events, as well as the International Program Committee that guaranteed the high quality of the papers. The organizers of the Edinburgh workshop were Joost Breuker, Aldo Gangemi, Daniela Tiscornia and Radboud Winkels, and the Program Committee included Trevor Bench-Capon, Richard Benjamins, Danièle Bourcier, Cristiano Castelfranchi, Rose Dieng, Caterina Lupo, Paulo Quaresma, Heiner Stuckenschmidt, Erich Schweighofer, Andre Valente and John Zeleznikow. The organizers of the Barcelona seminar were Pompeu Casanovas, Marta Poblet, Jesús Contreras and Richard Benjamins.

We would also like to acknowledge various publicly funded R&D projects, including SEKT (IST-FP6), Esperonto (IST-FP5), Netcase (PROFIT) and Iuriservice (PROFIT).

December 2004   V. Richard Benjamins (iSOCO, Spain)
                                                          Pompeu Casanovas (UAB, Spain)
                                                     Joost Breuker (UvA, Netherlands)
                                                         Aldo Gangemi (CNR, Italy)

Table of Contents

Part III Practice Papers: Information Retrieval and Applications

Law and the Semantic Web, an Introduction

V. Richard Benjamins[1], Pompeu Casanovas[2], Joost Breuker[3], and Aldo Gangemi[4]

[1]Intelligent Software Components (iSOCO),
Madrid, Barcelona, Valencia Spain
rbenjamins@isoco.com
[2]Autonomous University of Barcelona, Institute for Law and Technology (IDT),
UAB Sociolegal Studies Group (GRES),
08193-Cerdanyola, Barcelona Spain
pompeu.casanovas@uab.es
[3]University of Amsterdam, Leibniz Center for Law,
1000 BA Amsterdam Netherlands
breuker@lri.jur.uva.nl
[4]Laboratory for Applied Ontology (ISTC-CNR),
Viale Marx, 15, 00137 Rome Italy
gangemi@ip.rm.cnr.it

Abstract. In this paper, we introduce the role of Semantic Web technology for the legal domain. We will briefly discuss the current use of Information Technology in the legal domain, followed by an introduction to the Semantic Web. We then will put forward what we see as the particularities of the legal domain that need to be taken into account by technological solutions. Finally, we will explain how the articles in this volume contribute to the application of Semantic Web technology in the legal domain.

1 Introduction

The Semantic Web is an exciting new area of research and innovative applications that will transform the current web into the web of the next generation. The current web is basically made for human consumption; people easily can understand what web-pages are about and contain. The Semantic Web intends to enable also machines to understand -to some extent- what is in the Web; not only to improve human communication, but in particular to delegate more and more "intelligent" tasks to machines. Making machines more intelligent is one of the many fruits of research in Artificial Intelligence over the last decades.

Law, legal systems, and organizations have been subject to fundamental changes over the last decades, adding complexity to the legal fields. On the one hand, lawyering, sentencing and legal drafting have been increasingly growing. In the USA and in many European countries alike, there are three to four times more lawyers and legal professionals than in 1950 [1]. On the other hand, the production of legal rules - statutes, codes, rulings...- have followed the same inflationary path. This has led to a situation in which two of the main problems are handling the complexity and types of legal knowledge, and having reasonable ways to store, retrieve and structure a great amount of legal information.

V.R. Benjamins et al. (Eds.): Law and the Semantic Web, LNCS 3369, pp. 1–17, 2005.

The legal domain has been of interest to Artificial Intelligence since long. Pamela N. Gray pointed out in 1997 [2] that the theory and the tools of Artificial Legal Intelligence had developed in corresponding leaps, with the following progression of themes: (i) legal language, (ii) deontic logic, (iii) rule processing, (iv) case processing, (v) stratification of reasoning, (vi) procedural reasoning, (vii) co-ordination of multiple tasks.

Many legal expert systems have been built, but only a few made it to the market. For over more than two decades there is an active and productive community of researchers in the domain of AI & Law[1]. In the early eighties the research was particularly inspired by logic programming, fitting in an old philosophical tradition (starting with Leibniz) to ground legislation and legal reasoning in logical foundations. In particular some researchers saw a strong parallel between Prolog (or production) rules and legal rules [3] [4]. This parallel was not without problems as the logic suitable for normative reasoning appeared to require special features, which fostered new interests in deontic logics [5], [6] (see also the tri-annual workshop on deontic logics, DEON).

Another, less formal, approach was inspired by research in AI on case based reasoning, and it aimed analogical similarity between legal cases to enable the retrieval of relevant precedent cases [7], which fitted particularly but not exclusively the Anglo-Saxon legal traditions. The more applied orientation of AI in knowledge engineering had a strong impact on bringing AI & law to the market place, and a large variety of legal knowledge systems were developed. In particular the annual JURIX conferences provided the forum to report research results in this area of AI & Law.

Knowledge engineering was also the source for the growing interest in the development and use of legal ontologies [8] (see also Breuker, Valente & Winkels, this volume). This research is not only in line with the ambitions of the Semantic Web, but has been particularly undertaken with the aim to improve information retrieval of legal sources in general. A growing number of applied research projects, particularly as part of the European Framework Programme since the end of nineties, are concerned with the development of legal ontologies to put legal information retrieval on a more semantic footing (see also Section 4.2 below).

Legal professionals, be they judges or lawyers, handle information in order to take decisions. As such they are vulnerable to the Information Overload phenomenon. Moreover, increasingly more non-legal professionals have to deal with the Law due to increasing regulations in for example environmental protection and public security in buildings. The Semantic Web aims to enable machines to deal with information in an automatic way, and as such helps to reduce the information overload, while retaining the relevant information.

The Semantic Web is only in its infancy; currently the technological infrastructure is being developed and established. Important players include the W3C, lead by Tim Berners-Lee, many Universities and Research Institutions, and IT companies. Governments are investing significant amounts of money in this effort as well (e.g. EU, DARPA). Applying Semantic Web technology to support legal professionals in their

---

[1] In 1987 the Society for AI & Law was founded (http://www.iaail.org) and the Journal with the same name followed in 1992 (http://www.kluweronline.com/issn/0924-8463). The Society organizes a bi-annual conference (ICAIL). Moreover, also since 1987 there is the yearly JURIX Conference that started as a Dutch meeting of researchers and has grown now to an annual international conference on AI and Law (http://www.jurix.nl).

job is an exciting area of research, both for legal professionals and information re-searchers. There is a growing community of researchers working in this area. It is the aim of this book to provide an overview of the state of the field.

2 IT in the Context of Legal Applications

Let us first take a look at how information technology is currently used in the legal practice. We can distinguish between different legal professionals: judges, lawyers and other legal professionals such as in legal departments of organizations. A study of legal software applications showed that there are several types of applications, rang-ing from access to law text and jurisprudence (either online or on CD) to applications to manage law firms (e.g., time management, case management) [9].

We also have to take into account the different working styles and habits of legal professionals concerning IT, ranging from technophobes to computer enthusiasts. Studies show for example that the behaviour of Judges and Magistrates related to IT follows separate national patterns [10]. In Spain, e.g., they hardly use official email, moderately use the Internet and extensively consult legal databases on CD-ROM [11]. Sociological studies of the context and attitude of legal professionals are thus impor-tant to adapt IT tools to concrete users.

2.1 Software Applications for Legal Professionals

One class of commercial legal applications is dedicated to the management of law firms. Typical examples of such applications include Case Management, which is focused on the management of files, contracts, etc.; and Time and Invoicing, which is focused on management of time, planning, invoicing, etc.

A quick search revealed seventeen different products (in English) of those types of applications [9]. They basically help in the administrative management of law firms, but are not dealing at all with knowledge management (but see [12] for an update of possible applications for law using knowledge management tools).

Another class of applications relates to the consulting of legal databases (either online or on CD-ROM) such as law articles and jurisprudence (judicial rulings, sen-tences). Those databases aim to provide fast access to the content allowing different kinds of search criteria such as kind of ruling, appeal, date, summary, number of rul-ing, etc.

3 The Semantic Web

The Web has profoundly changed the way we communicate, do business, and perform our jobs. We can communicate at very low cost with almost anyone at anytime. We can initiate and (to some extent) conclude online business transactions. We have ac-cess to millions of resources, irrespective of their physical location and language. All these factors have contributed to the success story of the Web. However, at the same time, those success factors also cause the Web's main problems: information overload [13].

Many sources and reports provide estimations of how much money we lose due to information overload. E.g., "Two-thirds of 423 organizations surveyed in US and Europe suffer from Information Overload and have no time to share knowledge" (KPMG, 2000), and "Employees spend an average of 8 hours a week, or 16% of their workweek, looking for and using external information content. The salary cost alone to American business is $107 billion a year. There's a significant opportunity to companies to enable their employees to be more efficient and effective at putting external information to work for them" (Outsell Inc, 2001).

In our opinion, the technology of the current generation Web (including search engines, web portals, document management systems, etc.) has its limits. To be able to deal with the continuous growth of the Internet, intranets and extranets (in size, languages and formats), we need to exploit other information. This is where the Semantic Web comes in.

3.1 The Current Web

The current Web is based on HTML, which specifies how to layout a web page for human readers. Software has difficulties in understanding content in HTML since it has to "guess" the meaning. For instance, Fig. 1 illustrates what a user sees of a web page when he is looking for buying a CD of "Las Ketchup", and below the figure it shows how this is (partly) encoded in HTML.

Fig. 1. The current Web

```
<font face="arial, helvetica, sans-serif" size="+1"
color="#000000"><b><b>Las Ketchup</b></b></font><br>

<b>Retail Price: $13.98<br>Our Price: <font face="arial,
helvetica, sans-serif" color="#990000">$12.99<br></font>
```

It is clear that a lot of heuristics have to be used in order to extract the intended meaning. The Semantic Web aims to provide a solution to this problem. It is an extension of the current web in which information is given well defined meaning, better enabling computers and people to work in cooperation [14]. One of the ingredients for adding semantics to the web are ontologies (an ontology is an explicit specification of a conceptualization [15]). Ontologies thus represent meaning. Now, on the Semantic Web, instead of using HTML, we use an ontology web language such as OWL [16]. In such language, we use concepts and relations to describe meaning, whose semantics are anchored in publicly available ontologies. In the example above, we can imagine something like (not a realistic example):

```
<Artist>Las Ketchup</Artist>

Retail Price <Price> <Currency>$<Currency>13.98 </Price>

Our Price <Price> <Currency>$</Currency> 12.99 </Price>
```

where the relevant terms, such as `Artist`, `Currency` and `Price` are defined in ontologies for music and ecommerce. The main problem the Semantic Web faces is how to get the semantics into the web? Obviously, doing it manually is not very scalable (but see initiatives such as Wikipedia [17] and Open Directory Project [18] for interesting exceptions).

3.2 Technology of the Semantic Web

As evidenced by many ongoing research activities in the area, the Semantic Web is still under development and currently we can only see some applications [19]. Part of the technology is the so-called Semantic Web stack of languages, which is a layered architecture to adding increasingly more complexity and expressiveness to what we can represent on the Web. Fig. 2 illustrates the stack [20] [21]. The architecture starts with the foundations of URIs and Unicode, and on top of that includes the following languages [22]:

- XML provides a surface syntax for structured documents, but imposes no semantic constraints on the meaning of these documents.
- XML Schema is a language for restricting the structure of XML documents.
- RDF is a data model for objects ("resources") and relations between them, provides a simple semantics for this data model, and these data models can be represented in an XML syntax.
- RDF Schema is a vocabulary for describing properties and classes of RDF resources, with a semantics for generalization-hierarchies of such properties and classes.
- OWL adds more vocabulary for describing properties and classes: among others, relations between classes (e.g. disjointness), cardinality (e.g. "exactly one"), equality, richer typing of properties, characteristics of properties (e.g. symmetry), and enumerated classes.

The logic layer will provide an interoperable language for describing the sets of deductions one can make from a collection of data -- how, given the world we've now neatly described, we can make connections and derive new facts about it. The proof language will provide a way of describing the steps taken to reach a conclusion from the facts. These proofs can then be passed around and verified, providing short cuts to new facts in the system without having each node conduct the deductions themselves [23]. Trust refers to the reliability and the trustworthiness of a source. For instance, an online store with a history of spamming would probably not be trustworthy.

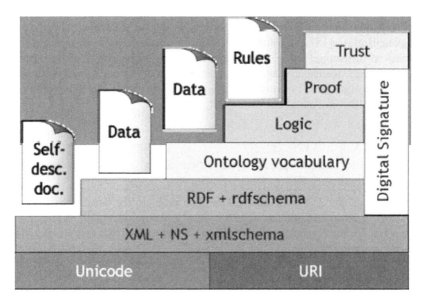

Fig. 2. Stack of Languages for the Semantic Web [http://www.w3.org/2000/Talks/1206-xml2k-tbl/slide10-0.html]

3.3 A Business Roadmap for the Semantic Web

We foresee that the evolution of the Semantic Web will follow a similar process as that of the Web, starting with small examples and applications, and ending in a multi billion business. We foresee the following–partially overlapping- stages in the process of commercially taking-up Semantic Web technology in business:

- Semantic Web applications in internal corporate settings (intranets with docs, emails, images, etc.).
- Semantic Web applications on the Internet with public information. Public organizations offering services for citizens will probably see little risk in applying this technology. See for example the project Esperonto [24], where this technology is applied to public organizations that have the mission to disseminate their information to a large public.
- Semantic Web applications between corporations (extranets).

Major issues to resolve before Semantic Web technology will be widely adopted in business concern security, trust and confidentiality of business-critical information. Moreover, several business and legal issues need further understanding before Semantic Web technology can and will be commercially exploited at the same level as the current web.

4 Law and the Semantic Web

The current state of legal Semantic Web applications appears still in an experimental phase, but the potential impact over the social and legal life is huge. As stated by the

Chairman of the ICANN Board Vinton G. Cerf [25, p. 25] in a recent Symposium on Technology-Driven Justice Systems we are still at the beginning: "the Internet and its World are early harbingers of the information-dense future to come".

Lawyers and legal researchers use to distinguish three different stages within the WWW development: (*i*) "Web publishing" (the provision of static information), (*ii*) "Web application" (the provision of computing applications), (*iii*) "Web Services" (the integration of business applications via the Internet regardless of differences in platforms) [26].[2] The quick growth of the Web and its multifunctional capabilities for commercial uses has lead to the vision of an "early period" (1970-1996, including Arpanet and NSFnet) and a "commercial period" (1996 to present), following the increasing numbers of commercial websites.[3]

But in the meantime, what it has definitely changed is law itself, legal needs and the way in which professionals represent them. In a global world, the creation of a new *lex mercatoria*, the expansion of law firm sizes, the consolidation of law firms as professionally managed business organizations and the leading position of interna-tionalized American and UK firms change the contexts of practicing law and the ways of litigation and conflict resolution. Poblet and Contreras [this volume] show the recent raising of "transnational legal networks" and their link to strategies of knowl-edge management. The expected percent growth of US law firms up to 2007 is 21%, with an expected value of 200 billion $. There is a dark side as well. Kingston, Schafer and Vandenberghe [this volume] base their work on fraud prevention in the growth of a global criminality.

This means that legal services are nowadays less a liberal profession than a mar-ketplace. And, eventually, the attitudes of citizens related to administration services (government and justice) are changing as well. E-Government and e-Court are not only developing fields of research, but a citizen demand [28]. In this sense, Web Ser-vices –the third stage of the Web- being designed to provide interoperability between diverse applications, may be completed through Semantic Web technology. The Se-mantic Web enables the accessing of Web resources by semantic content rather than by keywords, involving the automation of service discovery, acquisition, composition and monitoring [29]. This is what legal services require to overcome the "lag" pointed out by Richard Susskind between data processing and knowledge processing within the legal transitional field [30].[4]

It is difficult to assess the impact of the Semantic Web on the law and legal culture. To our knowledge, there are no reliable studies yet. However, we may foresee that the electronic exchange of legal data through XML standards and OWL will produce new legal environments and contexts of professional interaction in business and between

---

[2] A Web Service is a collection of protocols and standards used for exchanging data between applications. See http://en.wikipedia.org

[3] In December 1993, only 4.6 out of the 623 existing websites were. com websites. In January 1996, 50% of the 100.000 existing websites were already .com. In January 2000, 78% of the sites were commercial websites (out of a general population of 32.000.000.) [27].

[4] "We are great at getting information into systems and sending it around, but not so good at extracting all but only the information that we want. I call this the *Technology lag*. It is the all-important lag between what technologists call 'data processing' and 'knowledge process-ing'" [30, p. 91].

judges, prosecutors, lawyers, citizens and customers. This will happen in at least three different conceptual domains.

First, current concepts in jurisprudence such as "legal subject", "contract" and even "legal document" will probably change their traditional meaning through this enriched electronic exchange. For instance, might be considered a "legal subject" an intelligent agent? And, what about the static notion of "contract"? "A contract might be viewed not as a piece of paper or as an agreement made at a particular time and place, but as a continuing and ongoing process of collaboration" [31, p. 274]. It has been proposed the shifting from the notion of bilateral contract to a more flexible and shared notion of "network contract" (among multiparty partners) for the supply of goods and services [26, p. 251]. Moreover, it has been already noticed that XML tags themselves become a part of the contract. That is to say, XML leads to a creation of privacy metadata.[5]

Second, regulatory and self-regulatory concepts of the Internet might be revisited, because they cannot be considered as classificatory discrete entities anymore. With the evolution of the web, the standardization of regulation comes into scene. The domain of the Internet governance will not remain untouched. Think about the ICANN decisions about what is considered and what is not considered a "country", for instance. The extended use of ontologies will flesh out the way ontologies may be shaped and decided. It has been posed as a new problem in the legal literature the shift from technical standards, which regulate form, to technological standards that regulate user behaviour and, consequently, are substance-based [32] [33].

Third, the fact that the users' probable risk of loosing control increases at the same time that the Internet is going to its full potential has been repeatedly highlighted [34]. The Semantic Web may facilitate some necessary but contested practices such as Website deep linking[6], e.g. [35]. But what the Semantic Web applications are really challenging is not just security but the bulk of common sense notions that jurists and lawyers are mapping into the Internet regulations. Lessig's Creative Commons [36] [37], for instance, is a legal reactive answer to the US political intent to equate intellectual property to real property.[7]

Dan Hunter [38] has nicely shown that this kind of protective regulation is based on the metaphor of Internet as a physical place: "...we are enclosing cyberspace and imposing private property conceptions upon it. As a result, we are creating a digital

---

[5] XML standards for contracts are being created in US and EU within two bodies called LegalXML (US), LEXML (EU) and MetaLEX (http://www.metalex.nl). LegalXML (1998) is a collection of technical committees within OASIS (http://www.oasis-open.org), a not-for-profit consortium, developing open technical standards for the electronic exchange of legal data. LegalXML works on common law based contracts. LEXML is focused on civil law jurisdictions [31]. MetaLEX is an open XML standard for the markup of legal sources allowing for a rich variety of languages/legislations.

[6] Deep linking is the practice of creating a link to a web page that the owner of the targeted web page does not define as the proper page from which users should begin accessing the website [35]. The issue at stake here is not the practice in itself, but that users must agree and be aware of it.

[7] See [36] and http://creativecommons.org. This constitutes an answer to the 2001 judicial decision *Eldred vs. Ashcroft 537 U.S. 186 (Jan 15)* and to the extension of copyright protections contained in The Sony Bono Copyright Terms Extension Act (1998).

anticommon where suboptimal use of Internet resources will be the norm" (ibid. 439). The Semantic Web implementation may also deepen the USA/European gap on privacy, copyright and protection of sensitive data [39].[8]

4.1 Is the Legal Domain Special?

As the articles in this book show, the legal domain has several characteristics that make it an interesting application for Semantic Web technology. Some of those characteristics are shared by other domains where information is a critical asset of the profession. Other aspects are specific for the legal profession. One example of this is that the notion of information retrieval as *document* retrieval is not always sufficient in the legal domain. Often a particular question requires some deduction or inference before an appropriate answer can be given. In order words, "question-answering" seems more relevant than "information retrieval", as regulations may contain many different articles about the same topic and one can only assess whether something is permitted or not by understanding the full documentation. A rather detailed understanding is required, in particular, because regulations generally contain complex structures of exceptions.

For instance, the CLIME project [40] (Breuker *et al.*, this volume) was concerned with the knowledge management of about 15.000 legal norms about the construction, maintenance, and deployment of ships at sea. A particular topic – e.g. the presence and working of pumps on board – may be distributed over all "chapters" of these regulations. Simply retrieving these norms will not result in an understanding whether one is allowed to leave the harbour when a fire pump is not properly working. An underlying ontology serves here as knowledge base, exploited by an "assessment" problem-solving method, which enables question answering. In fact, except for legal professionals (e.g. legal drafters), the goal of consulting legal sources is almost exclusively to obtain insight whether some action or situation is legal or not, rather than obtaining the documentation itself. The income tax code by itself offers little support in deciding about alternative ways to fill in one's tax form.

4.2 Legal Ontologies

As mentioned earlier, ontologies can be seen as explicit specifications of conceptualizations [41]. In a simple version, this can be seen as representations of terminological knowledge: they form the semantic basis for intelligent services of the Semantic Web. As many of the articles in this book show, legal ontologies have been developed already far before the idea of the Semantic Web was put into W3C actions and standards. Ontologies have been used for legal knowledge management and as knowledge bases in legal knowledge systems. If the research and applications reported in this book do not explicitly mention how they operate in the Semantic Web, then this is due to the fact that the Semantic Web should *emerge* by using the technologies described in this book, i.e. the development of a "legal Semantic Web" is not dependent on special technologies to be developed, but on decisions of communities of legal

---

[8] "A strong conception of personal data as a commodity is emerging in the United States, and individual Americans are already participating in the commodification of their personal data" [39, p. 2125].

professionals and specialist users to install these services. Besides, in constructing legal information systems, the modelling of regulatory knowledge is a critical activity in many application areas, which are or will be typical for the Semantic Web: e-commerce, e-government, e-politics, codes of practice deployment, copyright management, enterprise knowledge management, security systems, service matching, etc.

Legal ontologies differ from ontologies in other fields of practice, like medicine or engineering in that they have to cover a wide range of (mainly) common-sense concepts that are part of physical, abstract, mental, and social worlds. Legal domains share complex and varied notions of norm and responsibility, but besides this legal "core", a legal domain refers to some world of social activities. This normative core has been traditionally the object of study in jurisprudence (legal theory). Particularly the work of Hohfeld (1919) is even at present an important source of reference and inspiration. In its normative view, law is concerned with overt behaviour, but in assigning responsibility to individuals, mental concepts like intention and predictability play a crucial role (see e.g. Lehmann *et al*, this volume). Moreover, as legal decisions have to be justified by reason (argument) and evidence, legal ontologies often also cover epistemological notions and issues, as is also visible in the core ontologies[9] of Law proposed so far[10], e.g. Fundamental Legal Conceptions [42], A-Hohfeld [43], Language for Legal Discourse [44], Functional Ontology for Law [8], Frame-Based Ontology of Law [45] [46], LRI-Core (Breuker *et al.*, this volume), Core Legal Ontology (Gangemi *et al.*, this volume)[11].

The core notions in regulatory, and especially legal, ontologies include: norm, case, contract, institution, person, agent, role, status, normative position (duties, rights, etc.), responsibility, property, crime, provision, interpretation, sanction, delegation, legal document.

To build and maintain legal ontologies, proper techniques and methods from ontology engineering have been used: conceptual analysis, knowledge representation, ontology modularization and layering, ontology alignment and merging, evolution and dynamics, multilingual and terminological aspects, etc. The papers in this volume describe a good sample of these techniques, and further examples can be found in the products of past or ongoing initiatives in the field, in particular the International Workshops on Legal Ontologies [40] [49], the two Workshops on Regulatory Ontologies [50] [51], and the site of the Legal Ontologies Working Group within the EU OntoWeb project [52].

4.3 Applied Research

Independently of the scope of Semantic Web applications, legal ontologies are being applied in a variety of settings, which present typical problems that are summarized here:

---

[9] A core ontology is an ontology covering the most central notions in a domain of application.

[10] We do not mention here the rich philosophical tradition, which only indirectly enters the process of legal ontology engineering.

[11] [47] contains a non-recent, but useful review of several core ontologies for Law. [48] contains a more synthetic but wider-ranged account of legal ontologies.

- Creation of regulatory metadata and content standardization (e.g. Legal-XML/LeXML/MetaLEX, ADR/ODR-XML, etc.) [53]. Ontologies can be used to metadata creation or standardization, and existing metadata and standards can be used as sources for ontology building. Ultimately, some envision a future ontology-driven legal data management.
- Information extraction from legal documents: patterns of textual chunks or of syntactic constructs can be matched against semantic patterns derived from legal ontologies.
- Regulatory compliance: case matching against existing jurisprudence, compatibility of norms from laws pertaining to different time, orderings or systems, for comparison or harmonization purposes.
- Modelling legal reasoning (from the typically reified ontological viewpoint): the epistemological aspects of Law have been pointed out as a necessary target for legal ontologies [54]. Therefore, case-based reasoning and reasoning with uncertainty may be hybridised with legal ontologies.
- Management of workflows based on legally-defined tasks.
- Decision-support for legal advice, eGovernment, eCommerce.

In terms of the technology take-up business roadmap, legal Semantic Web technologies typically involve two types of applications:

- Applications in internal corporate settings (e.g. knowledge management, intranets): e.g. CLIME (sea-ship "classification" (certification) [55], [40], IKF-IF-LEX [56], eCOURT (information management of criminal court cases [57], Breuker *et al*, this volume), E-POWER (drafting tax law [58] [59]).
- Applications with public information on the Internet such as JurWordNet [60].

4.4 Structural Legal Ontologies and Markup Standards

The Law is applied as stated in legal sources, therefore it relies on *documents*. Documents are the basic infrastructure for legal operations: they have a physical perspective (the support), a representational one (the language), and a cognitive one (the intended content): legal practice refers to those perspectives in each application case. Besides being able to represent such perspectives in legal ontologies, we need to access, index, and markup the source documents, and to keep track of the validity of their physical support, and of their interpretation.

In knowledge and information management, there is a large variety of types of documents and their structures. Documents may range from narrative texts (stories, histories, case descriptions, testimony) via "non-narrative" texts (reports, articles, handbooks, instructions) to fully pre-structured filled-in forms. Also they range from "primary sources of law", i.e., codes, statutes, regulations or court cases, the work products of many different types of sovereigns, either presently in force or of historical value, to instruments created to determine rights in private transactions, such as deeds or wills. "Legal text" can also refer to a scholarly writing on some law-related subject, such as an article in a law journal or a treatise. Legal documents cover this full range. Markup languages can be used for capturing information contained in legal documents. This is to be done in different ways:

- by the addition of several global attributes that carry basic information necessary to allow a text to be considered in its legal aspect,
- by the creation of tags to carry new elements that contain various types of legal metadata,
- by providing new legal-specific elements that reflect the specific structures found in legal text,
- by marking up relevant terms and text chunks with tags derived from legal ontologies.

Several projects have addressed these issues, starting with SGML tags [61] to ongoing projects like e-COURT, E-POWER, NormaInRete [62], LeXML [63], MetaLEX [69] [70] and LegalXML [64] and SEKT [65].

In SEKT what it is intended is the connection between markup documentary elements (sentences and rulings) and a repository of judicial experience to guide the queries. The proposal is to build up an ontology for professional legal knowledge (OPLK) (see[66] and Benjamins et al., this volume).

5 Content of This Book

We have divided this book into three parts. The first one (I) introduces the intellectual and social context. To our knowledge, the last book offering a comprehensive overview on the ontological commitments of the different trends and theories of law is fifteen years old [67] and, besides philosophy, from the social side of the law, it is not difficult to find on regular bases through the AI literature a number of papers asking for the incorporation of social sciences to the task of constructing legal ontologies [68]. In this regard, J. Aguiló-Regla's introductory work addresses the question of the changes in legal philosophy since the eighties, and offers a brief summary of the most recent frameworks. The next paper, by R. Alvarez, M. Ayuso and M. Bécue, reconstructs the everyday practices and habits of young Spanish judges using multidimensional exploratory techniques. Their work is closely related, as the reader will quickly realize, to the construction of Iuriservice, an iFAQ prototype for judicial assistance described in the last section of the book.

The second part of the book (II) covers legal ontologies and methodological issues related to the building of ontologies. In a way, the papers in this middle part summarize the efforts made over the last decade to grasp the increasing complexity of law and the legal knowledge. Therefore, they face the theoretical challenges implied in the epistemological and methodological domains.

J. Breuker, A. Valente and R. Winkels begin this section with a reflective paper on the FOLaw and the LRI-Core Ontology carried out since 1990 at the Leibniz Centre for Law (University of Amsterdam). They draw a broad picture in which the landmarks and the problems encountered in the main task of setting up the levels and dimensions of several ontologies mainly built from Dutch statutes are revealed and reflected. This starting point is enriched within the complementary paper by A.Valente on types and roles of legal ontologies. Valente summarizes and evaluates the existing ontological projects and makes some useful analytic distinctions aiming to avoid further intellectual confusions (e.g. between ontologies, knowledge representations and knowledge bases). A specific paper by J. Lehmann, J. Breuker and

B. Brouwer on the representation of causation for legal automatic legal reasoning completes the triad. This article offers a detailed ontological analysis of causation in common sense knowledge and law, one of the most difficult topics in legal theory.

The next two papers in the same section are related to the developments of DOLCE (Descriptive Ontology for Linguistic and Cognitive Engineering), originally the first module of the WonderWeb[12] Foundational Ontological Library. A. Gangemi, (Laboratory for Applied Technology, ICT-CNR) and M. T. Sagri and D. Tiscornia (ITTIG-CNR), concentrate on the ontological nature of the legal domain, and introduce the theoretical framework for a *constructive* ontology, the Core Legal Ontology (CLO). This article contains also a description of *JurWordNet*, an ontology-driven semantic lexicon, conceived as an extension of the Italian version of *EuroWordNet*. G. Boella, L. Lesmo and R. Damiano (COTA, University of Torino) present a model of norms, based on the behaviour of agents (agency). They characterize norms as constraints on behaviour, and they apply their ontological model to a specific case study (*fruits* and *goods*, following the Italian Civil Code).

This theoretical part ends up with two more contributions. The paper by O. Corcho, M. Fernández-López, A. Gómez-Pérez and A. López-Cima (Technical University of Madrid) aims to show how experts on the legal domain may develop their own ontologies following the ontology building methodology METHONTOLOGY, and using the ontology engineering workbench WebODE. Examples are borrowed from a class taxonomy proposed by Breuker. D. Bourcier's contribution may be seen as a counterpart of an automatic or semi-automatic method for ontological engineering. She addresses the question of the conceptual boundaries -how it is possible to take into account the dynamic and implicit dimension of legal discourses in the building of text-based ontologies? Bourcier's proposal consist of reaching pragmatic knowledge, e.g. through the notion of discretionary acts as a particular speech act of common knowledge.

The last part of the book (III) is reserved to several works focused on information retrieval and prototype applications. In this regard, G. Lame presents a general method relying on text analysis to identify components (concepts and relations among them) of an ontology for information retrieval. Her method has been tested on the 58 French Codes available on the Internet. J.Saias and P. Quaresma seek a similar purpose related to the Portuguese law. They present also a methodology for applying NLP techniques to create automatically a legal ontology (defined in OWL and using EVOLP+ISCO as a logic programming framework). Their method eventually merges an initial top-down ontological approach (from the Office of the Portuguese General Attorney) with a bottom-up semantic and pragmatic approach.

Finally, the closing section of this volume contains the description of three different prototype applications helping professionals to face the challenges of a globalised legal world.

Iuriservice is an intelligent Frequently Asked Question (iFAQ) system for newly appointed Spanish judges. V.R. Benjamins, P. Casanovas, J. Contreras, J.M. López-Cobo and L. Lemus are using an ontology based on the judges' everyday experience of handling cases in the so-called *on-duty* period (under the Spanish procedural law, this is the monthly week that they are on-guard and facing all kind of incoming prob-

---

[12] http://wonderweb.man.ac.uk/index.shtml

lems in the Spanish Courts). The authors call the practical knowledge needed to build the system an "ontology for professional legal knowledge" (OPLK).

NetCase is an intelligent system for cross-referral and case-forwarding to be used and implemented through transnational networks of law firms and lawyers. J.Contreras and M.Poblet show how the NetCase application implements several use cases that allows users to manage their skills and capacities. The most common one helps the user assigning a case to a law firm (selecting the best partners according to the features and complexities of the case). Both Iuriservice and NetCase are the result of the long term collaboration between iSOCO (Intelligent Software Components, S.A.) and the Sociolegal Studies Group (Institute for Law and Technology) at the Autonomous University of Barcelona.

Last, but not least, J. Kingston, B. Schafer and W. Vandenberghe, from the Joseph Bell Centre for Forensic Statistics and Legal reasoning (University of Edinburgh), describe the present status of the research on detection and prevention of financial fraud in the IST Project FF POIROT (Financial Fraud Prevention Oriented Information Resources using Ontology Technology). Their paper focuses on unauthorized online investment solicitation. They succeed in showing the nuances of a suitable ontology for this complex domain. The method used is that of "inference networks of law" (Wigmore charts, acyclic graphs for complex probabilistic reasoning tasks). They show the reusability of already existing ontologies (FOLaw, LRI-Core…) as well. However, to build a financial ontology, they complement them using SUMO (Standard Upper & Middle Ontology) and MacCarthy's REA (economic Resources, Events and Agents).

Acknowledgments

We thank Christoph Tempich and Denny Vrandecic for their detailed and useful comments on the final draft of the Introduction. This book has been published with support from the following Research Programmes: UE SEKT-IST-2003-506826; Spanish Government: SEC-2001-2581-C02-01; FIT-150500-2003 152,198,562.

References

1. Abel, R.L. (ed.): Lawyers: A Critical Reader. The New Press, New York (1997)
2. Gray, P. N.: Artificial Legal Intelligence. Aldershot, Dartmouth (1997)
3. Kowalski, R., Sergot, M.: Computer Representation of the Law, Proceedings of IJCAI-85. Morgan Kaufmann, Los Altos (CA) (1985)1269-1270
4. Kowalski, R., Sergot, M.J.: The use of logical models in legal problem solving, Ratio Juris, Vol. 2 n. 3, (1990) 201 – 218
5. Alchourrón, C, Martino, A.: A Sketch of Logic without Truth. In: Proceedings of the Second International Conference on AI and Law (ICAIL-89), ACM, New York (1999) 165-179
6. Sergot, A., Jones, M.: Deontic Logic in the Representation of Law: Towards a Methodology. Artificial Intelligence and Law Vol. 1 n.1 (1992): 45-6
7. Ashley, K and Rissland, E: A case based approach to modelling legal expertise. IEEE Expert, (1988) 70-77

8. Valente, A.: Legal Knowledge Engineering: A Modelling Approach. IOS Press, Amsterdam (1995)
9. Rodrigo, L., Blázquez, M., Casanovas, P. Poblet, M.: D10.1.1. Before Analysis. Case Study-Intelligent integrated support for legal professionals. State of the Art. EU-IST, IST-2003-506826 SEKT: Semantically Enabled Knowledge Technologies
10. Fabri, M.; Contini, F. (eds.): .Justice and Technology in Europe : How ICT is changing the Judicial Business. The Hague, Kluwer Int. Law (2001)
11. Ayuso, M. et al.: 2003Jueces jóvenes en España, 2002. Análisis estadístico de las encuestas a los jueces en su primer destino (Promociones 48/49 y 50). Internal Report for the General Council of the Judiciary, within the framework of the Project "Observatory of Judicial Culture", SEC-2001-2581-C02-01/02
12. Hokkanen, J., Lauritsen, M.: Knowledge tools for legal knowledge tool makers. Artificial Intelligence and Law Vol. 10 (2002) 295-302
13. Lawrence, S., Giles, C.L.: Accessibility of Information on the Web. Nature, July 8, Vol. 400 (1999) 107-109
14. Berners-Lee, T., Hendler, J., Lassila, O.: The Semantic Web. Scientific American, May 17, 2001
15. Studer, R.; Benjamins, V.R.; Fensel, D.: Knowledge Engineering, Principles and Methods. In: Data & Knowledge Engineering Vol. 25 n. 1-2, (1998) 161-197
16. http://www.w3.org/2001/sw/WebOnt/
17. http://en.wikipedia.org/wiki/Main_Page
18. http://dmoz.org/
19. See for example: http://www.w3.org/2001/sw/Europe/reports/chosen_demos_rationale_report/hp-applications-survey.html, http://challenge.semanticweb.org/, and http://elcano.isoco.net
20. Gómez-Pérez, A., Fernández-López, M., Corcho, O. Ontological Engineering, with examples from the areas of Knowledge Management, e-Commerce and the Semantic Web. Springer, London, Berlin (2003)
21. Davies, J.; Fensel, D.; van Harmelen, F. (eds). Towards the Semantic Web. Ontology-Driven knowledge Management. John Wiley & Sons, Chichester (2003)
22. From http://en.wikipedia.org/wiki/Semantic_web
23. http://www.xml.com/pub/a/2001/03/07/buildingsw.html
24. http://www.esperonto.net
25. Cerf, V.G.: Internet and the Justice System. 79 Washington Law Review 25 (2004)
26. Endeshaw, A.: Web Services and the Law: A Scketch of the Potential Issues. 11 International Journal of Law and Information Technology 251 (2003)
27. Caral, J.M.E.A: Lessons from ICANN: Is Self-Regulation of the Internet Fundamentally Flawed? 12 International Journal of Law and Information Technology (2004)
28. Sylverman, G.M.: Rise of the Machines: Justice Information Systems and the Question of Public Access to Court Records Over the Internet. 79 Washington Law Review (2004)
29. Davies, N.J., Fensel, D., Richardson, M.: The future of Web Services. BT Technology Journal Vol. 22 n. 1 (2004) 118-130.
30. Susskind, R.: Transforming the Law. Essays on Technology, Justice and the Legal Marketplace. Oxford, Oxford University Press (2000)
31. Mountain, D.: XML E-Contracts: Documents That Describe Themselves. 11 International Journal of Law and Information Technology 274 (2003)
32. Benoliel, D.: Cyberspace Technological Standardization: An Institutional Theory Retrospective. 18 Berkeley Technology Law Journal 1259 (2003)

33. Benoliel, D.: Technological Standards, INC: Rethinking Cyberspace Regulatory Episte-
    mology. 92 California Law Review 1069 (2004)
34. Biegel, S.: Beyond our control? Confronting the limits of our legal system in the age of
    cyberspace. MASS., The MIT Press (2002)
35. Dahm, A.L.: Database Protection vs. Deep Linking. 82 Texas Law Review 1053 (2004)
36. Lessig, L: The Future of Ideas: The Fate of the Commons in a Connected World. New
    York. Random House (2001)
37. http://www.creativecommons.org
38. Hunter, D.: Cyberspace as place and the tragedy of the digital anticommons. 91 California
    Law Review 439 (2003)
39. Schwartz, P.M: Property, Privacy, and Personal Data. 117 Harvard Law Review 2055
    (2004)
40. Winkels, R., Boer, A., Hoekstra, R.: CLIME: Lessons Learned in Legal Information Serv-
    ing. In: van Harmelen, F. (ed.): Proceedings of ECAI-2002. IOS Press: Amsterdam (2002)
    230-234
41. Gruber, T.R. A Translation Approach to Portable Ontology Specifications. Knowledge
    Acquisition 5 (1993) 199-220
42. Hohfeld, W.N. (1919). Fundamental Legal Conceptions as Applied in Judicial Reasoning.
    Cooke, W.W (ed.) New Haven,Yale University Press (1919)
43. Allen L.E, Saxon C.S.: Better Language, Better Thought, Better Communication: The A-
    HOHFELD Language for Legal Analysis. Proceedings of the Fifth International Confer-
    ence on AI and Law,(ICAIL-95), ACM, New York (1995)
44. McCarty, L.T: A Language for Legal Discourse: I. Basic Features. Proceedings of the
    Second International Conference on Artificial Intelligence and Law, ACM Press (1989)
45. van Kralingen, R.W.: Frame-based Conceptual Models of Statute Law. Kluwer Law Intl.,
    Amsterdam, (1995)
46. Visser , R.S.P. , Bench-Capon, T.J.M.: Ontologies in the Design of Legal Knowledge Sys-
    tems. Towards a Library of Legal Domain Ontologies. First International Workshop on
    Legal Ontologies, Melbourne Law School, Victoria (1997)
47. Visser, R.S. P., Bench-Capon , T.J.M.: A Comparison of Four Ontologies for the Design
    of Legal Knowledge Systems. Artificial Intelligence and Law 6 (1998) 27-57
48. Gangemi, A., Breuker J.: Section 5. Harmonizing Legal Ontologies. In: Deliverable 3.4.
    Harmonisation perspectives of some promising content standards. Ontoweb SIG on Con-
    tent Standards Legal Ontologies Working Group, Project IST-2000-29243 (2002)
49. Breuker, J., Gangemi, A., Tiscornia, D., Winkels, R. (eds.): ICAIL03 Wks on Legal On-
    tologies, Edinburgh, http://lri.jur.uva.nl/~winkels/legontICAIL2003.html (2003)
50. Jarrar, M., Salaun, A. (eds.): First Workshop on Regulatory Ontologies, OTM Workshops,
    Springer (2003)
51. Jarrar, M., Gangemi, A. (eds.): Second Workshop on Regulatory Ontologies, OTM Work-
    shops, Springer (2004)
52. http://ontology.ip.rm.cnr.it/onto/legontoweb.html.
53. Winkels, R., Boer, A., Hoekstra, R.: METAlex: An XML Standard for Legal Documents.
    In: Proceedings of the XML Europe Conference, London (UK) (2003)
54. Aikenhead, M.: Recycling law?. International Journal of Law and Information Technology
    4 (3) (1996)
55. A   Fourth   Framework   European   Project   IST   25414,   1998-2001,   see
    http://www.bmtech.co.uk/clime/index.html

56. Gangemi, A., Pisanelli D.M.; Steve, G. A.: Formal Ontology Framework to Represent Norm Dynamics. In: Second International Workshop on Legal Ontologies, University of Amsterdam (2001)
57. A Fifth Framewrok European Project IST 28199, 2000-2003. See http://www.intrasoft-intl.com/ecourt
58. A Fifth Framework European Project IST 28125. See http://www.lri.jur.uva.nl/~epower
59. Boer, A., Engers T. van, Winkels. R.: Using Ontologies for Comparing and Harmonizing Legislation. In: Proceedings of ICAIL2003, ISBN 1-58113-747-8, ACM Press, New York (2003)
60. http://www.ittig.cnr.it/Ricerca/UnitaEng.php?Id=11&T=4
61. Finke, N.D.: TEI Extensions for Legal Text. In: Text Encoding Initiative Tenth Anniversary User Conference (1997)
62. http://www.normainrete.it
63. http://www.lexml.de/mission_english.htm
64. http://www.legalxml.org/
65. A Sixth Framework European Project IST-2003-506826. SEKT: Semantically Enabled Knowledge Technologies. http://www.sekt-project.com
66. Benjamins, V.R., Contreras, J., Casanovas, P., Poblet, M., Blázquez, M., Rodrigo, L.: The SEKT Legal Use Case Components: Ontology and Architecture. 17th Annual Conference in Legal Knowledge and Information Systems. JURIX 2004. T.F. Gordon (Ed.) pp. 69-77
67. Amselek, P., MacCormick N.: Controversies about Law's Ontology. Edinburgh, Edinburgh University Press (1989)
68. Paliwala, A.: An Intellectual Celebration: A Review of the Jurix Legal Knowledge Based Systems Scholarship. Artificial Intelligence and Law 8 (2001) 317-335
69. Boer, A.; Hoekstra, R. and Winkels R. (eds.) Legal Knowledge and Information Systems. Proceedings of JURIX 2002, 1-10, Amsterdam, IOS Press (2002)
70. http://www.metalex.nl

Introduction: Legal Informatics and the Conceptions of the Law

Josep Aguiló-Regla

Departamento de Filosofía del Derecho, Universidad de Alicante,
Campus de Sant Vicent del Raspeig,
Ap. 99 E-03080 Alicante, España
josep.aguilo@ua.es
http://cervantesvirtual.com/portal/DOXA/

Abstract. This article shows how the first generalized developments of legal informatics in the Civil Law systems were coherent with the dominant conception of the Law during the 70s and 80s. Today, that conception of the Law is in crisis, and it is possible to talk about a change in the mentality of jurists as well. Both changes generate new spaces and further opportunities for legal informatics and for legal knowledge management.

1 Introduction

I have been away from the world of legal informatics for 14 years now. My last two papers on this issue date from 1990 [1] [2]. The first one focused on documentary languages and Thesaurus and I explored all the possibilities of linguistic coordination offered by the information retrieval systems to maximize the efficiency of the documentary searches. In the second one I introduced some proposals to modify the legislative drafting techniques in order to improve the automatic documentation of legislation.

To participate in the "International Seminar on Law and the Semantic Web" meant for me to come back to a world that —in my opinion— is a good testing bench for the validation of different proposals of general theory of Law.[1] In short, those proposals are constructions of structural and functional models of the Law, and informatics is a good validation test.

What has changed since? I am bound to answer that "everything has changed". Nonetheless, this sort of answer would probably end up by meaning almost nothing. Obviously, many technological changes have occurred. They have become pervasive and I can not see myself making any relevant contribution in this area. But I will try to analyse the changes occurred both in the mentality of jurists and in the conceptions of the Law within the Civil Law systems. In doing so, I will be able to show how the dominant conception of the Law in those years definitively shaped the first developments of legal informatics in Europe. I will conclude by arguing how the changes on the mentality of jurist (the change on the conception or on the paradigm of the Law) offer nowadays new opportunities for the development of legal informatics, especially of knowledge systems.

---

[1] I am grateful to Pompeu Casanovas for his very kind invitation to participate in the Seminar.

V.R. Benjamins et al. (Eds.): Law and the Semantic Web, LNCS 3369, pp. 18–24, 2005.

2 The First Generalized Developments of Legal Informatics

Legal informatics has formulated since its very beginnings a number of promises and a variety of projects. The emergence of informatics led vocational jurists to forecast a very promising future in the short term: they thought that a sort of new age for the Law was just breaking in. Just as the invention of the press brought about great changes to the Law, informatics was also called to be —according to these jurists— the booster of a new age for the Law. To be sure, this only holds true for those jurists who were "activist" of legal informatics (the vocational ones). The huge majority was more skeptical. As we will see, only two projects on legal informatics were almost unanimously embraced, none of them implying a qualitative change within the world of the Law.

Benjamins *et al.* have distinguished between the processing that stresses knowledge-result and the one that stresses knowledge-process [3]. Keeping this distinction in mind, it is not difficult to show what this change of mentality among jurists is about. During the 70s and the 80s, it was usual to distinguish between documentary legal informatics and management legal informatics. The former referred to information as a result. The idea was to document the legal system by considering it a set of documents (statutes, cases, etc.; "institutional results", so to speak). The corresponding institutional processes these documents were a result of function as mere identifiers of the documents to be included in the information retrieval system. One could say then that all the legal informatics was ancillary to the traditional theory of the sources of Law. Certainly, the documentation of the legal system (as a result or document) was meant to be a useful tool for jurists when fulfilling their particular tasks -namely, the processes of interpretation and application of the Law. However, these tasks did not fall under the scope of documentary legal informatics. Rather, they were the object of knowledge systems, much more theoretically than practically oriented at that moment. The research on documentary systems aimed at providing added value to the searches in two different senses. On the one hand, it intended to improve the quality of semantic searches by refining both the thesaurus (*a priori* and *a posteriori*) and the linguistic coordination included within the information retrieval equation. On the other hand, it aimed at establishing crossed references between different texts, seeking then to cover an aspect that was traditionally covered by legal dogmatics (or legal science). Still, the very idea of added value in the legal information was somehow problematic, since the main aim remained to document the legal system itself, the "positive Law". The mediations (the added value) were not part of the "legal system" itself, and in this sense they were considered as "influences". To be sure, there were many doubts on the very notion of added value. I recall from those years how the people in charge of the legal information retrieval systems nearly unanimously accepted the policy of maximising the efficiency of the documentation while minimizing the interpretative influence.

As for the information or knowledge as process, attention was paid to the automation of the different legal-institutional procedures. Procedures were seen as sequences of acts generating and processing information, and its automation was the realm of what was then called management legal informatics. The goal was not the automation of the decision, but the replacement of paper backup by computer backup and the rationalization of the information flows. Obviously, the development of this sphere of informatics was adapted to the institutional division of the State powers (legislative, executive and judicial). It was therefore common to talk about parliamentary informatics, administrative informatics, and judicial informatics.

Not surprisingly, the widespread acceptance of these approaches and orientations were in line with the dominant conception of the Law in the Civil Law systems: the Law as an objective system of norms and procedures. This conception impregnated legal thought to such an extent that to distinguish between legal statics (Law as norms or results) and legal dynamics (Law as acts or procedures) became commonplace. While these approaches are not false, they are somehow reductionist, since they entail a certain tendency to make legal operators invisible. One of the causes for a certain frustration of the expectations generated by the expert legal systems lies precisely in this invisibility of the legal culture. Furthermore, this conception of the Law has caused two main deformations of the legal method: one of them may be called a vice of excess and the other a vice of defect. *Grosso modo*, if we conceive the legal method as a set of operations that allow us to go from the generality of the norms to the individuality of a legal solution, and if we do accept that the central problem of the legal method is the rationality of legal solutions, then it is easy to show what these two deformations are about. The first one consists of a strong deductivism: basically, legal solutions are supposed to be the product of deductive operations, the product of subsuming the individual case within the general case established by the norm. From this point of view, to apply the Law is merely to "say" the Law [*dire le Droit*] for an individual case ("*juris-dictio*"). The second deformation consists of strong decisionism. General norms do not cause (do not determine) the individual solutions, so particular cases require making of a decision rather than finding a solution. The application of the Law is less a matter of method than a matter of power (*who* is the one to decide). The first deformation stresses the legal statics (there are deducibility relations among the norms), the second one stresses the legal dynamics (decisions are the product of acts of will). Surprising as it may seem, a number of jurists have simultaneously sustained these apparently incompatible attitudes. In fact, it became commonplace to argue that if the Law was determined or certain, the solution to the individual case was to be deduced; and subsequently when the Law was undetermined or uncertain, the solution needed to be discretionally decided (in these cases there was not indeed a solution but a decision). In short, from this point of view, legal statics corresponds to the rational moment of the Law, while legal dynamics correspond to the voluntarist (will) moment of it.

To sum up, the very first generalized developments of legal informatics in the Civil Law systems were coherent with this dominant image of the Law. To be sure, qualitative changes were not to be implied from those developments; and yet—though far from being negligible— quantitative changes such as availability and accessibility did happen. At present, this picture of the Law is clearly in crisis and we may talk about a change both in the mentality of jurists and in the dominant conception of the Law. Most likely, these shifts of mentality are independent from the technological changes that have occurred in our societies. Rather, the explanation should be found in political and social elements and in internal elements of the Law itself. In any case, what is most relevant to this exposition is that changes generate new spaces and opportunities for legal informatics and for legal knowledge management.

3   What Does This "Change of Mentality" Mean and What Consequences Does It Have on Legal Informatics?

As for the change of mentality of the jurists, I shall briefly refer to what has been usually referred to as the change of paradigm in legal thought. It can be summarized with the phrase "From the legalist conception of the Rule-of-Law to the constitutionalist conception of the Rule-of-Law". As regards the opportunities for legal informatics arising from this new mentality, I will focus on the implications emerging from the transition from a conception of the Law as enactments and/or procedures to a conception of the Law as a practice.

3.1   "From the Legalist Conception of the Rule-of-Law to the Constitutionalist Conception of the Rule-of-Law"

Law is considered to be an authority phenomenon. Undoubtedly, this feature makes the language used by the authority (enactments) as well as the ways of action used in the process of its formulation (procedures) remarkably decisive to the Law. This reaffirms the specific character of the legal language: jurists need to operate with the language provided by the authority (a distinctive character of legal knowledge, compared to other fields of knowledge, i.e. medicine). Again, this dependence on authority highlights the importance of the role that interpretation plays in the realm of Law. In other words, this subjection to authority is a necessary or defining property of the Law, but it does not imply the reduction of the Law to authority commands. In fact, this also underlies to a great extent the approaches of legal informatics retrieval systems. Still, it is necessary to point out that what has changed is not this connection to the authority but the conception of the authority itself: the Weberian idea that political legitimacy is simply formal and procedural. It appears that this conception of legitimacy and authority is coherent with the dichotomy expressed above between legal statics and legal dynamics and as a result it is in crisis too. The change of mentality takes place therefore by the modification of the conception of authority and of legitimacy, which entails a "substantivization" of legal reasoning. For a rule or an authority act to be valid, it must respect (be coherent with) certain principles and substantive values that, in a way -which is not worth explaining now- are previous to the authority decisions. This change in the conception of authority, Law, and validity has been referred to in many ways, but probably the most common one deals precisely with the change of paradigm mentioned before: the transition from the legalist conception of the Rule-of-Law to the constitutionalist conception of the Rule-of-Law. In the last decades, the great influence of the works of Ronald Dworkin [4] [5] [6], Jürgen Habermas [7], Robert Alexy [8] [9], Joseph Raz [10], Carlos S. Nino [11] [12] [13], Luigi Ferrajoli [14] [15], among others, illustrates this change. I shall briefly state here some of the determining features of this switch of paradigm:

a)   The assumption that the model of (only) rules is unsatisfactory in order to comprehend the structure of a legal system. This is due to the fact that along with rules, there are principles that play a determinant role [Dworkin; Alexy].

b) According to this, there are not only logical relations of deducibility among norms of a particular legal system but justificatory relations as well [Nino].

c) Consequently, there is a strong proclivity to the study of norms (rules and principles) not only from the point of view of its logical structure but also from the point of view of the role that each of them play (or intend to play) in practical reasoning [Raz; Nino].

d) The distinction between prescriptive and descriptive language has also weakened, so that the role that the science of law is meant to play nowadays is a more reconstructive, justificatory and practical one and can not be reduced to a descriptive and detached approach [Dworkin; Nino].

e) A strong tendency to break the isolation of legal reasoning in order to incorporate it (and its specificities) into the different spheres of practical reason, or the blurring of the venerable borders between law, morals and politics [Alexy; Nino].

f) A propensity for seeing the legal method under the scope of argumentative schemes, which implies that the justification of legal decisions cannot be reduced to mere obedience or rule following. This clearly relates to what was stated before as the "substantivization" of legal reasoning [Alexy; Ferrajoli].

g) The consideration that the Law is instrumental to the achievement of social changes beyond the mere obedience of rules. Furthermore this entails the incorporation of instrumental reasoning [Ferrajoli].

h) The conception of the Law (rules and principles) as a means of protecting and assuring certain values and goods, which leads to the incorporation of a value rationality (substantive reasoning) [Dworkin].

i) Therefore, the conviction that instances such as the principle of universalization, the principle of integrity or evaluative coherence, etc. confer a rational character to the social practice of justifying legal decisions [Alexy; Dworkin].

We could go on pointing out the main features of this model as an alternative to the legalist one, but I will not go further with it. Nevertheless, what I have put forward could lead us to think that this change of conception represents nothing but an obstacle to the development of legal informatics. Certainly, we may conclude that all of the main aspects outlined above involve an increase of the operations that are not subject of automation, since they cannot be reduced to rules (valuations, balancing, reasonability judgments, constraints in the scope of generality, etc.). In other words, the possibility of a wide acceptance of legal informatics systems could turn out to be chimerical. I will try to show why this is not likely to be the case, but quite the contrary: This change of mentality enhances the strong development of legal informatics.

3.2 "From the Law as Enactment and/or Procedure to the Law as a Practice"

No doubt, the mentioned change of mentality has not only meant a modification of the structural features of legal systems (kinds or types of norms), of the validity criteria, and of the conception of authority (the notion of legitimacy), but has also implied a revision of the reduction of Law to rules and procedures. Nowadays, it is usual to think of the law as a very complex and fluid social reality that overflows those limits and whose existence, structure and content fully depend upon the beliefs of the people that make use or operate with it (acceptants, participants or mere users). Therefore, the Law depends completely on its own practice. In other words, there is no opposition between its objectivity (rules and procedures) and its practice. The practice, the use of the "object" Law, contributes to shape that very object in a decisive way. That necessarily implies reconsidering the notion of "knowledge" as well as the notion of "added value" in the world of Law. Today, the assumption according to which there is only one positive Law and the cognitive needs of each jurist are identical and comprise having access to that Law has been completely overcome.

The expression "Law as a practice" seems a virtuous one, since it allows legal operators to be placed in an outstanding position. Once this is done, different groups of individuals emerge having very different informational needs. All this allows to "rip the corset" that the legalistic conception of Law had put upon legal knowledge and to the very notion of added value related to the positive Law.

Most likely, the informational needs of a judge are not the same as those of a regular citizen. Similarly, the needs of an experienced judge are different from the needs of a recently appointed one. This rupture of the unity of informational needs as well as the emergence of different kinds of agents modifies the relationship between the user and the informational system. From the notion of a particular "case" –where the positive Law is expected to give an answer—we move on to the notion of "problem" of a particular person with specific needs as well. In this sense, the notion of "Law as a practice" (from the "case" to the "problem") evidences the shift to a mentality much more instrumental than final, since it puts the emphasis on the individuals and their informational needs.

If everything stated here is true, then it seems obvious to me that new and hopeful possibilities for legal informatics and, specifically, for knowledge systems are arising in the European context. The increasing consciousness about the complexity of Law allows to track the projects on the path of utility for certain individuals rather than claiming an objectivity of the answers. It may be concluded from here that the conception according to which Law is something given and external to individuals (a set of general rules which solve any given case in advance) has to be given up.

References

1. Aguiló-Regla, J.: Lenguaje jurídico, lenguaje documental y thesaurus, Teoría (1990) 12-13, 31-65
2. Aguiló-Regla, J.: Técnica legislativa y documentación automática de legislación, Informatica e Diritto, January-April (1990) 87-110
3. Benjamins, R., Fensel, D., Decker, S, Gómez-Pérez, A. (KA)2: Building Ontologies for Internet: a Mid-term Report, International Journal of Human-Computer Studies 51 (1999) 687-712
4. Dworkin, R.: Taking Rights Seriously, Harvard University Press, Mass. (2002)
5. Dworkin, R.: A Matter of Principle, Harvard University Press, Mass. (1985)
6. Dworkin, R.: Law's Empire, Belknap Press of Harvard University Press, Mass. (1986)
7. Habermas, J.: Faktizität und Geltung. Beiträge zur Diskurstheorie des Rechts und des demokratischen Rechtsstaats, Suhrkamp (1994)
8. Alexy, R.: Theorie der Juristischen Argumentation, Suhrkamp (1978)
9. Alexy, R.: Theorie der Grundrechte, Suhrkamp, (1994)

10. Raz, J.: Practical Reason and Norms, Princeton University Press, New York (1990)
11. Nino, C.S.: La validez del Derecho, Astrea, Buenos Aires (1985)
12. Nino, C.S.: Fundamentos de Derecho Constitucional, Astrea, Buenos Aires (1992)
13. Nino, C.S.: The Constitution of Deliberative Democracy, Yale University Press, Yale (1996)
14. Ferrajoli, L.: Diritto e ragione: Teoria del garantismo penale, Laterza (1989)
15. Ferrajoli, L.: Los fundamentos de los derechos fundamentales, Trotta, Madrid (2001)

Statistical Study of Judicial Practices

Ramón Álvarez[1], Mercedes Ayuso[2], and Mónica Bécue[3]

[1]Dep. de Dirección y Economía de la Empresa, Universidad de León,
Campus de Vegazana s/n, 24071 León
dderae@unileon.es
[2] Dep. de Econometría, Estadística y Economía Española, Universidad de Barcelona,
Diagonal 690, 08034 Barcelona (corresponding author)
mayuso@ub.edu
[3] Dep. de Estadística e Investigación Operativa, Universidad Politécnica de Cataluña,
Pau Gargallo 5, 08028 Barcelona
monica.becue@upc.es

Abstract. The new technologies imply important changes for judges in documentation consulting and other working habits. Presently, the legal codes and
many judicial publications are being archived on electronic support and complex text and data bases are built up. How the judges are currently working and
which are their difficulties? Would an interactive network help them to resolve
the cases they face? These points and other many aspects of their daily activity
are better known through the answers of the judges in a survey through questionnaire. Multidimensional exploratory techniques are used to design typologies according to the whole of the answers relative to the documents consulting.
The authors use a survey to the young Spanish Judges to build up clusters of
judges in accordance to their working habits.

1 Introduction

The *Young Spanish Judges Survey 2002* has been designed in the context of a national
project[1] in order to better know the actual difficulties that the judges face. A special
interest was put on new technologies given that they have a strong impact in the resources they can use in their daily activity. Currently, the legal codes and many judicial publications are being archived on electronic support and complex text and data
bases are built up, which opens a large range of new interesting possibilities and implies the emergence of important changes in documentation consulting and other
working habits.

Which are the problems that the judges face in their professional activity, particularly when they are resolving judicial cases, which could benefit of a professional
network? How are they currently using the existing paper and electronic documentation about doctrine and jurisprudence? How do they use internet? The present global
behaviour and practice of the judges must be known in order to build up a well accepted interactive documentation and consultation network.

---

[1] Spanish Ministry of Science and Technology for the period 2001-2004.

V.R. Benjamins et al. (Eds.): Law and the Semantic Web, LNCS 3369, pp. 25–35, 2005.
© Springer-Verlag Berlin Heidelberg 2005

A special attention is given to the junior judges who are looking for assessment when facing difficulties and doubts in their first position. This collective is supposed to be particularly capable to benefit from new technological resources. However, the senior judges, besides they give a comparative reference level, provide an indispensable information about requirements, documentation, consultation, relationships and many kinds of useful resources due to their background experience.

In section 2, we present the sample design. Section 3 is concerned with the questionnaire. Then, section 4 gives some univariate results. In section 5 we explain the methodology used to build up a typology of the judges from their work on legal documents and jurisprudence. Section 6 offers a detailed presentation of the typology obtained and, finally, section 7 concludes with the main points that this study has underlined.

2   The Sample Design

To carry out the study, we have selected 129 judges with less than 4 years experience (junior judges) among a population of 352 judges in their first position (Spain, March 2002)[2]. Therefore, the documentation office of the Governing Body of the Spanish Judiciary (CENDOJ) provided us with the coordinates (court number, city,...) of all judges that had accomplished their training in the Spanish Judicial School (JSB), located in Barcelona, between 1997 and 1999.

To perform a comparative analysis, 139 senior judges were also selected. There is an oversampling of junior judges in order to obtain a good representation for this group. To extrapolate the results to the population, the sample is reweighted in accordance to actual experience (junior/ senior) and gender proportions[3].

An important aspect of the project was that people in charge of the interviews were the judges in training in the JSB. It was the best way to obtain a good quality of answers, taking into account their knowledge of the concepts. Besides, the judges in training could obtain information about what to expect in a near future. The judges volunteered to take part into the project. The interviews were conducted in March 2002 over the whole country. More details about the capture of information can be found in [1].

3   The Questionnaire

The questionnaire was an agreed work between professor-judges of the JSB, members of CENDOJ and the group of researchers. They were also assessed by the director of the *Spanish Judges and Magistrates Opinion Barometers,* survey regularly repeated since 1984. Although the main block of questions was directed to the professional problems that junior judges face in their first position, some questions were related to

---

[2] Judges from Basque Country were not included.
[3] In Spain in March 2002 there were 352 junior judges and 2352 senior, without including the Superior Courts (*Tribunal Constitucional*, *Tribunal Supremo*, *Audiencia Nacional* and *Tribunales Superiores de Justicia*).

the School, where junior judges stay for one year and half when they pass the Spanish public competitive exam.

The questionnaire was divided into two parts. The largest concerned the judge; the shortest, the judicial secretary. The objective was not only to know the principal characteristics of the judicial profession but also the working conditions. Questions about the judicial office were directed to the judicial secretary.

The part of the questionnaire concerning the judge tackles five fields:

- Training evaluation: in the university, in the Judicial School and through specific courses.
- Main problems found by judges in their professional activity.
- CENDOJ services concerning new technologies and documentation.
- Actionable, professional, institutional and social relationships.
- Professional evaluation.

25 open-ended questions complete the closed questions. The latter do not allow for a good approach to certain fields, in particular when they are badly known and for which it would be difficult to offer relevant items or fields which require spontaneous answers. It is well known that open-ended and closed questions cannot gather at all the same information [2]. In particular, the proposed items induce the answers. The individuals can be led to choose an item considered as "correct" because included, little prone to claim that no answer corresponds to their opinion or too concerned by giving satisfaction to the pollster leading them to choose an item. Furthermore, we cannot forget that the answer items cannot correspond to the actual perception of the interviewed individuals.

The treatment of these open-ended questions starts from the raw text, without neither precoding nor manual intervention. It constitutes an automatic tool for information extraction that relegates the subjectivity of the researcher to the later stage of the interpretation and puts forward features that are transparent to a classic reading.

In table 1, we summarize the main blocks of questions that we illustrate with some examples and the number of closed and open-ended questions.

4 Some Univariate Results[4]

Although the questionnaire was long, the level of response was high. Through the free answers, the judges explained the most important professional problems that they faced in their first position (14 non-responses); the most complicated civil and criminal cases they had to resolve (15 non-responses and 24 non-responses, respectively); as well as the characteristics of the civil and criminal cases that gave them more work (22 and 24 non-responses, respectively).

32,1% of the sample (18,9% junior judges, 34,1% senior) had a job concerning law before being a judge, and 22,4% of the sample (19,0% in the first subsample and 23,0% in the second) received additional specific courses. 90,7% of the sample (92,6% junior judges and 90,4% senior) evaluate the university as medium or good. The senior judges underline the quality of the teachers, while the junior claim for a more applied training.

---

[4] Weighted results.

Table 1. The questionnaire

Domains	Number of questions	Examples
Training evaluation	18 closed questions 3 open-ended questions	What is your opinion about training in the Law School? What changes do you suggest in the training at the Spanish School of the Judiciary? Did you use the continuous training of the Governing Body of the Spanish Judiciary during the last year?
Professional activity	13 closed questions 16 open.ended questions	What were the most complicated civil cases that you had to resolve during your first year as a judge? Could you define the criminal case that has given you more work? Do you comment a judicial case with someone else because you are worried about its resolution? Do you use Internet?
CENDOJ services	5 closed questions	Do you use the personal attention service of CENDOJ? Do you use legal databases?
Relationships	26 closed questions 4 open-ended questions	Do you think that people are right when they say that "*Justice is very slow*"? Do you have any professional communication with other judges?
Professional Valuation	7 closed questions 3 open-ended questions	In your opinion, what are the main personal and _rofesssional characteristics of judges in Spain? What does a "good judge" mean to you?

The second group of questions, mainly open-ended questions, was principally related to the difficult legal cases that the judges faced in their first position. The questionnaire focused on civil and criminal cases, which are the two kinds of cases that judges can deal with in their first position (see [3] for more information).

73,2% judges fully agreed with the design of a professional network in order to support documentation consulting (83,1% of the junior judges and 71,7% of the senior). 54,2% judges use Internet (60,6% of the junior judges and 53,2% of the senior). 56,7% of the sample "*sometimes*" take legal advice from other colleagues (72,7% of the junior judges and 54,3% of the senior). 23,7% "*frequently*" do it (11,8% in the first subsample and 25,5% in the second).

69,4% of the sample agree with people who think that "*Justice is slow*" but only 39,5% agree with those who say that "*judges do not listen*".

29,7% judges (34,5% of the junior judges and 28,9% of the senior) are completely satisfied with their career; 48,4% (54,7% of the first subsample, 47,5% of the second) are only partially satisfied.

71,2% senior judges are males and 28,8% females. However, 60,5% junior judges are females *versus* 39,5% males, which is in agreement with the data of the Spanish School of the Judiciary [4]. The remarkable increase of females in the judicial career is also underlined in the *Quinto Barómetro Interno de opinion de Jueces y Magistrados* [5].

5 Methodology to Build Up a Typology of the Judges

Aiming at better knowing the behaviour of the judges, such as described by their answers to the questionnaire, a good approach consists in building up a typology, that is to say, a partition of the judges into clusters.

The adopted strategy combines multiple correspondence analysis (MCA) and cluster analysis methods ([6], [7], [8], [9]), in such a way that MCA only constitutes a preprocessing step.

Multiple correspondence analysis (MCA) is concerned with large data sets in which individuals are described by qualitative variables. MCA aims at describing similarities between individuals, on the one hand, and at offering a balance of the relationships between variables (and/or modalities), on the other hand. The latter includes a visualisation of the similarities between modalities and also a summary of the qualitative variables by a small number of quantitative variables, the principal coordinates vectors, linked to the whole of the studied variables. For more information about MCA, see [10], [11], [7].

Then, cluster analysis allows for gathering the individuals from the principal coordinates vectors, generally considering only those that conserve an important proportion of inertia. Among the different clustering methods, hierarchical clustering, using generalized Ward's criterion, is convenient when operating from the principal axes coordinates (Lebart *et al.*, 1995, pp. 170-176 [7]; Escofier and Pagès, 1998, pp. 35-42 [11]). After cutting the hierarchical tree, some k-means iterations are realized to consolidate the obtained partition.

This combined methodology presents various advantages. First the principal axes are very stable with respect to sampling, which is not the case in cluster analysis methods that can give results notoriously different when changing a small number of individuals [9]. To loose a part of the information by keeping only the first principal axes is far from being an inconvenient: so, random fluctuations, that could shade important phenomena, are eliminated, given that the principal axes method acts such as a filter ([6], [7]) and preserve only the useful information. Another advantage comes from a quicker processing to build up the clusters, due to the reduction of the dimension of the table.

Once the clusters are built up, the individuals belonging to a same cluster present similarities that must be pointed out in order to know which aspects are in the origin of the observed groupings (active variables) but also which features, not used in the clusters building, also differentiate them (illustrative variables). So, for every cluster, the frequency of each modality is compared to its frequency in the whole sample, by using a statistical indicator. Then, the modalities are ranked according to the value of this indicator, whose different values constitute mutual references; the modalities linked to the smallest values are overlooked.

Among the illustrative information, the open-ended questions play a specific role. The open-ended questions are used to obtain specific results, not equivalent to those obtained by closed questions, to collect opinions that cannot be summarized in a few words, to valuate the level of interest of the respondent (giving an extensive and argued answer or, on the contrary, a laconic answer) to take into account the language level and pick up nuances such as the personal implication. Their treatment goes through the identification, by using a statistical criterion, of the over and under represented words in the whole answers of each cluster and also of the original answers that can be considered as typical answers of every cluster [6].

This global strategy supplies clusters of individuals about which much information is given, allowing for understanding their behaviour and opinion and for linking the difficulties that the judges find with all the aspects of their activity. The information will stand out from the accumulation of complementary information.

6   Results

6.1   Active Questions

We are aiming at creating typologies of the respondents mainly depending on the use of the documentation by the judges. The selection of the active questions must reflect this choice. So, the questions about the domains in which the problems appear, the lack of time they have to resolve them and the consults to colleagues, juridical data bases, occupational data bases and doctrinal publications are chosen as active (Table 2).

Table 2. Active questions

- I feel better with civil cases (yes/not)
- I feel better with criminal cases (yes/not)
- Do you have enough time to study the cases (5 levels)?
- Do you comment the legal cases with some professional in a direct interview? (yes/not)
- Do you comment the legal cases with some professional by phone? (yes/not)
- Do you consult:
Jurisprudence on paper publications? (yes/not)
Jurisprudence on electronic data bases? (yes/not)
Documentation about doctrine? (yes/not)
- Do you use internet? (yes/not)
- Do you think that a telematic network is useful as a support to take decisions? (yes/not)
- Do you use the documentation centre of the CGPJ?
- How do you value a telematic network as a support to take decisions? (5 levels)
- How often do you use (5 levels):
The central library of the CGPJ?
The electronic data bases of the CGPJ?
Documents about doctrine?
The CGPJ web?
Paper publications of the CGPJ?

6.2   Clusters Description

Description by the Closed Questions. Following the strategy described above, four clusters are obtained, described in tables 3 (closed information) and 4 and 5 (open-ended questions). For this description, we use the active variables, listed on Table 2 and also all the other variables as supplementary variables. As explained in the methodological section, for every cluster we compare the frequency of each modality in the cluster and in the whole sample. In this sense, we take into account, in the cluster description, those modalities having a percentage of responses higher than in the whole sample. When the difference is not statistically significant, this modality does not appear in the description.

We can summarize the most important features below.

They think that domestic and youth violence can have a great impact in their profession. We must note that the junior judges are dominant in this cluster (61% of the cluster) and so, we find a generation effect. However, there is an important group of senior judges, also used to new technologies, and it would be interesting to study this subgroup to check how they adapted their working habits.

Table 3. Description of the clusters from active and illustrative modalities overrepresented

Domains	Cluster 1	Cluster 2	Cluster 3	Cluster 4
Junior/ senior	46 junior, 72 senior judges (junior judges overrepresented)	13 junior, 33 senior judges	33 junior, 39 senior judges	11 junior, 21 senior judges
Training Evaluation	Trained in the Spanish School of Judiciary, give a positive valuation to the training periods in the official legal institutions, to the experiences during the second year and to the attention received from the tutor-judge. Trained in telematic resources by CGPG services, showing a positive valuation	Postgraduate training in work matters law		Postgraduate training in civil rights Postgraduate training in criminal law No training in telematic resources
Professional activity	Use internet Consult jurisprudence by using databases and not paper documents Give a positive valuation to a possible telematic network, considered as helpful to take decisions.	Do not use internet Consult and read documents relative to doctrine frequently Consult jurisprudence by using paper documents Give a negative valuation to a possible telematic network, considered as useless to take decisions Prefer work matters	Do not use internet Do not consult documents relative to doctrine Do not consult jurisprudence by using data bases Prefer criminal cases, do not like laboral cases	Do not use internet Do not consult jurisprudence by using data bases Non-response to the questions about telematic network

Table 3. (*Continued*)

Present and future problems in professional activity	Agree with the assessments "*yes, the subject to justice feels as if he was not listened*", "*the subject to justice has a lack of information*" In the future, expect impact on their work coming from domestic and youth violence	Do not agree with the assessments "*yes, the subject to justice feels as if he is not listened*", "*the subject to justice has a lack of information*" Non-responses about possible problems which could have an impact in their future work	In the future, expect some impact on their work coming from drugs and domestic violence	Non responses to the questions of this block
CENDOJ services	Use the CGPJ web Consult jurisprudence data bases very frequently Consult electronic publications and electronic publications of the CGPJ Use of the library on line of the CGPJ Use the central library of the CGPJ Use the documentation centre of the CGPJ Positive valuation of the legal documentation center of the CGPJ	Do not use the CGPJ web Consult electronic publications of the CGPJ very seldom. Do not use the library on line of the CGPJ Use the central library of the CGPJ Read doctrine very frequently Consult jurisprudence data bases very frequently Consult paper publications of the CGPJ very frequently Very positive valuation of the legal documentation center of the CGPJ	Do not use electronic documents Do not use CGPJ web Do not use CGPJ libraries on-line Do not use the central library of the CGPJ Do not use paper publications of the CGPJ Infrequent use of jurisprudence data bases Dot not use CENDOJ services Read sometimes documents about doctrine	Non-responses to the questions of this block

In the second cluster, the senior judges are dominant (71,7%). This group also consults frequently doctrine and jurisprudence, but using alternatively paper and electronic databases. They are not used to electronic resources. More than average are reluctant to a professional telematic network. They do not give their opinion about future problems that will have an impact in their activity.

The third cluster, half senior judges/ half junior, concentrates the individuals who consult little doctrine and no jurisprudence. They do not use internet and only sometimes the central library or the paper publications of this institution. They prefer criminal cases and, in the future, expect some impact from drugs and domestic violence.

In the fourth class, no answers were given to the active questions.

Table 4. Words used at least 5 times in the whole of the answers to the question "What does a good judge mean to you?"

Nouns: *law, justice, judge, citizen, case, issue, society, resolutions, court, actionable, person, work, reality, problems, conflicts, decision, function, sense, responsibility, ability, service, knowledge, conscience, quality.*
Verbs: *to have, to resolve, to listen, to be, to know, to apply, to carry out, to try, to serve, to have time.*
Adjectives: *common, hardworking, good/very good, responsible, personal, legal, professional, social, trained, impartial, human, prudent, honest, just, reliable, balanced, decisive, technical, reasonable.*

Table 5. Excerpt of the characteristic free answers of every cluster

Cluster 1:
- *To know how to listen, to understand, and to resolve*
- *An objective person, reasonable and hardworking*
- *Who makes frequent use of common sense*
- *Person with a good technical training but with capability to face the problems*
- *A person with a good legal training. Very prudent and calm. Honest, with ability for a permanent training*
- *Someone who works and tries to be just*
- *A person technically qualified and with common sense*
- *A person who achieves his/her work well*

Cluster 2:
- *that tries to administrate justice*
- *The judge who is independent of the parties, of the political power*
- *Balanced, comprehensive, somewhat distant*
- *Who speaks taking into account the actionable and tries to explain the reasons why the claim is overruled or not*
- *Has common sense and knows about law*
- *Analyses meticulously and exhaustively the contributed evidence*
- *hardworking, friendly and very integrated in the society*
- *Honest and honestly administrating justice without any pressure*

Cluster 3:
- *Coherent person*
- *Person who assumes his/her responsibility and does not put forward his/her personal vision*
- *Somebody who resolves according to his/her conscience*
- *Person responsible and professionally conscious*
- *Person with common sense, sacrificed to his/her profession*
- *As any other profession, he/she must be responsible*
- *Person in charge of the work, very prudent, very balanced , friendly with people*

Cluster 4:
- *Non responses*

Description by the Open-Ended Question "What Does a Good Judge Mean to You?". We want to point out that the question *"What does a good judge mean to you?"* interested the judges. Table 4 shows the words used at least 5 times by all the respondents and table 5 presents the differences between the clusters according to this question through excerpts of the answers considered as typical of the clusters.

In cluster 1, the respondents mainly value the ability to work (*ability to face the problems, a person who works, who achieves well his/her work,…*), a good training (*to know, good technical training, a good legal training, technically qualified…*) and some personal qualities (*honest, prudent, objective, human, just…*).

Cluster 2 underlines, as main characteristics for a good judge, those directly related to the justice administration. Thus, we can find that a good judge *"tries to administrate justice"*, *"is independent …"*, is *" balanced, comprehensive …"*, *"not influenced by anything or by anybody"*, *"honest and honestly administrating justice without any pressure"* or *"analyzes meticulously and exhaustively the contributed evidence"*.

The respondents from cluster 3 reveal that a good judge must have personal characteristics, however not directly related to his/her personal training or his/her ability to work. These characteristics indicate that a good judge needs to be *"coherent"*, *"responsible"*, *"independent"*, *"prudent"*, *"resolving in accordance to his/her conscience"*, *"not putting forward his/her personal vision"*, *" having common sense"*.

In cluster 4, there are, as in the case of the closed questions, many non-responses to this and other open-ended questions.

7   Conclusions

The methods used in this analysis belong to the exploratory multidimensional statistical methods field. The approach that these methods offer allows us to underline different features present in the data and can orientate posterior researches and/or lead to issue new hypotheses. For instance, the answers to the open-ended question, relative to their own "good judge" perception, reveal us that many aspects of the judges' work habits are linked to the global vision that they have concerning their profession, which advises for a global approach of their practice. From the typology, we can also deduce that the documentation consulting practice is extended among the judges (mainly those in clusters one and two) and not particularly linked to experience. It is consulted through internet resources more by junior judges than by senior, although part of the latter are already used to all kind of electronic supports and part of the former are, besides their training, reluctant to use this kind of tools. So, it would be interesting to study both subgroups: the senior judges used to new technologies in order to check how they adapted their working habits; the junior reluctant to these tools in order to understand why they avoid their use. Furthermore, we should wonder if through both ways of consulting documentation and jurisprudence they are aiming at the same information.

Acknowledgements

Thanks are given to Spanish grants SEC2001-2581-C02-01/02 and FEDER.

References

1. Ayuso, M., Becue, M., Alvarez, R., Valencia, O., Alvarez, M., Hernández, M. L., Santolino, M.: Análisis Estadístico de las Encuestas a los Jueces en su Primer Destino. Report de Resultados n° 1, Escuela Judicial de Barcelona (2002)
2. Lebart, L., Salem, A., Berry, E.: Exploring Textual Data. Kluwer (1998)
3. Ayuso, M., Becue, M., Alvarez, R., Valencia, O., Alvarez, M., Hernández, M. L., Santolino, M.: Jueces en España en su Primer Destino – 2002. Report de Resultados n° 2, Escuela Judicial de Barcelona (2004)
4. EJB: Datos Estadísticos-Promoción n° 50, Curso 1998-1999. Dossier Escuela Judicial de Barcelona (2000)
5. Demoscopia: Quinto Barómetro Interno de Opinión (Encuesta realizada a una muestra estadísticamente representativa de Jueces y Magistrados). Consejo General del Poder Judicial (1999)
6. Lebart L. : Les Enquêtes et la Statistique. In: Grangé, D., Lebart, L. (eds.) : Traitements Statistiques des Données d'Enquête, Dunod París (1994) 1-19
7. Lebart L., Morineau A., Piron M.: Statistique Exploratoire Multidimensionnelle. Dunod París (1995)
8. Morineau, A. : Le "Thémascope" ou Analyse Structurale de Données d'Enquête. In: Grangé, D., Lebart, L. (eds.) : Traitements Statistiques des Données d'Enquête, Dunod París (1994), 135-159
9. Roux, M. : Clasification des Données d'Enquête Statistique. In: Grangé, D., Lebart, L. (eds.): Traitements Statistiques des Données d'Enquête, Dunod París (1994), 91-112
10. Benzécri, J.: L'Analyse des Données. Dunod París (1973)
11. Escofier, B., Pagès J.: Analyses Factorielles Simples et Multiples; Objectifs, Méthodes et Interprétation. Dunod París (1988, 1998)

Use and Reuse of Legal Ontologies in Knowledge Engineering and Information Management

Joost Breuker[1], André Valente[2], and Radboud Winkels[1]

[1] University of Amsterdam, Leibniz Center for Law,
Faculy of Law, P.O. Box 1030, NL 1000 BA Amsterdam, Netherlands
{breuker, winkels}@lri.jur.uva.nl
[2] Knowledge Systems Ventures,
7707 Boeing Ave, Los Angeles, CA 90045, USA
avalente@ksventures.com

Abstract. In this article we present an overview of legal ontological modeling over a period of more than a decade. Most of the research reported concerns results from mid-size (European) projects aimed at the development of legal reasoning and information management tools and systems. In these projects we developed ontologies for several legal or regulation domains. However, the main thread of this article is provided by fundamental research performed by us or under our supervision (e.g. PhD theses by [1], [2], [3]), leading to more abstract legal 'core' ontologies and legal reasoning architectures. The major insights we have obtained from these experiences can be summarized as follows:

- Legal sources contain and assume non-legal, common-sense based domain knowledge. Therefore, a legal core ontology should be rooted in highly abstract common sense concepts as a foundational ontology. This notion is worked out in the *LRI-Core ontology*, presented in this article.
- What remains as typical legal knowledge to be modelled is normative and legal responsability knowledge. However, in this article we only summarize our work in this area, refering to [4] and to [5] on these issues.
- As law and legal theory is focussed on questions of justification, legal (core) ontologies, e.g. *FOLaw*, are epistemological frameworks, describing legal reasoning, rather than legal ontologies, explaining knowledge resources.

1 Introduction

This article presents insights acquired during more than a decade of development, use and reuse of legal ontologies at the Leibniz Center for Law (LRI) at the University of Amsterdam. These ontologies have been constructed in various projects concerned with the development of legal knowledge systems and legal information management. These insights provide a framework rather than a methodology for modeling legal knowledge and reasoning. Results and experiences in the projects are used to illustrate this framework. Although this framework is operationalized by reusable legal knowledge system architectures (e.g. *ON-LINE* [4], TRACS [6], [2]), the focus of this article is on discussing the conceptual views on legal knowledge and reasoning.

V.R. Benjamins et al. (Eds.): Law and the Semantic Web, LNCS 3369, pp. 36–64, 2005.

In the projects a large variety of legal domains have been analyzed and modeled: traffic regulations; tax –, criminal –, and administrative law; international treaties on trade, and safety at sea. To enable reuse of these ontologies in a library and to abstract the common legal denominators of these legal domains, much effort has been spent in finding a unifying view on legal domains. The goal is to support the modeling of ontologies in new legal domains. In this paper we will discuss two proposals for a legal **core ontology**: FOLaw [4] and more recently: LRI-Core. FOLaw has proven to be a good modeling support for building legal knowledge systems, because it reflects an understanding of types of knowledge and dependencies in legal reasoning. However, when applied to ontology based management of legal information services, the support is very limited: in Section 5 we will explain why and what views have lead us to develop this new LRI-Core ontology.

An ontology describes how some domain is 'committed' to a particular view: not so much by the collection of the terms involved but in particular by the way these terms are structured and defined. This structure tells us "what a domain is about". For instance, medical domains are about malfunctions of humans. These malfunctions are often diseases, i.e. processes; they are classified in (multiple) taxonomies, and associated with sets of typical symptoms, and with treatments ([7, 8]; more recently: [9]). In the next section (Section 2) we will make such an analysis for legal domains.

The article is further structured as follows. We will give a short overview of ontological commitments that can be found in legal theory. Next we will introduce our 'functional ontology of law' and see that it is rather an epistemic framework than a detailed ontology. From there on we will explore what is in a true ontology of law; what are typical and unique elements of law? When we have identified them, we will see them put to use in several applied R&D projects. Finally, we will discuss the current state of our work and draw some conclusions.

2   What is Law About?

An ontology makes explicit the views one is committed to in modeling a domain. Modeling is taken here in the broad sense that includes the notion of understanding. A major and typical problem from jurisprudence (legal theory) occurs already in the use of the term "law". In the title of this section we avoided any commitment to whether we mean '*the* law' or 'laws'. Indeed, the problem of what counts as the unit of law is already one of the fundamental questions in jurisprudence and is called the *individuation* problem:

> "Classifying laws in logically distinct categories has always been one of the major tasks of legal philosophy ... The classification of laws presupposes a solution to the more fundamental problem of the individuation of laws, i.e., an answer to the question 'What is to count as one complete law?" [10–page 825]

There are two extreme views. The first one takes all legally valid statements in legal sources (legislation, precedence law, etc) as a whole: the law. The assumption is that in principle the individual statements constitute a coherent whole. This is the predominant view in jurisprudence and legal philosophy (see also Section 3). Whether this coherence is an actual concern for the legal system (i.e., the law should be the object of proper knowledge management), or whether it is 'genetically' built-in by the constraints provided by fundamental, 'natural' legal principles, is a long and classical debate in legal theory.

However, the other extreme takes all legally valid statements as being individual laws. *In extremo* this view is incorrect, if only because at least one other legal (meta-)statement that is concerned with the validity of other legal statements: we need law about law, and this dependency is a serious concern of legal scholars (see e.g. [11]).

Legal theory is in the first place concerned with justifying law, so legal scholars will not easily take validity statements in law as a side issue

Law is theoretically very much concerned with the 'version' control of legislation, but in practice the means to control which is the current, valid version are not very sophisticated and not foolproof; let alone to assess whether some legal statement was valid at some point in time in the past. In constructing legal reasoning or information systems, knowledge engineers simply assume that the legal source to be modelled is a legally valid one. In the rest of this article we leave this meta-level issue in legal reasoning aside (see [12] further on this issue).

The coherence of law in a legal system as postulated by many legal scholars is in the first one that should evade contradictory outcomes for assessing legal cases: the law should not contain serious contradictions (exceptions are not considered to be contradictions; see Section 2.1). However, we usually mean by coherence more than only 'not contradictory': there should also be no conceptual 'gaps': two unrelated statements do not contradict one another but they do not form a coherent text. This lack of 'semantic coherence' [13] is exactly the problem one will find in modelling legislation. The normative statements that make up the bulk of legislation refer to some domain of social activity, but do not describe this domain. The individual normative statements qualify certain kinds of situations as illegal. By another meta-level law that states that anything that is not forbidden by law is allowed – the default of all national legal systems – in principle no statements are required that fill the set of situations that are not illegal. A legal source is therefore incomplete and It means that a knowledge engineer has to reconstruct and reverse engineer the social domain some legal source is about. In the next section we will illustrate this principle for the domain of traffic.

2.1 Distinguishing Normative and World Knowledge: TRACS

"Can you develop a computer program that can check if the new traffic regulation (RVV-90) is consistent and complete?" This apparently innocent question, posed by a government agency concerned with traffic safety, SWOV [1], triggered a decade of research at our institute. The question is highly similar to the verification of software.

Different from a 'normal' text or a computer program, the individual articles have no semantic coherence. The individual articles in the RVV-90 refer to situations in traffic, but there is no (discourse) structure that connects the statements. Therefore, it will be hard to assess whether a regulation is complete. Viewed as a text, the RVV-90, and for that matter (almost) any regulation, is full of gaps as it is not intended that one statement can and should be related to a next one. This kind of incompleteness can only

---

[1] Stichting Wetenschappelijk Onderzoek Verkeersveiligheid; Foundation for Research on Traffic Safety.

be detected when one has reconstructed the model of the domain the legislator had in mind when drafting a regulation. Even then it is hard to assess whether the legislation covers all situations intended, because the intentions of a law are only in an abstract and incomplete way specified.

One may, for instance, observe that the RVV-90 does not talk about children, while they are the most endangered species in the traffic jungle. The question is whether these kinds of gaps are accidental (and non-intended), or due to the limited role of law, or whether there simply is no real gap. One may argue that children have insufficient control or understanding to 'obey' the law. Also: they are subsumed (implied) in the RVV-90 under pedestrian, etc. There are indirect ways to establish this covering or completeness. The first one is to use constraints (requirements, goals). One of the aims of the RVV-90 is to avoid collisions, i.e. if there is a collision, at least one participant should have trespassed at least one norm. The other one is to compare the same situation under two different codifications. For instance, the legislator has indicated in which respects the RVV-90 is aimed to be different (an improvement) from the previous version. At the end of this section we will elaborate on this issue.

If it is difficult to assess the completeness of a regulation, consistency is another problem, as can be illustrated by the first normative statements in the RVV-90:

Art 3.1 Vehicles should keep as much as possible to the right
Art 3.2 Two bicyclists may ride next to each other

Article 3.1 describes an obligation and 3.2 a permission to a subset of drivers: the drivers of bicycles. In fact, it is not so easy to see how 3.2 is an exception to 3.1. It requires some complex spatial reasoning ('right', 'next to') to see that the left-hand bicyclist violates article 3.1, because she leaves the right bicyclist between her and the side of the lane. [2] This exception is a normative conflict and therefore a logical inconsistency. This inconsistency can be repaired by applying meta-rules, such as the principles that provide priority to the more recent, the higher and the more specific norm.

Exceptions are intended. They are used to limit over-generalizations of more generic norms, in the same way as we still want to classify penguins under birds despite the fact that they lack one of the essential characteristics of birds: that they can fly. [3] There is a way

---

[2] In fact, the exception is even more subtle because the left-hand bicyclist is also held to keep still as much as possible to the right, i.e. the exception is not a license for this bicyclist to take any position in the lane next to the right-hand bicyclist.

[3] This is the typical example to illustrate the need for non-monotonic reasoning in normative (deontic) reasoning. However, this analogy between exceptional birds and normative exceptions does not necessarily imply that normative reasoning with exceptions is really non-monotonic. The conflict resolution, implied by the principle that a more specific normative statement overrides a general one, suggests so, but a closer look at what the conflict resolution means is that there is no retraction of beliefs of what is the case in the world. The case remains unchanged. It is only that there are conflicting normative qualifications about the case. The typical view in jurisprudence and AI & Law is that the conflict is resolved by putting priorities to applicable, conflicting norms: not to withdraw norms or facts about the case. Article 3.a is still valid for the left-hand bicyclist: she still has to keep as much as possible to the right. Despite this observation, most researchers assume that normative reasoning is non-monotonic because one has to 'withdraw' some conclusion (one of the two qualifications).

to get rid of normative exceptions without affecting the normative qualifications intended by the code [14]. We may be able to see exceptions as "not really inconsistencies" in law, but the problem remains that we cannot distinguish on formal grounds between intended and non-intended exceptions. In fact in the TRACS project [15, 16] we have found out that the RVV-90 contains many non-intended exceptions which are often hidden in the (implicit) normative structure of a regulation. We should add that normative conflicts, or more precise: "conflicts of disaffirmation" are not the only kind of inconsistencies that may occur in regulations. [17] also distinguishes "compliance conflicts". These conflicts are between mandatory norms (obligations and prohibitions) which are not jointly realizable. For instance, a bus driver may be obliged to keep the time-table, but at the same time speed-limits may prohibit him to be able to comply with the time-table norm.

TRACS is a prototype knowledge system aimed at verifying the Dutch traffic regulation RVV-90. TRACS is a kind of policeman that assesses all possible traffic situations the RVV-90 may distinguish. The situation generator (or recognizer) constructs a a combination of traffic participants and traffic actions on some configuration of roads. These situations are generated by an ontology that represents the definitions and axioms of the terms involved. This 'world' knowledge base allows one to infer, for instance, all possible spatial relations: e.g.

```
equivalent(left-of(car-A,bicycle-B),right-of(bicycle-B,car-A))
```

These were used to match with the set of regulations, coded in terms of the traffic ontology so that the legal consequences could be derived. The RVV-90 was never completely tested but in a long series of test trials many errors were found: the most notable one was the fact that the tram was not allowed to run on the tram-way (see [2] for all details). The essential issue here is that this ontology of traffic terms plus an ontology about spatial terms was sufficient to test the core of the traffic regulation. The major categories of this ontology were roles (drivers), vehicles, actions, and parts-of-road. The spatial ontology is a very simple, abstract one and consisted of axioms of terms of orthogonal directions and positions in a two dimensional world.

3   Ontological Commitments in Legal Theory

Legal theories usually contain elements of an ontology, but they are normally framed under some specific theoretical goal which lies beyond the ontology itself. For instance, Hart's theory intends to explain how legal systems evolve; Kelsen's goal was to demonstrate the difference between laws and morals; yet both propose very specific views on what competence is behind legal phenomena, and what primary concepts are used to represent law.

Kelsen. In his last work ('General Theory of Norms' [11]), Kelsen proposed four basic types of norms: command, empower, permit and derogate. Commanding norms command (prohibit, obligate) a certain behavior. Empowering norms associate roles with the power to posit and apply norms under certain restrictions. Permitting norms refer to what he called the positive sense of permission. Kelsen argued that we may permit behavior in the sense that this behavior is neither prohibited nor commanded, in which case we have a negative or *weak*) permission. In contrast, permitting norms use a positive sense of permission, in which behavior is actively allowed. Kelsen sees permitting norms as always an exception to a command, i.e. it occurs when there is a commanding norm about a certain behavior, and this command is then derogated by the permitting norm. Kelsen points out that the difference between commanding and prohibiting on the one hand, and permitting (positively) and empowering on the other, can be mapped onto the distinction between observing/violating and applying a norm. Only a norm which commands (or prohibits) a certain behavior can be observed or violated. Norms that permit or empower cannot be violated or observed; only applied or not. Finally, derogating norms "repeal of the validity of [...] another norm". Kelsen stresses that a derogating norm does not repeal another norm, but its validity: a derogated norm still exists, but it is no longer valid.

Hart. The Hartian distinction between *primary* and *secondary rules* (norms) has become a quasi-standard in legal theory. Hart's distinction, carefully detailed in his 'Concept of Law' [18], draws a line between a first level which refers to human behavior and a second, meta-level of the first, which contains knowledge *about* primary norms. These secondary rules may belong to three types: (i) rules of adjudication, that can be used to determine authoritatively whether a certain primary rule has been violated or not; (ii) rules of recognition which define, directly or indirectly, which rules are the valid ones, and can therefore be applied; (iii) rules of change, which define how rules are to be made, removed or changed. These distinctions point out three functions of secondary norms: to provide support for solving conflicts (adjudication), to specify the limits of the legal system (recognition) and to specify how the legal system can change in time (change).

Bentham. Bentham's theory is divided in two parts [19]. The first is a logic of imperation which uses four basic operators: commanded, prohibited, non-commanded and permitted.[4] These are in fact interdefined, resulting in only one of the four as primitive. The second part is a logic of obligations and rights in which he defines three primitive concepts: obligation, right to a service and liberty. These are also interdefined based on obligation, which Bentham sees as an obligation someone has to the effect that something (some state of affairs) occurs. Therefore, we are left with only two atomic concepts: commanded and obligation.

Hohfeld. Hohfeld's theory is considered a landmark in American jurisprudence [22]. An interesting (and unusual) aspect of Hohfeld's theory is that rights and other positional concepts that represent legal relations are considered primitives. There are two groups of interrelated legal relations or positions. The first group is composed by right, duty, no-right, privilege and has a strong normative flavor. These concepts are closely related to Bentham's concept of right, obligation and liberty. The second group consists of power, liability, disability and immunity. These concepts are more closely related to legal competences and legal responsibilities.

3.1 Legal Theory in AI and Law

There are a number of studies in AI & Law which have used ontological assumptions drawn from legal theory in the manner we propose in this article. Allen and Saxon

---

[4] A logic of imperation — an idea also mentioned by Austin [20] — was later developed in more detail by Hofstadter [21], but it is presently considered to be superseded by deontic logics.

(e.g. [23, 24]) have developed a 'language for legal relations' (LLR) in which they have transformed the Hohfeldian ontological primitives into about forty relations ('cascading propositions'), taking the notion of duty as primitive. Hamfelt [25] proposed and implemented a representation of legal knowledge in which Hart's primary and secondary rules were mirrored in meta-levels of a logic programming formalism. [1] has formalized normative legal knowledge mainly on the basis of legal theoretical concepts from Kelsen and Hart. This is also the perspective on legal normative knowledge we take here.

There is also work which has an ontological flavor, but which has not been based on legal theory. For example, McCarty's Language of Legal Discourse [26] can be seen as an ontology of Law, where his 'modalities' play the role of knowledge categories and are linked together with a formal (logical) presentation. Also, the research in deontic logics as a basis for normative reasoning sometimes uses ontological assumptions from or is applied to legal theory — see for instance [27, 28]. Kelsen's view on norms as descriptions of an ideal world can be seen the basis of deontic logic. Deontic logic provides interpretations for the terms 'obligation', 'prohibition' and 'permission'. Indeed some form of deontic logic is often proposed as a formalism for automated normative reasoning. Because (standard) deontic logic is intractable, and gives rise to pseudo-paradoxes, all kind of extensions and simplifications have been developed. In fact, [1] has shown that deontic logic does not make the necessary distinction between the normative status of a situation and the normative operator of a norm. By making this distinction a much simpler and tractable inference mechanism has been formally defined and implemented. Van Kralingen ([29]) uses the theory of Brouwer ([30]) as a starting point for what he sees as the core elements of law: norms, actions and (legal) concepts.

From this overview of legal theoretical studies we conclude that for over a century the main interest has been on the normative aspects of legal knowledge. [5] These studies deal with concepts like rights, permissions, obligations, etc. and their interrelations. However, this ontological perspective on the normative core business of law has resulted rather in epistemological views on legal reasoning, as exemplified in studies in deontic logics (e.g. [32]), than in a comprehensive view of what (categories of) concepts make up law (see also [33] for the way ontological and epistemological views are intertwined in views on normative knowledge.)

4   Knowledge Typing and Dependencies in Legal Reasoning: *ON-LINE* and *FOLaw*

Although the combination of world and normative knowledge makes up the resource for reasoning in legal domains, this is only part of the story. In the mid-90ies, André Valente constructed a core ontology that distinguished also other types of knowledge [1, 4]. This core-ontology, called *FOLaw*, served a number of purposes. The first one was to distinguish the various types of knowledge in legal reasoning, and in particular those types that are typical for legal reasoning. Related to this role it also explained the dependencies between these types of knowledge in legal reasoning. This typing and its dependencies could easily be translated into an architecture for legal reasoning: *ON-LINE*. The sec-

---

[5] A notable exception is the work by [31] on legal causation (see also [5] in this volume).

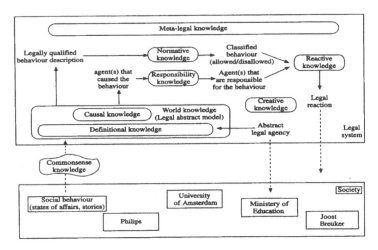

Fig. 1. FOLaw: a functional ontology for law [Valente, 1995]

ond role is the typical core-ontology role: to organize and index libraries of domain ontologies and to support knowledge acquisition to construct new ontologies.

The ontology is a functional ontology. This means that the roles the legal system plays in society are taken as point of departure. A legal-sociological view is taken, rather than a perspective from the law itself, as in most legal theoretical studies. There is a secondary notion of functional involved: *FOLaw* identifies the dependencies between the types of knowledge, which indicate the roles that types of knowledge play in the reasoning. These two views on 'functional' are not independent. One may see the reasoning as to some extent simulating the social roles, in the same way as reasoning about physical systems consists to a large extent of simulating physical processes.

We will give here a summary description of *FOLaw*. Figure 1 provides the comprehensive picture of dependencies of the various types of knowledge in legal reasoning. At the same time it also expresses the role of the legal system as controlling the actual social behavior of individuals and organizations in society.

4.1   *FOLaw*'s Types of Knowledge in Legal Reasoning

The major types of knowledge we have distinguished are *normative knowledge, world knowledge, responsibility knowledge, reactive knowledge, creative knowledge* and *meta-legal knowledge*

Normative Knowledge. Normative knowledge is the most typical category of legal knowledge, to such an extent that to many authors 'normative' and 'legal' are practically the same thing. The basic conception of norm used in the ontology is largely derived from [11]. A norm expresses an idealization: what ought to be the case (or to happen), according to the will of the agent that created the norm. This view on norms is a generally accepted one, but it should be noted that this view does not make norms different from any abstraction. A model is also an idealization with respect to reality. What has been easily overlooked is that the idealization is motivated by desirability; not by a match between model and reality. Norms limit possible behaviors and the assumption is that this subset of possible behaviors is a better world (from the perspective of politics). This implies also that this possible world is conceived in good correspondence with reality and that the norms refer to agent based activities that can be driven by intention, and not make wrong assumptions about physical and intentional processes.

Meta-Legal Knowledge. As stated above, we take the perspective that the law is defined on the basis of individual norms: e.g. individual articles in a regulation. The difference between the standard defined by the normative system on the one hand and the standards defined by the norms on the other hand is fundamental to understanding the role of normative knowledge in law, and it is accounted for by knowledge *about* individual norms. This distinction is captured by defining the categories of primary norms and meta-legal knowledge. Primary norms are entities that refer to agent caused, human behavior, and give it a normative status. This normative status is, in principle, either *allowed* (legal, desirable, permitted) or disallowed (illegal, undesirable, prohibited). However, each norm refers only to a few types of behavior, in the sense that it is only able to provide a status if applied to some types of situations (cases). For the remaining types of cases, the norm is said to be *silent*.

There may be a difference between the normative status given by a single norm and the one ultimately given by the normative system as a whole. Individual norms may conflict: if that is intended then some norm may be an exception to another norm. In order to solve these normative conflicts, meta-legal knowledge is applied. Typical conflict resolution is provided by meta-legal rules that state for instance that the more specific rule should be applied rather than a more general one: *"lex specialis derogat legi generali"* expresses this age old wisdom in law. Meta-legal knowledge is not only used for solving conflicts between norms. Another function is to specify which legal knowledge is *valid*. Validity is a concept which can be used both for specifying the dynamics of the legal system and its limits. A valid norm is one that belongs to the legal system (cf. [34]).

World Knowledge. By its very nature, law deals with agent caused behavior in the world. Therefore, it must contain some description of this behavior. For instance, in order to describe how the world should (ought to) be, norms must describe how things can be. In addition to adopting a category of legal knowledge which describes the world, we propose that this knowledge constitutes a structured model of some domain of law. For instance in a traffic act, the world of traffic is assumed to operate in a certain way, and the legislator may pose constraints – norms – on this behavior. A car may drive on all sides of a road, but the legislator (in most countries) obliges us to take the right hand side. Implicitly, the legislator has some model in mind of how traffic operates and can operate. The behavior in this world has to be modeled. This model is a generic one: how things (may) work, are done, or may be done in general if there are no normative limitations. In principle, the legislator has to foresee all possible types of situations and label these as allowed (desirable) or not. Thus, the term *legal abstract model* or LAM is used as a synonym for world knowledge when its model character is to be stressed.

The legal abstract model is an interface between the real world and the legal world. Its role is to define a model of the real world which is used as a basis to express normative and other categories of legal knowledge. The bulk of the LAM consists of definitions of concepts that represent entities and relations in the world, i.e. it is to be viewed as an *ontology*.

Apart from describing the world, what is behavioral reasoning used for in law? We propose that this description of possible and relevant behaviors is built around the concept of *cause*, in order to allow the assignment of responsibility of an agent for a certain case. Causal knowledge, however, refers or uses a static description of the world (e.g. to model world states). Accordingly, we propose that the world model is actually composed of two related types of knowledge: terminological or *definitional knowledge* and *causal knowledge*. The definitional knowledge (ontology) is used by the normative knowledge to describe the ideal world they define. The causal knowledge is used by the responsibility knowledge to describe who or what have caused a given state of affairs, and can thus be considered responsible for it.

Responsibility Knowledge. Responsibility is the intermediary concept between normative and reactive knowledge, since a reaction can only occur if the agent is held responsible for a certain norm violation. Responsibility knowledge plays the role of linking causal connections with a responsibility connection — i.e. that connection which makes an agent accountable for a norm violation and possibly subject to legal reactions (see also Section 4.1). As [31] point out, however, responsibility does not have "any implication as to the type of factual connection between the person held responsible and the harm" — that is, causal connections are only a "non-tautologous ground or reason for saying that [an agent] is responsible" [31–pag. 66]. There are two basic mechanisms which are used in responsibility knowledge. First, the law may establish a responsibility connection independent of a causal connection — i.e. a *responsibility assignment*. This can be seen in a rule used in e.g. French, German or Brazilian law, by which parents are held responsible for the the damage done by their children even if there is no specific causal link between their attitudes or actions and the damage. That is, the parents are held responsible even though they have not necessarily caused the damage. Second, the law may limit the responsibility of an agent under certain circumstances, disregarding some possible causal connections — i.e. a *responsibility restriction*. For instance, in England a man is not guilty of murder if the victim dies more than one year after the attack, even if the death was a consequence of this attack. Other well-known factors that may influence the establishment of responsibility connections in law are *knowledge* and *intention*.

We refer here further to the work of [3] (see also [5] in this volume) who has worked out the relation between (physical and agent) causation and the various notions of responsibility of law; Lehmann has specified this in a foundational ontology that defines the notions of causality and causation.

Reactive Knowledge. To reach the conclusion that a certain situation is illegal (based on normative knowledge), and that there is some agent to blame for it (responsibility knowledge) would be probably useless if the legal system could not react toward this agent. That knowledge that specifies which reaction should be taken and how is what we call *reactive knowledge*. Usually this reaction is a sanction, but in some situations it may be a reward. The penal codes, which are usually a fundamental part of legal systems of the Romano-Germanic tradition, contain basically responsibility and reactive knowledge only.

Creative Knowledge. A legislator may indirectly create some entity that did not exist before in the world, using what we call *creative knowledge*. It is usually stated in imperative terms, designating an agency that previously did not exist as part (or not) of the reality from a certain point of the time on. The creative function has a somewhat exceptional (or even abnormal) status if compared to the other ones. In this case, the law not only wants to classify or to react over certain agents that already exist in the real world, but attempts to create a new agent.

4.2   In Search of Ontological Foundations of Law

We have used the framework of *FOLaw* as a lead for fundamental research [35, 3], and as the basis for practical applications and architectures for legal reasoning (e.g., *ON-LINE* [4]). The CLIME project [6] was aimed at the construction of a legal information server. The try-out domain were international rules for safety and environmental care at sea, and the rules for ship classification (certification): in total about 15,000 different articles. This CLIME information server has two modes of operation. The first mode is typical information retrieval, where keywords (in phrases) are matched against terms in the rules. A large ontology (over 3,500 concepts) allows the elaboration of the keyword-terms by implied terms. The second, more expensive and experimental mode is in fact a question answering one. The CLIME system assesses whether a case, e.g. results of the inspection of a ship, or legal questions during the design of a ship, complies with the rules or not. The applicable (violated or 'potentially' violated) articles provide the justification and focus for the answer. An overview of CLIME and an evaluation of its results can be found in [36]. Other applications of the *FOLaw* framework (annex architecture) are reported in [37] (PROSA, a training system for solving legal cases); in the KDE project [7] the ontologies of CLIME have been re-used [38].

These results about the use and re-use of *FOLaw* also show its limitations. In developing the legal domain ontologies it turns out that the major effort in modeling is in the world knowledge. This is not surprising, given that the initial analysis about the content of legislation as in the TRACS project already revealed that world knowledge is the driving force in legal reasoning systems. More theoretically, it appears that law does not have its own ontological foundation. When legal philosophers discuss the ontological assumptions in law and legal reasoning, it is invariably about normative knowledge. This is different from other knowledge based fields of practice like medicine [39] or engineering [40], which have abstract ontological foundations in notions about physics, mathematics, etc. Jurisprudence and legal philosophy are primarily concerned with the *justification* of law and legal systems, rather than the *explanation* of the working of law and its relation to social reality. This is not to blame jurisprudence. The explanation of

---

[6] CLIME was an European project (IST 25414, 1998-2001): see http://www.bmtech.co.uk-/clime/index.html).

[7] KDE, for Knowledge worker Desktop Environment is a European IST project (IST 28678,1999-2001); see www.lri.jur.uva.nl/kde).

social reality is the concern of sociology, political and management science, etc. Explanations are models and these are grounded in ontological commitments. However, justification –which is derived from the term *ius* (law)– is the domain of epistemology; the study of what we can know and believe.

4.3 Epistemological Frameworks and Ontologies

Epistemology is about reasoning, argument and evidence, while ontology is concerned with modeling and explaining the world. Therefore, it is no surprise to see that 'core ontologies' about law are rather epistemic frameworks [41, 42]. [3] and [33], who make the same classical philosophical distinction between epistemology and ontology, construct 'ontologies' that mix both ontological and epistemological entities. In [43] we argue that this mixing up is theoretically not very clean, but the practical consequences may be a limitation of re-use and problems in interoperability. We want to maintain this classical distinction between ontology and epistemology. Epistemology is concerned with valid reasoning to arrive at justified conclusions. Of course, this reasoning is dependent on content: on the understanding (modeling) of the world, so the relationship is very intimate. However, the relationships between concepts is different from a perspective of ontology than from a perspective of epistemology. Typical epistemological terms, like hypothesis, evidence, conclusion, data can be reified as concepts in an ontology, but the epistemological relations are different. For instance, by using evidence on the basis of data a hypothesis may be confirmed and lead to a conclusion. So there are dependency relations between these reasoning states and these dependencies constitute argument structures or problem solving methods. However, this is not the way these terms are related in an ontology. Hypothesis and conclusion are roles in a problem solving method, while (empirical) evidence is a relation between states of a problem, as conveyed by these roles, and data. The backbone structure of an ontology consists of subsumption and mereological abstraction hierarchies, while epistemological structures are built from dependency and consistency relations between problem abstractions and data abstractions. Therefore *FOLaw* is rather to be viewed as an epistemological framework than as a core structure of legal ontologies. It can easily be re-written as a high level CommonKADS inference structure, as can be found for instance in [44]. [8]

5 Ontologies for Reuse: *LRI-Core*

If *FOLaw* is not sufficiently detailed and is rather an epistemological framework, there is a need for a new approach for constructing a core ontology for law. *FOLaw*, based upon notions of Kelsen, Hohfeld and Hart, has shown us two distinctive sets of concepts that are typical for law. (1) normative terms (and their definitions and axioms), and (2) responsibility terms (liability, guilt, causation, etc), which confirms what we have found in legal theory. An ontology of normative terms has been worked out by [1]. A foundational ontology that relates responsibility issues to agent– and to physical causation has

---

[8] It is curious to note that the first two authors of this article have worked on the design and content of this CommonKADS PSM library, but have not noticed this close formal correspondence.

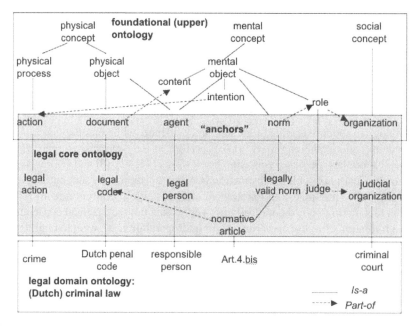

Fig. 2. LRI-Core layers: foundational and legal core share 'anchors' (high level concepts typical for law)

been constructed by [3]. Responsibility and norms may be notions that are typical for law, but they are not exclusive for law. The research of [45] (see also [46], this volume) shows that the terms of French law cannot be distinguished from common-sense terms, on the basis of statistical clustering methods. In other words, it appears that the law does not have a specific vocabulary, as is the case in other professional domains. If it is hard to find terms that are exclusive for law, we may be able to find terms that are still typical for law. The law is aimed at social activities. That means that notions of role, social position, and other social relationships and actions, in particular communicative ones, play a dominant role in domains of positive law. Property relationships, damage, individuality are some other recurring themes in law. Also law relies heavily on documentation and procedure. However, these typical, but not exclusive concepts in law are founded deeply in *common-sense*. That means that for modeling and understanding some legal domain we should be able to include notions about agents, actions, processes, time, space, etc, i.e. some foundational ontology appears to be indispensable on top of a core ontology of the *typical* legal terms, because the concepts of law are spread over almost the full range of common-sense. This means that a core ontology of law that covers these concepts that are typical for law should be grounded in some foundational ontology. Figure 2) sketches how *LRI-Core* is a legal specialization of some highly abstract common-sense concepts. In this section we will explain the perspective from which the common-sense grounding of *LRI-Core* is constructed, and present an overview of the main conceptualizations. In Section 6 we show how *LRI-Core* is applied to an ontology of (Dutch) criminal law.

We could not simply start with one of the currently available foundational or "upper" ontologies (e.g. Sowa's [47],or the IEEE-Standard Upper Ontology (SUO) [9] [48]) because their focus is rather on describing the physical and formal-mathematical world: not the social/communicative world which is more typical for law. These ontologies are 'revisionary' in the sense that they take ontology to represent our modern, scientific and formal insights as a point of departure, which is divergent from the 'naive' or 'folk' theories that make up common-sense. The upper part of the CYC [10] ontology and DOLCE [49, 50] are claimed to have a common-sense view, but this common-sense view is rather arbitrarily based upon personal intuition than on empirical evidence. For the construction of *LRI-Core* we have been inspired by results from studies in cognitive science: in particular evolutionary, neural and developmental psychology. Examples of how empirical evidence may support 'revisions' or 'folk' conceptualizations, are the following. In *LRI-Core* we will present in this section, space has two different meanings: 1) it refers to the *size* (extension) of physical objects, and 2) it refers to *positions* in space. This distinction is reflected by neural activation of different parts of the cortex [51]. On the other hand, contrary to common-sense wisdom, neurological evidence shows that we act before we decide to act in many circumstances, cf. [52]. This finding is so contrary to our common-sense intuitions that it would take a major overhaul of our folk psychology to make this part of our common-sense. However, common-sense is not an evolutionary given and fixed collection of conceptualizations: cultural revisions occur. For instance, although the notion of energy was introduced in physics just over a century ago, over the years it has become an undeniable part of our common sense conceptualizations. Another reason for not starting from already available foundational ontologies is that these do not very well cover the concepts typical for law such as roles, mental objects and processes, documents, social and communicative actions, etc. Extensions of DOLCE do, as one can see in the article by Gangemi *et al.*} in this volume, but DOLCE was not available yet when we started development of *LRI-Core*. Moreover, like all other researchers in this area (and philosophers over the ages), we did not agree with the solutions proposed by these ontologies. The disagreement is not only due to a lack of grounding in evidence about common-sense distinctions. We also made a number of design choices which are different from other foundational ontologies. Some of these are:

- We do not make the distinction between 'perdurant' and 'endurant' entities as in Sowa's ontology and in DOLCE. In principle all concepts are endurants, i.e. all concepts are 'timeless'; all instances are perdurants (occurrences).
- Mental concepts are not "non-physical" concepts (DOLCE); the mental world is an analogon of the physical world with an intentional perspective.
- Energy is virtually absent in other ontologies. In *LRI-Core* it plays an important role in defining mental and physical processes.
- The notion of role covers in *LRI-Core* most social concepts, where in other ontologies role is rather a relationship (Sowa) or

---

[9] http://suo.ieee.org, A merged version of these ontologies, called SUMO, is available at http://ontology.teknowledge.com/

[10] www.cyc.com

The foundational layer of *LRI-Core* is not meant to be a fully worked out stand-alone foundational ontology. It contains relatively few concepts: we expect no more than about three-hundred concepts. Only those concepts that have a legal significance are fully worked out (the 'anchors' in Figure 2). The other concept are intended as a coherent coverage. *LRI-Core* is currently still under active development, it is expressed in OWL-DL, using the OWL-Plugin of Protégé [11]. A first version of *LRI-Core* has been developed and used to support knowledge acquisition in the e-Court project (see Section 6). In the next subsection we will present a short overview of *LRI-Core*.

5.1   Principles and Main Categories of *LRI-Core*

The top of *LRI-Core* consists at the moment of five major categories: each referring to a 'world'. These five are: physical and mental concepts, roles, abstract concepts and terms for occurrences. Most likely we have to add a sixth category: life (see below). These categories follow from an assumed evolution of human (and animal) conceptualizations of reality. Primary conceptualizations are inspired by moving and sensing, i.e. real-life interactions with the *physical* world. The complexity of this causal world is reduced when we take a 'teleological' stance with respect to life, in particular on living organisms of the same species. A teleological or intentional stance implies that the actions of agents are assumed to be motivated by goals. Teleological reasoning works 'backward', i.e. it allows reasoning from end-states (goals) to current states. This is less complex than the branching of possible worlds in causal, forward reasoning. Living creatures seek the maintenance and reproduction of life.

As human beings (and to some extent other higher mammals as well) discovered their own *mental* life, i.e. consciousness and self-awareness, the need arose for models of mental processes and objects. Awareness not only enables us to handle our own reasoning and emotions, but also to understand those of our fellow creatures in order to plan social activities and to communicate. Self-awareness enables 'reification', the building of metaphors that makes up *abstract* conceptualizations. These considerations convinced us that the mental world can be conceived as an intentional metaphor of the physical world, i.e. our mental life is made up of objects and processes. The categories we use to understand our own and other people's mental events mirror those of the physical world. The emergence of conscious planning and prediction of behavior has led to the conceptualization of *roles* that make up social organization. *LRI-Core* has thus been equipped with the following main categories: *physical, abstract* and *mental* concepts, and *roles* [12]. Finally, *LRI-Core* knows about a fifth category: *occurrences*. Strictly speaking, occurrences are not part of an ontology, as we will explain below. Figure 3 presents the top two layers of the ontology.

Occurrences. An ontology should not be structured according to the *way* things occur in physical, mental, or fantasy worlds, but rather to *what* the things 'essentially' are.

---

[11] See http://protege.stanford.edu

[12] One may argue that we have omitted another major category: life, or rather agent hood. Indeed, the distinction between non-living physical objects and living ones (agents) is crucial in common-sense. We have not (yet) investigated this category.

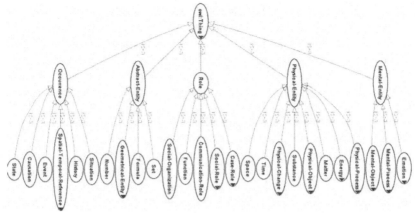

Fig. 3. LRI-Core, top two layers

Ontology has a Platonic flavor in the sense that it specifies the ideas with which we understand a/the world as it passes by. Making sense of the world means that we build models of current, past, and even to some extent, future situations. The structure of entities occurring in a world is different from the (abstraction) structure of generic concepts that make up an ontology. The concepts defined in an ontology enable us to recognize entities and their relations as they occur in the world. A simple example may illustrate this distinction. A functional ontology of furniture may distinguish as major categories objects one can sit on (chairs, banks); objects one can put objects on for immediate access (tables, desks), and objects for storing objects (cupboards, shelfs). So far so good, but the furniture in my room does not exhibit this structure at all. The structure to capture is in the first place a spatial one, i.e. dealing with positions. The distinction between these two views on furniture is not simply the distinction between instances and concepts, as one may imagine the generic spatial structure of a typical office versus a typical living room. Again, these structures, or rather frameworks or models, are different from those in an ontology of furniture. Note that we have met already another kind of framework: the epistemological ones, which we wanted to distinguish from ontologies in Section 4.3. In principle, as argued above, in a clean ontology there is no place for frameworks or generic models. Both can be part of a knowledge base, but for purposes of clarity and re-use one would like to keep them apart.

Ontologies define and deliver the building blocks for the construction of interpretations of actual situations and histories: partial models of real or imaginary worlds. Histories describe the life line of individual entities, and situations are diachronic spatial structures of objects and processes. The distinction between situation models and the concepts we use to identify the elements (parts) of situations, is obscured in ontologies that make a fundamental distinction between occurrents (perdurants) and continuants (endurants) (e.g. Sowa, DOLCE). Perdurants are entities that have parts that change with time or place. "For example, the first movement of the (execution of) a symphony is a temporal part of it." ([53–p. 20]. Indeed the execution of a symphony has temporal parts, but the concept of symphony itself has not. One may hold that all entities (instances, individuals) that exist are perdurants. Even a stone, a typical 'endurant' in these ontologies is in the execution of its life-line also perduring. Originally part of a rock, a stone may end up as sand on a beach, gradually spreading its parts spatially. However, when we take the concept of first-movement-of-a-symphony, or (pars-pro-toto) a symphony, there is nothing of temporal parts, even if the score represents a temporal sequence. The notion of symphony, once created, remains an 'eternal' concept. It does not differ from our notions of a process or a physical object. Strictly speaking, all entities in situations are endurants; all concepts are perdurants.

The distinction between a concept and its occurrence is particularly relevant where mental concepts (here: entities) get executed. For instance, plans, norms and roles and their execution (respectively, their observation) may show divergences that can be marked as 'bad' or even illegal. A divergence can only be identified if a mental plan, norm or role still exists so that it can be compared with actual behavior (or its memory or recording).

The category of occurrences in *LRI-Core* captures those strictly temporal aspects related to the *execution* of scenarios involving objects and processes. This means that events are occurrences, but processes are not. Where processes contain the explanation of the changes they cause, events only describe a discrete difference between the situation before and after the event took place: they describe the input-output of the execution of a process, and happen 'in' time. All this does not reduce the need for terms to talk about occurrences in general. For instance, above we have used terms like situation, event, history and entity. These terms refer to occurrences in an abstract sense that can legitimately be part of an ontology that defines concepts. Therefore, LRI has a category of 'occurrences'.

The distinction between real occurrences and ontology is reflected in a major distinction in human memory. Psychological research has identified two types of 'declarative' memories. The distinction between semantic memory and episodic memory is well established (see e.g. [54]). Semantic memory corresponds with our knowledge about the world, i.e. ontology; episodic memory contains memories of events (occurrences). Semantic memory emerges in child development earlier than episodic memory: we have to know before we can understand events and situations.

Physical Entities. The physical world evolves around two main classes: physical objects and processes. Objects are bits of matter, which in turn is typed by its substance. Objects have mass, extension, viz. form and aggregation state (limiting form). The existence of objects expresses the notion that matter (in particular solid matter) is what renders the physical world relatively stable and observable. Physical situations are usually described by the arrangement of instances of physical objects.

This intuition does not exist for the second major class that governs the physical world: process. Processes consume energy to change objects, or parts of objects. Though energy is a naively problematic concept (See [55]), its use has become widespread to such an extent, that it has conquered its place in common sense. Particularly the fact that electricity can be converted in many types of energy has enabled the common acceptance of this 'revisionary' concept. Processes are described by the changes they bring about. Change is an inherently temporal concept, belonging to the realm of occurrences. Through interaction, processes can cause one another, leading to series of events that only stop at some equilibrium: in general conceived as that there are no interactions at all. In *LRI-Core*, processes are typed according to two views: (1) formal change (transformation, transduction and transfer) and (2) the kinds of (properties of) objects involved. (e.g. movements are the change of position of objects; chemical processes change the substance of objects, etc.). A third property is whether a process produces or consumes energy; the default is the latter.

The concept of process is often used as synonymous to action and activity. LRI-Core defines actions as processes that are initiated by an agent acting as actor. Notwithstanding the intricacies of mental (or agent) causation ([56]), the action itself is strictly physical: i.e. some muscle movement. The mental perspective implied by agent-causation is that actions are intended: they are preceded by some kind of intentional decision to act. Many ontologies use the term process to cover both processes and actions. Business processes, to give an example, consist of actions. By abstracting out the agents one may see the work in an organization as anonymous processes, but they do not exhibit the same causal gluing as in physical processes. For instance, business processes are planned and controlled, i.e. initiated by (supervising) agents. The analogy for planned activities is the causal design of a device. Devices funnel causal chains of processes in such a way that they exhibit intended behavior, expressed as the functions of a device.

Mental Entities. Conceptions of the mental world have a strong analogy to the physical world. We conceive the mind as consisting of (mental) objects, like concepts and memories, which are processed by mental processes that transform or transfer these objects. Memories are retrieved; concepts are formed. Moreover, these mental objects may be aggregations of more elementary objects. Memories consists of multi-media representations of situations experienced; thoughts are made of more elementary parts like concepts.

The contents (substance) of these objects are representations. The conceptual content of thoughts is intended by propositional attitudes, like belief, desire, norm etc. Mental objects are processed or stored in containers (such as the mind) which in turn can have parts, e.g. memories. Mental processes like thinking, memorizing, imaging are operations on mental objects. The equivalent of physical energy in mental processing is the concept of emotion: the forces that make us focus our mental energies.

There is however, an important difference between the mental and the physical. Where physical processes are governed by causation, mental processes are controlled by intention. If that is the case, we would rather use the term 'action' for these processes. Thinking is thought to be an action, as we assume that we have full control over our thoughts and can decide about what we are thinking. However, where our mind escapes our conscious intentions, as e.g. in getting in uncontrollable emotional states, or in forgetting an appointment, we rather take a physical than an intentional stance. Despite this subtle difference, we keep the term mental process to cover both, as we want to reserve the term action for agent-caused processes.

The outcome of a mental process can be the intention to act, for instance according to a structure of primary actions: a plan. These actions can be aimed at bringing about both physical and mental changes, e.g. changing the mental state of another agent. Such intended mentalistic actions are acts of communication (which also need some physical medium to transfer the intended mental state). Speech act is the most common of these actions.

The role of mental conceptualizations is extremely important in understanding and communicating with other people. Their primary use lies in their role as building stones of models of the minds of other people: user-models. The intentional stance means that we attribute intentions and intention directed mental processing and belief to other people and to some extent animals (or even computers, [57]).

Roles. Roles cover functional views on physical objects (devices), on agent behavior or on mental processes. In particular, social behavior and social organizations are explained as (consisting of) roles. Typical mental roles are epistemological ones. For instance conclusion, evidence and hypothesis are roles in problem solving processes and can therefore also be categorized under mental classes [58]. From a role perspective, functions are roles of physical objects, e.g. we may use objects for non-intended functions.

Roles are entities in the mind, they do not 'really' exist. Roles are idealizations: we may not play a role correctly. An important distinction should be made between playing a role and the role itself: "agents can act, and roles cannot" [59]. Correcting incorrect role playing does not mean that we change the role: we change our behavior. Like plans and processes, roles in ontologies are often confounded with their execution, in the same way as the execution of a symphony may be confounded with the symphony itself. The original meaning of the term role refers to a role of paper that contained the text of an actor in a play. Also the role-taker (some agent) and the role are often confounded, which may become obvious when we identify a role with a person. These kinds of confusions have made conceptual modelers aware of the tricky issues about roles (see e.g.[60]).

Roles are often viewed as relationships ([47, 60, 61]). Indeed, social roles have mutuality and complementarity. No students without teachers; no parents without children; no speakers without hearers, etc. In theory of law, a related view exists about the mutuality of legal positions: i.e. rights and duties [22, 11]. For instance, if citizens have the obligation to vote, the government has the duty to enable this voting. Nevertheless, this complementarity of roles might not be of enough importance to grant their representation as relationships in an ontology. The ontology may specify such relationships, but the primary notion of role is as a concept.

This becomes clear when we look at roles as concepts, i.e. at what roles *mean*. Roles are behavioral requirements on role execution and on qualifications of role taking. These requirements are prescriptions, i.e. they are normative. In modern society many roles have formal requirements enforced by *law*. Legislation addresses actors by the roles they play [13]. If actual behavior deviates from the norms attached to these roles we violate the law. Violations are based upon the distinction between the prescription (role) and role performance. Therefore, in court, it is the actor of the role who is made responsible: as a person; not as a role. Even the fictitious concept of legal-person for social organizations turns into concrete responsibilities of the liable persons who have mis-performed their roles.

Abstract Entities. As all concepts are abstractions, one may argue that a separate abstract world is difficult to see. However, common sense knows about a (small) number of proto-mathematical concepts, such as collections, sequences and count-numbers (positive integers). We know about geometric simplifications such as line, circle, square,

---

[13] An exception to this rule is in criminal law.

cube, etc. [62] even argue that these common sense notions are the real roots of our mathematics. Nonetheless, these kind of semi-formal abstractions do not play a very central role in law, and therefore *LRI-Core* is thinly populated with abstract classes.

The role of the concepts defined in *LRI-Core* is illustrated in the next section, where we present fragments of an ontology of Dutch criminal law, as developed in the e-Court project.

6   An Ontology of Criminal Law: *OCL.NL*

The e-COURT project was aimed at the semi-automated information management of documents produced during a criminal trial: in particular the transcriptions of hearings. The structure of this type of document is determined by the debate/dialog nature of these hearings, but also by specific, local court procedures. Besides tagging its structure, it is also important to identify (annotate) content topics of a document. These vary from case descriptions (e.g., in oral testifying) to topics from criminal law (e.g., in the indictment).

The case descriptions have a strong common-sense flavor, but the legal professionals who are the main intended users are primarily interested in the (criminal) legal aspects of a case. We developed an ontology that covers Dutch criminal law, whose major structure we will discuss below. As the e-COURT solutions are aimed to work for most European countries, in principle one has to develop such an ontology for every jurisdiction that intends to use e-COURT. This Dutch ontology was intended to work as a reference for the development of similar ontologies of Italian and of Polish criminal law.

We can illustrate the use of 'anchors' in the *LRI-Core* ontology with parts of the ontology for Dutch criminal law (OCL.NL). In Figure 4 the boldface terms are terms from *LRI-Core*. *LRI-Core* knows about the distinction between a person as a lifetime identity and roles that a person may perform. Roles are taken by persons who are agents. Agents are both physical and mental objects: dependent on the context of use the physical or the mental properties of an agent are selected. This solution is more elegant than assuming that an agent has a body and a mind. That is the Cartesian solution. The two views on 'agent' correspond better with a more unified view of the identity of an agent [63, 64].

In Figure 5 a selection of typical legal roles in criminal (procedural) law is presented. In *LRI-Core* we distinguish between social roles and social functions. Social functions

```
agent
|     person
|     |     natural person
|     |     juristic-person
|     |     |     company
|     |     |     association
|     |     |     foundation
|     collection-of-agents
|     |     group
```

Fig. 4. Agents in Dutch Criminal Law (OCL.NL) (excerpt)

```
role
|    social-role
|    |    legal-role
|    |    |    juridical-role
|    |    |    |    judicial-role
|    |    |    |    |    judge
|    |    |    |    |    |    judge-presiding
|    |    |    |    |    prosecution-role
|    |    |    |    |    |    public-prosecutor
|    |    |    |    |    defense-role
|    |    |    |    |    |    defense-counselor
|    |    |    |    |    defendant
|    |    |    |    |    |    principal-defendant
|    |    |    |    |    |    accessory-defendant
|    |    |    |    |    |    offender
|    |    |    |    |    |    |    convict
|    |    |    |    |    witness
|    |    |    |    clerk-of-court
|    |    |    |    lawyer
|    |    |    |    the-Regent
|    |    |    |    the-State
|    |    |    public-servant
|    |    |    owner-of-goods
|    |    |    owner-of-rights/duties
|    |    |    |    creditor
|    |    |    |    debtor
|    social-organization
|    |    legal-organization
|    |    |    public
|    |    |    |    Ministry-of-Justice
|    |    |    |    courts-by-jurisdiction
|    |    |    |    |    criminal-court
|    |    |    |    |    administrative-court
|    |    |    |    courts-by-level
|    |    |    |    |    cantonal-court
|    |    |    |    |    court-of-appeal
|    |    |    |    |    Supreme-court
|    social-function
|    |    public-social-function
|    |    |    jurisdiction
|    |    |    |    public-prosecution
|    |    |    criminal-investigation
|    |    |    |    forensic-investigation
```

Fig. 5. roles and functions in Dutch Criminal Law (OCL.NL) (excerpt)

are external roles of organizations. Social roles make up the functional internal structure of an organization. In these figures we cannot show multiple classification, nor other relations between classes than subsumption. For instance, an organization has social

mental-object
| juridical-mental-object
| | legal-norm
| | judicial-mental-object
| | complaint
| | accusation
| | judicial-decision
| | | verdict
| | | | conviction
| | | | acquit
| | | | final-verdict
| | juridical-qualification
| | | deontic-qualification
| | | | deontic-legal-role-attribute
| | | | | right
| | | | | duty
| | | | | authority
| | | | deontic-modalities-of-norms
| | | | | permission
| | | | | obligation
| | | | | prohibition
| **reasoning-role**
| | **evidence**
| | | testimony
| | | | eye-witness-testimony
| | | forensic-evidence
| | **problem-solving-role**
| | | **solution**
| | | **problem**
| | | **problem-solving-method**
| | **argumentation-roles**
| | | **debate-argument-role**
| | | | accusation-position
| | | | defense-position
mental-process/action
| **internal-mental-processes**
| | **reasoning**
| | **communicative-mental-action**
| | testifying
| | interrogating   .
| | **argument**
| | **dialog**
| | | **dialogical argument**
| | | | dispute
| | | | | judicial-dispute

Fig. 6. Mental objects, processes and states in Dutch Criminal Law (OCL.NL) (excerpt)

functions and 'has-as-parts' social roles. This is not the only view on the composition of an organization. The hierarchy of authority is another one, but this hierarchy maps onto the roles: authority is a mental entity: to be precise a 'deontic-legal-role-attribute' Figure 6 presents some of the major categories of the mental world.

In this representation of the mental world we have skipped some views. Some mental legal objects, such as 'accusation' are in fact (illocutionary) acts. In legal discourse an accusation is really treated as an object, i.e. it is the (content; sometimes the literal surface structure) text that is referred to. However, its meaning is indeed the act of accusation, so it should inherit properties of mental objects and those of (illocutionary) mental actions. Legal procedures may objectify or 'reify' these actions.

Many objects of the mental world are reifications of epistemological roles. Terms like 'reason', 'evidence','explanation', 'problem', 'dispute' etc. come from the vocabulary of reasoning methods and are concerned with assessing the (trust in) the truth of (new) beliefs. As stated in the Introduction, law is particularly with justifying legal decisions, so roles in argumentation and reasoning play an important role in legal discourse in general. Note that these terms are not part of Dutch criminal law, except some global terms like 'evidence' and 'doubt'. We have added some because they occur frequently in court discourse.

The hard core of the OCL.NL consists of actions. There are two major types: the criminal actions themselves (called 'offenses'). These are of course the actions executed by the person who is successively acting as suspect, defendant, and eventually convict (if true and proved. . .). On the other side, the convict may be at the receiving end of the 'punishment' actions, that are declared by the legal system etc. Crime and punishment are the keys to criminal law that is synonym to penal law.

6.1   Use of Ontologies in Legal Information Retrieval

The ontologies of criminal laws are used in e-COURT to support the information retrieval of information contained in the hearing session documents. Criminal law is only part of the discourse in these sessions, but an important part. Another part consists of descriptions of 'what has happened' for which only full blown common sense (CYC) or superficial but extensive ontologies like Wordnet may play a role in information retrieval. Thus far we focus on the criminal legal terms, because the primary type of users are legal professionals.

In e-Court, two user modes of search are used: basic and advanced. The basic search mode allows meta-data and/or keyword search by specifying values for one or more meta-data fields and/or keywords. The advanced search mode includes possibilities to use linguistic weights and quantifiers with the keywords, to select the language of the query and the searched documents; to choose particular document sections of interest. In this subsection we describe the specific additional information management functions that are supported by ontologies.

Annotation and XML Tagging of Legal Documents. In information management the emphasis has been on archiving and retrieving documents by their formal, syntactic characteristics. These structures are abstracted in meta-data: RDBM schemas, DTDs for XML-tags, XML-Schemata, etc. This works fine as long as the structures are rather fixed and the occurrence of parts ('sections') is easy to identify in an automatic way. The criminal trial *hearing* documents in e-COURT are not the typical kind of documents that are handled by information systems. Hearing documents reflect in the first place oral, often 'spontaneous' **dialog** from the court room. The role of ontologies in indexing the e-Court hearing documents is threefold:

- The first role is an indirect one: the ontologies provide the structured vocabulary for meta-data descriptions and maintain consistent use and semantic distinctions. The XML-Schemata only provide 'syntactic', structural information, but the ontologies (expressed in OWL/RDFS) enable semantic coherence and verification.
- The identification of dialog-turns can be (almost) fully automated by the use of simple voice-recognition devices that have only to distinguish voice characteristics of the participants in the dialog. However, all other tagging of documents has to be done by hand by the transcribers of the hearing recordings. An ontology browser supports this activity.
- The e-COURT system indexes all documents. A number of these indexed terms correspond with terms of the ontologies. In this way we can link documents automatically with some semantics, i.e. one may gather what the document is about, which is functionally equivalent to (XML)-tagging the document with these

Query Expansion. The set of keywords used in a query can yield unsatisfactory results because the actual use of terms in a document may not correspond to what the user has in mind. This is obvious in the use of synonyms. However, also more abstract terms may be used to denote a more specific object: e.g. *killing* (synonym: *manslaughter*) for *murder*. A reference to a *murder* may be missed because in the document the terms *killing* and *manslaughter* are used. The reverse may also be relevant in information retrieval. The user may search for the *weapon* that is used in a particular criminal case, but may not know what kind of weapon exactly was used. By browsing a taxonomy of weapons (e.g. as part of an ontology of terms in criminal law) she may specify the query further. We have observed that users of legal information retrieval systems have a tendency to *under-specify* the cases they present. They do not provide all potentially relevant facts, and they use terms that are too general. Therefore the system may miss potential exceptions in the set of norms, and the user may deduce a wrong normative assessment of her case. Having a user interface that explicitly allows for specification of used terms may help. Another solution is to have the system return potential exceptions as well as norms that exactly match the case at hand ([34]). In both search modes (basic and advanced) the ontology repository is consulted for subsumed or subsuming terms with respect to the keywords given.

Expansion by Subsuming Classes By adding terms for searching that are superclasses of the already specified terms, the search is directed also to the more general, abstract terms. In searching documents that contain regulations (laws, statutes, contracts) where applicable provisions are often formulated in generalized and abstract terms, this IR strategy is in fact the only one to avoid false negatives (i.e. missed applicable provisions). In the CLIME project this strategy has been implemented [36].

Expansion by Subsumed Classes The example of the search for a *weapon* above shows the problem when the user is searching for a subclass of a term she may well know. There are two possibilities. The user may allow all subsumed terms to participate as keywords in the search (which may lead to an explosive return of candidates) or she may have already restricted the set of possible documents and have a look at those *weapons* that occur as indices of these documents. In fact, the example is typical for the kind of searches where one is looking for additional, very specific information that should answer a question.

Disambiguation of a keyword term is another role of ontologies in information retrieval. Classical ambiguity consists of terms that have different meanings but the same 'orthography'. Except for orthographic coincidences, most ambiguous terms in fact share meaning, besides their differences. Disambiguation occurs in the context of use and is a matter of 'degree'. There may be little ambiguity in the term *car* as an isolated term, but there is little overlap in what it implies between the mechanic's and the salesman's view of *cars*, even if they work for the same company. In ontologies persistent, but context (role) dependent ambiguity is represented as **multiple classification**.

Except for disambiguation and selective use of terms of subsumed classes, the additional terms are added as disjunctive keywords to the query set, which means that the set of documents that is returned – the *'result set'* – may have increased exponentially. One may find more correct returns, but one must be prepared for a large amount of false positives: the classical problem of information overload we try to avoid and for which the major web stakeholders (at least the W3C) see the solution in the semantic web technology. It appears there is not a free lunch at the web, nor at e-COURT that seeks the same solutions. There are two methods to cope with this problem. The first one is to have the user refine his query. However, this is often a problem because the user may not have enough information to do this.

A second solution consists of *(re)organizing the result set*. The typical problem in (WWW) information search is that the number of returned documents may be unmanageably large and heterogeneous. The cause of much heterogeneity is the fact that a term may have multiple senses/views. In particular, the legal (criminal) domain is full of multiple views as we explained in Section 6, so we expect that disambiguation may occur by not only matching the indices of the returned documents with the keywords, but also have a second filtering/clustering where we also match indices with associated terms in the ontologies, i.e. the *value(-class)* and other related terms in the ontologies.

7   Discussion and Conclusions

The research reported here covers a long period – about fifteen years – of a number of mid-size (European) projects. In this article we have only pursued and discussed the views and results related to the development of a core ontology that identifies the main concepts that are typical for law. This guided tour has revealed that in fact the law has only a few of those concepts. Legal theory, but also work in AI & Law indicate that the most typical ones are concerned with normative knowledge (deontic terms) and with notions about legal responsibility [3]. Already at the start of our investigations in the TRACS project that was about traffic regulations we found that by far the majority of terms referred to the common-sense world of traffic; the only exception were the already mentioned deontic terms. Does this mean that law is a typical common-sense domain?

The answer is 'yes' and 'no'. The 'no' is explained by the fact that the legal world knowledge (LAM, in terms of Valente's *FOLaw* [1]) is a filtered and adapted version of what may have started as a common-sense. It should be noted that we have not divided up law in the way it is universally conceived and taught at law school, where the first distinction is between private and public law, and public law covers such legal domains as administrative law and criminal law. In each of these domains of law one will find concepts that may have evolved from common-sense, but which have received a typical and exclusive meaning in law. Moreover, as in all domains of professional practice, new concepts may have been developed. The understanding and use of the current state of these legal-domain specific concepts is for instance what legal education is about. A major reason for the evolution of legal terms in specific domains of law is in the first place due to the fact that the power of law is limited: it cannot command the physical world (so what is desirable in law is always a subset of what is possible). Therefore, only those concepts and relations are object of law that can be affected by human conscious (and individual) intervention. A second reason is that common sense terms may get refined and redefined in such a way that they correspond better with principles of law. A third reason is that law transpires the views and goals of the recent and current politics.

Therefore it appears that within legal domains much common-sense is filtered, 'cleaned' and transformed into a layer only understandable and usable for legal professionals. However, this is only part of the story. The legal system needs a close correspondence between the common sense view of the world and its terminology. This is not only required for drafting legislation, but particularly for citizens to understand the law and for interpreting cases. Cases are accounts of what has happened and they are cast in narrative discourse: events that are connected by causes and intentions (reasons). Therefore, a mapping between legal and common-sense concepts has to be maintained. All this is to say that a core ontology for law in general has problems in covering this large area of world knowledge and has to resort in a first approach to common-sense foundational ontologies. We have also identified terms which are not exclusive, but still very typical and well elaborated for law: document, document-structure, role, etc. are central terms in law and may be grounded in a core ontology that imports these notions from a still high level and simple foundational (common-sense) ontology.

References

[1] Valente, A.: Legal knowledge engineering: A modelling approach. IOS Press, Amsterdam, The Netherlands (1995)

[2] den Haan, N.: Automated Legal Reasoning. PhD thesis, University of Amsterdam (1996)

[3] Lehmann, J.: Causation in Artificial Intelligence and Law: a modelling approach. PhD thesis, University of Amsterdam (2003)

[4] Valente, A., Breuker, J., Brouwer, P.: Legal modelling and automated reasoning with ONLINE. International Journal of Human Computer Studies **51** (1999) 1079–1126

[5] Lehmann, J., Breuker, J., Brouwer, P.: CAUSATIONT: causation in AI & Law. In: this volume. (2004)

[6] Breuker, J., Den Haan, N.: Separating world and regulation knowledge: where is the logic? In: Proceedings of the third international conference on AI and Law, Oxford, ACM (1991)

[7] Clancey, W.: Heuristic classification. Artificial Intelligence **27** (1985) 289–350

 [8] Patil, R.: Artificial intelligence techniques for diagnostic reasoning in medicine. In Shobe, H., AAAI, eds.: Exploring Artificial Intelligence: Survey Talks from the National Conferences on Artificial Intelligence. Morgan Kaufmann, San Mateo, California (1988) 347–379

 [9] Rector, A.: Medical informatics. In Baader, F., Calvanese, D., McGuinness, D., Nardi, D., Patel-Schneider, P., eds.: Description Logic Handbook. Cambridge University Press (2002) 415–435 http://www.cs.man.ac.uk/ franconi/dl/course/dlhb/dlhb-10.pdf.

[10] Raz, J.: Legal principles and the limits of law. The Yale Law Journal **81** (1972) 823–854

[11] Kelsen, H.: General Theory of Norms. Clarendon Press, Oxford (1991)

[12] Boer, A., van Engers, T.: A knowledge engineering approach to comparing legislation. In Wimmer, M., ed.: Proceedings of the Conference on Knowledge Management in E-Government, Springer (2003)

[13] Van Der Velden, W.: Coherence in law: a semantic and deductive explanation. In Brouwer, B., Hol, T., Soeteman, A., Van Der Velden, W., De Wild, A., eds.: Coherence and Conflict in Law, Deventer, Boston / Zwolle, Kluwer Law and Taxation Publishers / W.E.J. Tjeenk Willink (1992) 257–287 Proceedings of the Third Benelux-Scandinavian Symposium in Legal Theory, Amsterdam, January 3-5, 1991.

[14] Winkels, R., Haan, N.D.: Automated legislative drafting: Generating paraphrases of legislation. In: Proceedings of the Fifth International Conference on AI and Law, College Park, Maryland, ACM (1995) 112–118

[15] Den Haan, N., Winkels, R.: The Deep Structure of Law. In Prakken, H., Muntjewerff, A., Soeteman, A., eds.: Legal Knowledge Based Systems: The Relation with Legal Theory – Seventh International Conference on Legal Knowledge-based Systems Legal Knowledge-Based Systems, JURIX–1994, Koninklijke Vermande (1994) 43–54

[16] Breuker, J., Petkov, E., Winkels, R.: Drafting and validating regulations: the inevitable use of intelligent tools. In Cerri, S., Dochev, D., eds.: Artificial Intelligence: methodology, systems and applications. Springer (2000) 21–34

[17] Lindahl, L.: Conflicts in Systems of Legal Norms: A Logical Point of View. In Brouwer, B., Hol, T., Soeteman, A., Velden, W.V.D., Wild, A.D., eds.: Coherence and Conflict in Law, Deventer, Boston / Zwolle, Kluwer Law and Taxation Publishers / W.E.J. Tjeenk Willink (1992) 39–64 Proceedings of the Third Benelux-Scandinavian Symposium in Legal Theory, Amsterdam, January 3-5, 1991.

[18] Hart, H.: The Concept of Law. Clarendon Press, Oxford (1961)

[19] Bentham, J.: An Introduction to the Principles of Morals and Legislation. Athlone Press, London (1970) Edited by J. Burns and H. Hart.

[20] Austin, J.: The Province of Jurisprudence Determined. Weidenfeld and Nicolson, London (1954) edited by H.L.A. Hart.

[21] Hofstadter, A., McKinsey, J.: On the logic of imperatives. Philosophy of Science **6** (1939) 446–457

[22] Hohfeld, W.: Fundamental Legal Conceptions as Applied in Legal Reasoning. Yale University Press (1919) Edited by W.W. Cook, fourth printing, 1966.

[23] Allen, L., Saxon, C.: More IA needed in AI: Interpretation assistance for coping with the problem of multiple structural interpretations. In: Proc. of the Third International Conference on AI and Law, Oxford (1991) 53–61

[24] Allen, L.: The language of legal relations, RLL: useful in a legal ontology toolkit? In Visser, P., Winkels, R., eds.: Legal Ontologies: proceedings of the ICAIL-97 workshop. ACM, New York (1997) 47 – 60

[25] Hamfelt, A., Barklund, J.: Metaprogramming for representation of legal principles. In: Proceedings of Meta'90. (1990) 105–122

[26] McCarty, T.: A language for legal discourse I. basic structures. In: Proc. of the Second International Conference on AI and Law, Vancouver, Acm (1989) 180–189

[27] Alchourrón, C., Bulygin, E.: Normative Systems. Springer-Verlag, Wien (1971)

[28] Alchourrón, C., Bulygin, E.: The expressive conception of norms. In Hilpinen, R., ed.: New Studies in Deontic Logic. D. Reidel (1981) 95–124

[29] Kralingen, R.W.V.: Frame-based Conceptual Models of Statute Law. PhD thesis, University of Leiden, The Hague, The Netherlands (1995)

[30] Brouwer, P.: Samenhang in Recht: een analytische studie (coherence in law). Wolters-Noordhoff (1990)

[31] Hart, H., Honoré, T.: Causation in the Law. Second edition edn. Oxford University Press, New York (1985)

[32] McNamara, P., Prakken, H., eds.: Norms, logics and information systems; new studies in deontic logic and computer science, IOS-Press, Amsterdam (1999)

[33] Mommers, L.: Applied legal epistemology: building a knowledge-based ontology of the legal domain. PhD thesis, University of Leiden (2002)

[34] Winkels, R., Bosscher, D., Boer, A., Breuker, J.: Generating exception structures for legal information serving. In Gordon, T., ed.: Proceedings of the Seventh International Conference on Artificial Intelligence and Law (ICAIL-99), ACM, New York (1999) 182–189

[35] Lehmann, J., Breuker, J.: On defining ontologies and typologies of objects and processes for causal reasoning. In Pease, A., Menzel, C., Uschold, M., Obrst, L., eds.: Proceedings of IEEE Standard Upper Ontology, Menlo Park, AAAI-Press (2001) 31 – 36

[36] Winkels, R., Boer, A., Hoekstra, R.: CLIME: lessons learned in legal information serving. In Harmelen, F.V., ed.: Proceedings of the European Conference on Artificial Intelligence-2002, Lyon (F), Amsterdam, IOS-Press (2002)

[37] Muntjewerff, A., Breuker, J.A.: Evaluating PROSA, a system to train legal cases. In Moore, J., Redfield, C., Johnson, L., eds.: Artificial Intelligence in Education. FAIA-Series, Amsterdam, IOS-Press (2001) 278–290 ISSN:0922-6389, ISBN:1 58603 173 2.

[38] Jansweijer, W., Van Der Stadt, E., Van Lieshout, J., Breuker, J.: Knowledgeable information brokering. In Stanford, B., Kidd, P., eds.: E-bussiness;: key issues, applications and technologies. IOS-Press (2000)

[39] van Heijst, G., Schreiber, A.T., Wielinga, B.: Using explicit ontologies for kbs development. International Journal of Human-Computer Studies **46** (1997) 183–292

[40] Borst, P., Akkermans, J.M., Top, J.L.: Engineering ontologies. International Journal of Human Computer Studies **46** (1997) 365–406

[41] Van Kralingen, R., Visser, P., Bench-Capon, T., H, V.: A principled approach to developing legal knowledge systems. International Journal of Human Computer Studies **51** (1999) 1127–1154

[42] Hage, J., Verheij, B.: The law as a dynamic interconnected system of states of affairs: a legal top ontology. International Journal of Human Computer Studies **51** (1999) 1034–1077

[43] Breuker, J., Hoekstra, R.: Epistemology and ontology in core ontologies: FOLaw and LRI-Core, two core ontologies for law. In: Proceedings of EKAW Workshop on Core ontologies, http://sunsite.informatik.rwth-aachen.de/Publications/CEUR-WS/, CEUR (2004)

[44] Breuker, J., Van De Velde, W., eds.: CommonKADS Library for Expertise Modeling: reusable problem solving components. IOS-Press/Ohmsha, Amsterdam/Tokyo (1994)

[45] Lame, G.: Construction dÕontologie à partir de textes. Une ontologie de droit dédié à la recherche dÕinformation sur le Web. PhD thesis, Ecole des Mines, Paris, Http://www.cri.ensmp.fr/ (2002)

[46] Lame, G.: Using NLP techniques to identify legal ontology components: Concepts and relations. In: this volume. (2004)

[47] Sowa, J.F.: Knowledge Representation: Logical Philosophical, and Computational Foundations. Brooks Cole Publishing Co, Pacific Grove, CA (2000)

[48] Pease, A., Niles, I.: IEEE Standard Upper Ontology: A progress report. Knowledge Engineering Review **17** (2002) 65–70 Special Issue on Ontologies and Agents.

[49] Gangemi, A., Guarino, N., Masolo, C., Oltramari, A.: Sweetening WORDNET with DOLCE. AI Magazine **24** (2003) 13–24

[50] Massolo, C., Borgo, S., Gangemi, A., Guarino, N., Oltramari, A., Schneider, L.: The WonderWeb foundational ontologies: preliminary report. Technical Report Deliverable D17, version 2, ISTC-CNR (Italy) (2002)

[51] Pinker, S.: How the mind works. Penguin Books (1997)

[52] Wegner, D.: The Illusion of Conscious Will. Bradford Books, MIT Press, Cambridge, Massachusetts/London, England (2002)

[53] Gangemi, A., Guarino, N., Masolo, C., Oltramari, A., Schneider, L.: Sweetening ontologies with DOLCE. In Gomez-Perez, A., Benjamins, V., eds.: Proceedings of the EKAW-2002, Springer (2002) 166–181

[54] Tulving, E.: Concepts of human memory. In L.Squire, Lynx, G., Weinberger, N., McGaugh, J., eds.: Memory: organization and locus of change. Oxford University Press (1991) 3–32

[55] Hayes, P.J.: The second naive physics manifesto. In Hobbs, J.R., Moore, R.C., eds.: Formal Theories of the Common Sense World. Ablex Publishing Corporation, Norwood (1985) 1–36

[56] Kim, J.: Mind in a physical world: An essay on the mind-body problem and mental causation. In: Representation and Mind. MIT Press (1998)

[57] Dennett, D.: The Intentional Stance. MIT-Press (1987)

[58] Breuker, J.: Components of problem solving. In Steels, L., Schreiber, G., van de Velde, W., eds.: A Future for Knowledge Acquisition: proceedings of the EKAW-94, European Knowledge Acquisition Workshop, Berlin, Springer Verlag (1994) 118 – 136

[59] Pacheco, O., Carmo, J.: A role based model for the normative specification of organized collective agency and agents interaction. Journal of Autonomous Agents and Multi-Agent Systems **6** (2003) 145–184

[60] Steimann, F.: On the representation of roles in object-oriented and conceptual modelling. Data and Knowledge Engineering **35** (2000) 83–106

[61] Masolo, C., Vieu, L., Bottazzi, E., Catenacci, C., Ferrario, R., Gangemi, A., Guarino, N.: Social roles and their descriptions. In: Proceedings of Knowledge Representation Workshop. (2004)

[62] Lakoff, G., Núñez, R.: Where Mathematics Comes From. Basic Books (2000)

[63] Strawson, P.: Individuals: an essay in descriptive metaphysics. Routledge (1959)

[64] Damasio, A.: Looking for Spinoza. Putnam (2003)

Types and Roles of Legal Ontologies

Andre Valente

Knowledge System Ventures,
7707 Boeing Ave, Los Angeles, CA, USA
avalente@ksventures.com

Abstract. In this paper, we propose a number of basic types and roles of ontologies, and use them as a basis to analyze several legal ontologies in the AI
and Law literature. We discuss some dimensions in which to distinguish types
of ontologies, for example considering their level of structure. We propose five
main roles of ontologies in general: (a) organize and structure information; (b)
reasoning and problem solving; (c) se-mantic indexing and search; (d) semantics integration and interoperation; and (e) understanding the domain. We then
discuss example of works that have exploited each of these roles in the AI and
Law literature. Further, we discuss some of the consequences of using ontologies to play each of these roles in terms of the level of structure of the knowledge represented in the ontologies, the kinds of knowledge representation formalisms they use, and the reasoning methods they employ.

1 Introduction

There is a growing body of research and practice in constructing legal ontologies and
applying them to the law domain, as evidenced for instance by recent workshops on
Legal Ontologies [1,2]. The research area has been growing in importance in the last
few years, fueled by the rise of the Semantic Web as a source of legitimacy and as a
focus of applications. The Semantic Web can be seen as a challenging application of
existing techniques from Knowledge Representation and Reasoning, Knowledge
Engineering, etc..

Looking at that body of work, however, one would be forgiven for struggling to
understand how these works are connected. There are two main problems. First,
different authors mean different things by the term "ontology". As a consequence, the
ontologies proposed vary significantly in the way they are represented. These differences are significant in that they make it hard to compare different ontologies if they
have different types – like the proverbial comparison of apples and pears. A second
problem is that ontologies are used in very different ways. This makes their application also hard to compare or contrast.

In this paper, we will attempt to look at the practice of AI and Law and understand
what kinds of ontologies are built, how they are used, and how these uses determine
in part the type of ontology – which KR formalisms are used, how expressive or
structured the ontologies are, and what finds of reasoning are used. We will not try to
judge the value of the different choices, but instead focus on understanding the conse-

V.R. Benjamins et al. (Eds.): Law and the Semantic Web, LNCS 3369, pp. 65–76, 2005.

quences of these choices. In particular, we will try to show how certain choices in use or structure are connected to other choices in how the ontology is represented.

This paper is organized as follows. In Section 2, we discuss different meanings of the term ontology and focus on defining types of ontologies based on the way they are represented or structured. In Section 3, we outline a number of basic *roles* or *uses* of ontologies and discuss examples in the AI and Law literature of works that have exploited these roles. In Section 4, we discuss some of the consequences of using ontologies to play each of these roles in terms of the level of structure of the knowledge represented in the ontologies, the kinds of knowledge representation formalisms they use, and the reasoning methods they employ. In Section 5, we discuss related work, and in Section 6, we present our conclusions.

2 Ontologies and Types of Ontologies

The term ontology was borrowed from Philosophy, where it meant a description of the nature of being (a "theory of existence"). The meaning of the term in AI is not quite the same (and is closer in many ways to an epistemology). The most frequently quoted definition is "a specification of a conceptualization" [3], which is rather vague. AI practitioners in general (and AI & Law practitioners in particular) have a rather malleable view of what constitutes an ontology.

We have discussed in earlier works what we believe are the minimum requirements for something to be named and ontology [4,5]. However, the goal here is not to impose or defend any one such interpretation. Instead, our aim is to examine the practice of developing and using ontologies in AI and Law research to understand what types of ontologies are created, and how they are used.

To do so, we will introduce in this section some basic dimensions through which we can interpret and explain the different types of ontologies and their uses. Notice that while in this article we will apply these concepts to legal applications, the concepts apply to all work with ontologies in AI in general.

2.1 Ontologies, Knowledge Representations and Knowledge Bases

A key source of confusion in ontology discussions is the (lack of) distinction between ontologies, knowledge representations and knowledge bases. A knowledge base is some representation of terms (concepts, relations, etc.) in some formal language, usually logic. A knowledge representation is a one such formal language. The term ontology is normally not used for domain-independent knowledge representations (e.g., first-order logic), but instead for specialized, domain-dependent formal languages.

In practice, we have found that some researchers develop ontologies that are knowledge bases, while others use them as a knowledge representation or as a foundation for one. It can be argued that both are interchangeable, that is, given an ontology in knowledge base form (e.g., in Ontolingua [3] or KIF [6]) one could create a corresponding knowledge representation by creating commands to define each of the classes of things defined in that ontology. However, one key distinction is that an ontology as knowledge representation formalism implies the existence of some sort of specialized inference mechanism or calculus, which is not necessarily the case with knowledge bases (although these assume some generic reasoning mechanism e.g. first order logical reasoning).

Another related issue is that some claim that not all knowledge bases are ontologies, that ontologies are somehow special kinds of knowledge bases (or representations). That is certainly in the philosophical origin of the term –ontology meaning a theory of being or at least some specification of what can be found in a domain). This implicit characteristic is also found in the origins of ontologies in AI as mechanisms for knowledge sharing and reuse [3]. In these first papers, ontologies were assumed to be reusable and thus should be free of application-specific or reasoning-specific commitments. Unfortunately, as argued by Valente et. al. in [7] this is never the case. All ontologies are built with some application in mind, and their very usability depends on commitments that are biased towards the types of reasoning the ontology is supposed to support.

2.2 Knowledge Structure

Another important distinction to make about ontologies how much *structure* they contain. The term structure here means how many types of (formal) relations that are defined between terms, which is a measure of how many fundamental distinctions can be made. Ultimately, structure means complexity, both in the sense of computational or inferential complexity (more structured languages are harder to compute) and in the sense that the ontologies are richer entities.

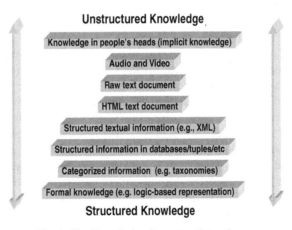

Fig. 1. The Knowledge Structure dimension

Valente and Housel [8] proposed a framework called KSS (Knowledge Structure and Services) as a way to analyze, compare, and select Knowledge Management tools. Part of the framework defines a *knowledge structure dimension* that shows the levels of formalization or structure in the ways knowledge is represented (Figure 1).

From top to bottom, we increase the formalization and precision of knowledge, while from bottom to top, we accommodate more informality and ambiguity. Knowledge forms towards the top end are relatively easy for people to create and update, while knowledge forms towards the bottom end demand more knowledge engineering and incremental analysis.[1]

The specific levels of knowledge structure shown in Figure 1 are relevant examples, rather than fixed layers – for instance, there are many levels of structure within the "formal knowledge" level. The reader should feel free to map/add other types of documents, knowledge bases, etc. to the list. The levels shown in the picture are, from the least structured to the most structured:

- *Knowledge in people's heads* is intrinsically non-formalizable – yet, many organizations rely on this kind of knowledge and the support of tools to find out who knows what where inside an organization.
- *Audio and video* contain multiple "streams" of knowledge such as music voices, faces and objects. Humans have a much easier time than machine in interpreting and indexing this kind of knowledge, but recent advances have been made to improve automated management of this type of knowledge.
- A *raw text document* is the formal equivalent of an audio track. Its complexity is comparable natural language, and it is hard for machines to process.
- In contrast, an *HTML document* with markup tags can display the texts' structure. Patterns and regularities in the document structure can aid in interpreting the content. For example, there are now tools that "wrap" structural patterns in HTML text into semantic descriptions. This can allow, for example, to discover based on placement inside a document that a certain HTML markup contains the name of a country, or the arrival time of a flight.
- *Structured documents* using formats like XML (or its ancestor, SGML) explicate the semantics implicit in HTML markups. For example, an XML document may contain a tag such as <country name> USA </country name> that indicates that "USA" should be understood as the name of country.
- The next kind of knowledge structure is *"tuples" of data*, the essence of information stored in databases. For example, databases may contain lists of relationships between countries and their populations. Most databases are made for efficient storage and retrieval of this kind of information, but as a result, they are usually unreadable by human eyes. Recently, there has been a trend to use XML documents as a readable form of databases. For example, a sequence of tags can contain a <population> tag inside a <country> tag to indicate a relationship between the country and its population.

---

[1] An interesting consequence of this trade-off is that we frequently encounter systems that index highly unstructured knowledge by building more structured descriptions of the content as "proxies" for the original content. For example, because it is very hard to recognize faces or voices directly, many tools that manage audio and video knowledge employ simpler forms of knowledge to index the content, such as keywords, categories or close-captioned text.

- *Categorized information* has roughly the same level as structured information in databases. Taxonomies such as the ones we use in biology are examples of categorized information. This kind of knowledge is used extensively by directory sites such as Yahoo to provide taxonomies of concepts, ideas or subjects.
- *Formal knowledge* is used here in the mathematical sense, meaning logical statements such as theorems and equations. This kind of knowledge can be used in a very rigorous way to make sure all semantics are explicit and rules are followed.

The way this dimension is useful to analyze ontologies is to recognize that different ontologies are more structured than others. Indeed, one can think of different expressions of the same ontology (or at least the same underlying conceptualization) in different levels of structure. For example, an ontology they can be expressed with progressively more structure in English, in an XML file, in a database schema (or even just a database), and finally to expressions in formal logic. This is important because there is a correlation between the use of the ontology and the level of structure used to express it, as well as between the level of structure and the formalism used to express the ontology.

3 Roles and Uses of Ontologies in AI and Law

We propose that five main uses or roles for ontologies can be identified: (a) organize and structure information; (b) reasoning and problem solving; (c) semantic indexing and search; (d) semantics integration and interoperation; and (e) understanding the domain. Below we briefly present each of these roles in general and discuss examples of legal ontologies that exercise that role.

3.1 Organize and Structure Information

The basic role of ontologies in this case is to organize and structure information in the domain. Ontologies here are tools to describe things or phenomena in the domain of interest. The ontology thus plays the role of *vocabulary*, answering two main questions: (a) which terms can be used? (i.e., ontology as a *lexicon*); and (b) which (valid) sentences can be expressed (i.e. ontology as a *grammar*) say?

In AI & Law, this role is shown in the use of ontologies to define legal vocabularies. These are typically used to define the terms used in regulations. In this way, the ontologies are not so much legal ontologies but representations of the world or domain the law is working on, e.g. taxes, crime, traffic, immigration, etc.

Two examples of this use are Gangemi, Sagre and Tiscornia's Jur-Wordnet ontology [9], an extension to the legal domain of the quasi-standard top ontology Wordnet [10], and Asaro et. al.'s Italian Crime Ontology [11], a schema for representing the vocabulary used in Italian criminal law.

3.2 Reasoning and Problem Solving

The basic role of ontologies in this case is to represent the knowledge of the domain so that an automated reasoner can represent problems and generate solutions for these problems. The ontology here works as the *structure of the knowledge base*. This use is found in the many expert systems (problem solvers) and decision making systems developed in AI & Law. Examples are Boer, Hoekstra and Winkels' CLIME Ontology [12], that is the basis for a legal advice system for maritime law, and Zeleznikow and Stranieri's ArgumentDeveloper [13], which was used (post-facto) in connection with several legal knowledge-based systems.

In using ontologies for this role, secondary goals are to create knowledge bases that are reusable, efficient, explainable, modular, etc. Indeed, one can argue that the use of ontologies in AI comes from research in the late eighties and nineties that aimed at improving knowledge engineering by attacking these roles by creating "well-structured" knowledge bases that would not only solve the problem at hand but be more maintainable, easier to extend, etc. In this sense, ontologies in this use are very much an engineering tool.

This role of ontologies implies the use of an *inference engine* that is used to conclude specific goals. An interesting problem that arises is the introduction of an *inference bias*. Valente et. al. [7] argue that ontological choices are strongly influenced by the purpose of the ontology. That is, the same knowledge will be structured or formalized differently depending of how it will be used by the reasoner in reaching the desired conclusions in a specific context. This indicates that reusability is a good idea, but it can never be accomplished completely. Indeed, we believe the inference bias is both *inevitable* and *positive*. It is positive because tailoring the ontology to its use privileges use before reuse. It is inevitable be cause no formulation will be completely neutral. Indeed, an example presented in [7] showed that correct logical definitions may not be computationally useful depending on the inference engine. Therefore, we are better off embracing rather than avoiding the inference bias, making it explicit as a design criterion in formulating ontologies.

3.3 Semantic Indexing and Search

The basic role of ontologies in this case is to represent the contents of documents or other "soft" knowledge sources (picture, movies, etc.). The ontology here works as a *semantic index of information,* that enables semantic search for content.

Law and legal practice produce vast amounts of knowledge in the forms of documents, charts, schemas, etc. There is a key need to organize and be able to find these documents. Ontologies can be used to represent and search semantically the content of documents – to go beyond word or keywords.

The traditional example that shows the need for this use of ontologies is the existence of multiple meaning of words – e.g., "sun" as the computer company or the star. Ontologies can be used to disambiguate these natural language meanings. Ontologies can also be used in a more intentional way, as a mechanism for creating annotations – i.e., allowing a person to semantically mark content so it can be found later.

An example of this use is the work of Benjamins et. al. [14], who created an application to retrieve FAQ questions about legal procedures that included an ontology-based interface for query and retrieval. Other examples include the work by Sais and Quaresma on using ontologies to query legal texts [15], and the work by Leary,

Vandenberghe and Zeleznikow [16] on an ontology for financial fraud that is used for representing financial fraud cases primarily for retrieval purposes.

3.4 Semantic Integration/ Interoperation

The basic role of ontologies in this case is to support applications to exchange information electronically. The ontology here works as an *interlingua* that defines a (narrow) vocabulary to be used to interchange information.

This use is less common in the legal domain, and unfortunately we have not found any articles relating this kind of work. We believe there is potential for this type of use in law enforcement, e.g., organizations exchanging information about criminals. There is also a lot of use in quasi-legal situations such as in complex systems in large bureaucracies that need to interoperate (e.g., the European Union). Since they can be seen as a semantic information schema, these ontologies may reuse parts of ontologies created for other uses.

3.5 Understand a Domain

The basic role of ontologies in this case is to provide a view of what a domain is about – to try to make sense of the variety of knowledge in that domain. The ontology here works as a *map* that specifies what kinds of knowledge can be identified in the domain.

This type of ontology can be used as a basis for designing specialized representations. Because it tries to get close to the nature of the domain, it frequently connects and draws from theories of that domain (e.g., theories of law). These types of ontologies have been called *core ontologies* [17].

An example of this type of ontology is the Functional Ontology of Law created by Valente and Breuker [4,5,18]. It defines a number of functional roles legal knowledge may play, namely (a) world knowledge, (b) normative knowledge, (c) responsibility knowledge, (d) reactive knowledge, (e) creative knowledge and (f) meta-legal knowledge.

Other notable examples of core ontologies of law are Mommers' knowledge-based model of law [19], McCarty's Language of Legal Discourse [20] and van Kralingen and Visser's Frame Ontology [21,22]. Core ontologies may also focus on a subset of law, for example Lehman's ontology of legal causality [23].

Some of these core ontologies are also used or at least designed for supporting reasoning and problem solving. For example, Valente's Functional Ontology of Law was used as a basis for a legal problem solving in the ON-LINE architecture [18]. Also, Viser's ontology was used in part for constructing the legal KBS FRAMER, that performs assessment tasks on the Dutch Unemployment Benefits Act [24].

3.6 Summary of Examples

Table 1 presents a summary of the examples of legal ontologies we used in this section.

Table 1. Summary of legal ontologies in the literature, their types and roles

Ontology or Project	Application	Type	Role
Valente and Breuker's Functional Ontology of Law [4,5,18]	General architecture for legal problem solving	Knowledge base in Ontolingua, highly structured	Understand a domain, reasoning and problem solving
Mommer's Knowledge-based Model of Law [19]	General language for expressing legal knowledge	Knowledge base in English, very lightly structured	Understand a domain
Van Kralingen and Visser's Frame Ontology [21,22]	General language for expressing legal knowledge, legal KBSs	Knowledge representation, moderately structured (also as a knowledge base in Ontolingua)	Understand a domain
McCarty's Language of Legal Discourse [20]	General language for expressing legal knowledge	Knowledge representation, highly structured	Understand a domain
Lehman, Breuker and Brower's Legal Causation Ontology [23]	Generally expressing causal legal knowledge	Knowledge base in English, very lightly structured.	Understand a domain
Benjamin et. al.'s ontologies of professional legal knowledge [14]	Intelligent FAQ system (information retrieval) for judges	Knowledge base in Protégé, moderately structured	Semantic indexing and Search
Lame's ontologies of French Codes [25]	Legal information retrieval	NLP-oriented (lexical) knowledge base, lexical, lightly structured	Semantic indexing and Search
Leary, Vandenberghe and Zeleznikow's Financial Fraud Ontology [16]	Ontology for representing financial fraud cases.	Knowledge base (schema) in UML, lightly structured	Semantic indexing and search
Saias and Quaresma's ontologies of legal texts [15]	Semi-automatic creation of ontologies from text	Lexical knowledge base in OWL, moderately structured.	Semantic indexing and search
Gangemi, Sagre and Tiscornia's Jur-Wordnet [9]	Extension to the legal domain of Wordnet	Lexical knowledge base in DOLCE (DAML), lightly structured	Organize and structure information
Asaro et. al.'s Italian Crime Ontology [11]	Schema for representing crimes in Italian law	Knowledge base (schema) in UML, lightly structured	Organize and structure information
Boer, Hoekstra and Winkels' CLIME Ontology [12]	Legal advice system for maritime law.	Knowledge base in Protégé and RDF, moderately structured.	Reasoning and problem solving.
Zeleznikow and Stranieri's ArgumentDeveloper [13]	Several legal knowledgebased systems	Knowledge representation, moderately structured	Reasoning and problem solving.

4 Consequences for Knowledge Representation Formalisms and Reasoning

There is a relatively close correspondence between the role or use of an ontology and its type, particularly the level of structure. In general, ontologies for reasoning and problem solving normally have moderately to highly structured ontologies. In contrast, ontologies used for semantic indexing and for organizing and structuring information have moderate to light structure. Interestingly, core ontologies (used for understanding a domain) vary considerably – some are highly structured and some are very lightly structured. This is in part because some of these ontologies are meant as theoretical exercises (sometimes of a philosophical or legal theoretical nature), while others are designed to be a basis for applications. Naturally, the more theoretically-oriented ontologies (e.g. Mommer's [19] or Lehman's [24]) have less structure than the ones used for applications. Another way to look at this relationship is that the core ontologies built with application bias really have a mixed use: they are moth core ontologies and ontologies for reasoning and problem solving (for instance, that is explicitly the goal of Valente's Functional Ontology of Law [4,18]).

As one would expect, there is some relation between the type of ontology (and its level of structure in particular) and the representation language used to encode it. Lightly structured ontologies are frequently represented as trees, taxonomies, fact assertions (e.g., in RDF), sometimes even in English (e.g., Mommer's Knowledge-based Model of Law [19]). In contrast, highly structured ontologies are represented using formal knowledge representation languages, usually based on first-order logic, description logic, or frames, such as Ontolingua, DAML, OWL, KIF and Protégé.

However, we found out that the use of a formal KR language does not necessarily mean the ontology is highly structured, since one can use very little of the representation power of such languages. That is, it is possible to use a description language such as OWL or Protégé but only use class inheritance relationships, in practice constructing a simple taxonomy. For example, Jur-Wordnet [9] is represented in DAML but has no logical descriptions and instead largely relies on assertions in RDF using a handful of relations.

For this reason, there is little correspondence between the KR language used and the type of reasoning adopted – when the KR language is an overkill very few (if any) of its reasoning mechanisms are actually used. Also, KR languages are frequently used without the use of corresponding reasoners. Indeed, some of the most frequently used languages (Ontolingua, Protégé) do not have readily available reasoners.

In contrast, there does seem to be a close correspondence between the level of structure of the ontologies and the types of reasoning employed. Lightly structured ontologies frequently use only simple inheritance or taxonomic reasoning, with is-a relations. Moderately structured ontologies sometimes use mechanisms such as class or frame reasoners, and simple class reasoning. Highly structured ontologies tend to use more of the full arsenal of first-order and description logics, such as instance classification and rule-based reasoning.

5 Related Work

Several other authors attempted to draw distinctions of types of ontologies or roles of ontologies. For example, Davis et. al. [26] discussed roles of knowledge representations. He proposed five roles. First, a knowledge representation is a surrogate, a mechanism we use to reason about the world instead of acting directly upon it. Second, it is a set of epistemological commitments, i.e., a specification of the terms in which the world is to be seen. Third, it is a fragmentary theory of reasoning, that specifies what reasoning is, which inferences are valid and which are recommended. Fourth, it is a medium for pragmatically efficient computation. Fifth, it is a language in which we say things about the world. It can be argued that ontologies are embodiments of Davis' second roles, that is, they focus on knowledge representations as an expression of a set of epistemological commitments. In that sense, Davis' roles are orthogonal to those we presented here. Also, as discussed in section 3, ontologies may be embodied as a knowledge representation (language), but that is not necessarily so.

Another paper that dealt with an analysis of different legal ontologies is [27], where Visser and Bench-Capon use dimensions such as epistemological adequacy, operationality and reusability. While there might be correlations between these dimensions and the dimensions of type and use employed in our analysis, the analyses are fundamentally different in that (a) Visser and Bench-Capon are interesting in comparing how good ontologies are, while we have refrained from such focus, and (b) they focused specifically on core ontologies, that have a specific use. This is reflected in the fact that Visser and Bench-Capon proposed one specific set of criteria that is biased towards the use as core ontologies and might not be applicable or equally relevant for other applications (e.g., epistemological adequacy may be of little relevance in semantic indexing applications).

Similar ideas to the knowledge structure dimension used here have appeared in other places. For example, Nicola Guarino, in an OntoWeb5 report [28], talks about levels of ontological precision, varying from a glossary to a thesaurus to an axiomatized theory.

6 Conclusions

There are many types of (legal) ontologies being developed and used by practitioners in AI and Law. They vary in form, structure, and use. We defined a number of dimensions for form and structure, as well as some types of use, and analyzed a number of works in AI and Law that developed or used legal ontologies. We found out that the use biases both the form and the structure. The use or role of ontology has implications for how to build the ontology, what contents it will have, how much structure will it contain, what representation language it uses, and how much emphasis is put on usability and reusability. The dimensions described in this paper can help identify some of these implications and better understand the variety of legal ontologies available.

References

1. LegOnt 2001: Proceedings of the Second International Workshop on Legal Ontologies. Amsterdam, the Netherlands. URL http://www.lri.jur.uva.nl/jurix2001/legont2001.htm.
2. LegOnt 2003: Proceedings of the ICAIL 2003 Workshop on Legal Ontologies & Web based legal information management. Edinburgh, 2003. URL: http://www.lri.jur.uva.nl/~winkels/legontICAIL2003.html
3. Gruber, T.: A translation approach to portable ontologies. Knowledge Acquisition, 5(2):199-220, 1993.
4. Valente, A.: Legal knowledge engineering: a modelling approach, Amsterdam: IOS Press. 1995
5. Valente, A. and Breuker, J.: "A functional ontology of law." In G. Bargellini and S. Binazzi, editors, Towards a global expert system in law. CEDAM Publishers, Padua, Italy, 1994.
6. Genesereth, M.: Knowledge Interchange Format (KIF). URL http://www-ksl.stanford.edu/knowledge-sharing/kif/.
7. A. Valente, T. Russ, R. MacGregor and W. Swartout. "Building, Using and Reusing an Ontology of Air Campaign Planning." IEEE Intelligent Systems, 14(1), pages 27—36, January/February 1999.
8. A. Valente and T Housel. "Analyzing and Maximizing ROI in Knowledge Management Tools." Knowledge Management Magazine, 2002.
9. Gangemi, A., Sagri, M.T. and Tiscornia, D.: "Metadata for Content Description in Legal Information". In Proceedings of the ICAIL 2003 Workshop on Legal Ontologies & Web based legal information management. 2003.
10. Fellbaum, C.: WordNet: An Electronic Lexical Database. Bradford Books, May 1998.
11. Asaro, C., Biasiotti, M.A., Guidotti, P., Papini, M., Sagri , M.T and Tiscornia, D.: "A Domain Ontology: Italian Crime Ontology". In Proceedings of the ICAIL 2003 Workshop on Legal Ontologies & Web based legal information management. 2003.
12. Boer, A., Hoekstra, R. and Winkels, R..: The CLIME Ontology. Proceedings of the Second International Workshop on Legal Ontologies. Amsterdam, the Netherlands, 2001
13. Zeleznikow, J. and Stranieri, A.: An Ontology for the Construction of Legal Decision Support Systems. Proceedings of the Second International Workshop on Legal Ontologies. Amsterdam, the Netherlands, 2001
14. Benjamins, V.R., Contreras, J., Casanovas, P., Ayuso, M., Becue, M., Lemus, L. and Urios, C.: Ontologies of Professional Legal Knowledge as the Basis for Intelligent IT Support for Judges. In Proceedings of the ICAIL 2003 Workshop on Legal Ontologies & Web based legal information management. 2003.
15. Saias, J. and Quaresma, P.: Using NLP techniques to create legal ontologies in a logic programming based web information retrieval system. In Proceedings of the ICAIL 2003 Workshop on Legal Ontologies & Web based legal information management. 2003.
16. Leary, R.M., Vandenberghe, W. and Zeleznikow, J.: Towards a Financial Fraud Ontology; A Legal Modelling Approach. In Proceedings of the ICAIL 2003 Workshop on Legal Ontologies & Web based legal information management. 2003.
17. Valente, A. and Breuker, J.. Towards Principled Core Ontologies. In: B. Gaines and M. Musen, editors, Proceedings of the Tenth Knowledge Acquisition for Knowledge-Based Systems Workshop (KAW'96), pages 33/1—33/20, Banff, 1996.
18. Valente, A. and Breuker, J.. Legal Modelling and Automated Reasoning with ON-LINE. International Journal of Human-Computer Studies, 51(6), pages 1079-1125, December 1999.
19. Mommers, L.: Applied legal epistemology. Building a knowledge-based ontology of the legal domain. Ph.D. Thesis, 2003.

20. McCarty, L.T.: A Language for Legal Discourse, I. Basic Features, Proceedings of the Second International Conference on Artificial Intelligence and Law, pp.180-189, Vancouver, Canada, 1989.

21. Kralingen, R.W. van: Frame-based Conceptual Models of Statute Law, Computer/Law Series, No. 16, Kluwer Law International, The Hague, The Netherlands, 1995.

22. Visser, P.R.S.: Knowledge Specification for Multiple Legal Tasks. A Case Study of the Interaction Problem in the Legal Domain, Leiden University: Ph.D. thesis, 1995.

23. Lehman, J., Breuker, J. and Brower, B.: "Causation in AI & Law". In Proceedings of the ICAIL 2003 Workshop on Legal Ontologies & Web based legal information management, 2003.

24. Visser, P.: FRAMER: Source Code of a Legal Knowledge System that performs Assessment and Planning, Reports on Technical Research in Law, University of Leiden, Leiden, The Netherlands, Vol. 2, No 1., 1995

25. Lame, G.: "Using text analysis techniques to identify legal ontologies' components". In Proceedings of the ICAIL 2003 Workshop on Legal Ontologies & Web based legal information management. 2003.

26. Davis, R, Shrobe, H., and Szolovitis, P.: What is Knowledge Representation?, AI Magazine, 14(1):17-33, 1993.

27. Visser, P. and Bench-Capon, T.: A Comparison of Four Ontologies for the Design of Legal Knowledge Systems, Artificial Intelligence and Law Journal, Volume 6, Issue 1, 1998.

28. Guarino, N.: OntoWeb WP3 Content Standardization Month 18 report, available online at http://www.ontoweb.org/workshop/ontoweb4/Ontoweb4_files/WP3Report(M18).ppt.

$CAUSATIO^{NT}$:
Modeling Causation in AI&Law

Jos Lehmann[1], Joost Breuker[2], and Bob Brouwer[3]

[1] Laboratory for Applied Ontology, Institute of Cognitive Science and Technology,
Italian National Research Council, Rome, Italy
jos.lehmann@istc.cnr.it
[2] Leibniz Center For Law, Faculty of Law,
University of Amsterdam, Amsterdam, The Netherlands
breuker@lri.jur.uva.nl
[3] Department of Jurisprudence, Faculty of Law,
University of Amsterdam, Amsterdam, The Netherlands
p.w.brouwer@uva.nl

Abstract. Reasoning about causation in fact is an essential element of attributing legal responsibility. Therefore, the automation of the attribution of legal responsibility requires a modelling effort aimed at the following: a thorough understanding of the relation between the legal concepts of responsibility and of causation in fact; a thorough understanding of the relation between causation in fact and the common sense concept of causation; and, finally, the specification of an ontology of the concepts that are minimally required for (automatic) common sense reasoning about causation. This article offers a worked out example of the indicated analysis, which comprises: a definition of the legal concept of responsibility; a definition of the legal concept of causation in fact; CausatiOnt, an AI-like ontology of the common sense (causal) concepts that are minimally needed for reasoning about the legal concept of causation in fact.

1 Introduction

This article presents the most relevant results of an AI&Law-like research project [1, 2], which was envisioned as part of the Functional Ontology of Law (FOLaw, in the following) [3], between 1991 and 1997 at the Department of Computer Science and Law of the University of Amsterdam. Between 1998 and 2003 the project was realized at the same department, recently renamed Leibniz Centre for Law. The central topic of the reported investigation is the *representation of causation for automatic legal reasoning.* By expanding FOLaw's with modules for Causal and Responsibility knowledge, the main purpose of this study is the definition of an analytical model of the concepts (and the conceptual relations) used in legal reasoning when assessing causation in a case description. Such a model may be used as a basis for automatic legal reasoning. In this sense the link between the research presented in this article and AI research is Ontology,

V.R. Benjamins et al. (Eds.): Law and the Semantic Web, LNCS 3369, pp. 77–96, 2005.

the most philosophical subfield of Artificial Intelligence, which has steadily been growing for the last fifteen years.

The paper is structured as follows. Section 2 concentrates on the legal (theoretical) concept of responsibility and on the notion of ground for the attribution of legal responsibility. One of such grounds is causation in fact. Section 3 concentrates on the legal theoretical notion of causation in fact. Three main legal theoretical approaches to causation in fact are presented: causal maximalism, causal minimalism and Hart and Honoré's approach. This last approach is chosen as our legal theoretical point of reference on matters of causation in fact. Section 4 presents a preliminary analysis of the ontological elements that are implicit in Hart and Honoré's proposal (i.e., physical, agent, interpersonal and negative causation) and the philosophical biases of our proposal (cognitivism, singularism, functionalism, agentism, formalism). Section 5 presents CausatiOnt[1], an ontology developed as a basis for modeling physical and agent causation. For reasons of conciseness, we do not present *all* the ontology nor a fully worked out application of the ontology to the canonical example used in this paper. Our overall concern in this paper is to show how, through philosophical analysis, a well founded legal theoretical treatment of the notions of responsibility and of causation in fact may be turned into (the fragments of) a rich AI-like ontology of causal concepts. The full specification and application of CausatiOnt would require a paper on its own and, to achieve it here, we should cut short on the legal theoretical foundations of the ontology. But this would undermine exactly the interdisciplinary approach that characterizes this paper. Therefore, for a fully specified treatment of CausatiOnt the interested reader is referred to chapter 3 of [1]. Finally, Section 6 draws some conclusions.

2   Legal Theory on Responsibility

The present section elaborates on the legal (theoretical) concept of responsibility and on the notion of ground for the attribution of legal responsibility. Consider the following example:

> *Example 1 (The air rifle). In breach of a statute forbidding the sale to an infant under the age of 16 of dangerous weapons, the defendant sold an air rifle and ammunition to a boy of 13. The boy's mother told the boy to return the weapon to the defendant and get a refund: on the defendant's refusal to take the rifle back, the boy's mother took it from the boy and hid it. Six months later the boy found it and allowed a playmate to use it, who shot and accidentally wounded the plaintiff, destroying the sight of one eye. (Henningsen v. Markovitz (1928) 132 Misc. 547, 230 NYS 313)*

The dramatic development of the events described in Example 1 raises a general question of responsibility. This is due to the fact that the final event described

---

[1] From CAUSATIon ONTology, indicated as $_{CAUSATI}O^{NT}$ in headings and captions throughout this article.

in the example is a harmful one. It is mostly - even though not exclusively - about undesirable events that people seriously ask themselves: "Who made this happen? Who is to blame?". As shown at more length in [1, 2], the legal practice normally relies on an assumption of consistency and of uniformity of application (of any given norm). Therefore the attribution of legal responsibility requires detailed (and preventive) analyses concerning the *explicit* criteria that should be used by a court when blaming someone for the harm inflicted on someone else. It is precisely such longing for consistency that raises tough problems concerning the criteria of legal responsibility attribution.

A legal case presents two main types of elements, which may play a role in attributing responsibility: the *factual elements*, which contain information for establishing the chain of causation and which, therefore, make it possible to attribute the responsibility of the harm to the person(s) who caused it; the *legal elements* of the case, which contain information for identifying the person(s) who may be held responsible for the harm, based on so called considerations of legal policy. As observed in [4] (p. xlviii), most legal theoretical treatments of legal responsibility are not neutral with respect to the roles that either causation or legal policy play in the attribution of responsibility. In order to overcome such lack of a neutral ground of confrontation, Hart and Honoré propose to see legal responsibility as described by three main elements: a definition of the legal concept of responsibility, the legal grounds for the attribution of legal responsibility and, finally, the types of cases that arise from combining different grounds. These form together a general framework for treating issues of responsibility, without requiring any strong commitment about the role of causation or of legal policy.

2.1   The Legal Concept of Responsibility

Hart and Honoré [4] (p. xliii) reduce the notion of legal responsibility to the legal status of someone who is subject to a legal punishment or a sanction.

Definition 1 (Legal Responsibility). *Legal responsibility is the liability of a person to be punished, forced to compensate, or otherwise subjected to a sanction by the law.*

The definition above does not give any indications regarding what a person must have done in order to be held legally responsible. Hart and Honoré limit the concept of legal responsibility to the purely legal aspects of this notion and they reduce legal responsibility to the legal status that a person acquires (i.e. the liability to certain disagreeable consequences). This approach has three advantages:

1. It binds the notion of legal responsibility to the notion of *liability*, marking a clear distinction between legal responsibility and any other form of responsibility (e.g. moral responsibility, political responsibility, etc.). This is due to the very meaning of liability: the liability of a person may be seen as the person's relation with a (judicial) authority. Such authority has the power to make decisions that directly affect the person and her future.

2. Through 1, it binds the notion of legal responsibility to the notion of *account-ability* of the person. In order to be liable, a person must be accountable, which depends on whether the person satisfies the criteria of accountability fixed in the law. These criteria usually refer to the physical and psychological capacity of a natural person to have control on her actions and/or to stand trial. Typical examples of such criteria are age or mental sanity.

3. It shields the definition of legal responsibility from the (legal-theoretical) debates about the existence of necessary and/or sufficient conditions for legal responsibility. Hart and Honoré propose instead to see such so-called conditions as *grounds*, which are used in *attributing* legal responsibility, rather than as defining conditions of legal responsibility itself.

2.2   Grounds for Responsibility Attribution

The grounds for responsibility attribution do not have the status of logical or strictly rational conditions ([4], p. xliv). They rather are widely accepted requirements, which generally grow out of tradition and that are progressively codified by legislators in the Law. The difference between a logical condition and a requirement may be understood in terms of the (Kantian) difference between analytic statements (logical conditions) and synthetic statements (requirement). Such requirements should therefore be left outside the definition of legal responsibility.

Definition 2 (Grounds for Legal Responsibility Attribution). *Grounds for the attribution of legal responsibility to a person for a given harm are: the conduct of the person; the causal connection between the conduct of the person and the given harm; the fault legally implied by the conduct of the person.*

Definition 2 revolves around the notion of conduct. This is not further defined by Hart and Honoré, but it can be quite safely taken as indicating the intentional or unintentional behavior of a person throughout the events under analysis. Furthermore, the definition considers both factual and legal elements as grounds for the attribution of responsibility. This is in accordance with Hart and Honoré's intention of giving equal consideration to causation in fact and legal policy in their framework definition of legal responsibility. In Example 1 an instance of conduct is the combination of the seller's sale of the rifle and his later refusal to accept it back; an instance of fault is the seller's breach of the mentioned statute; finally, an instance of a causal connection is the relation between the shooting and the blinding of the victim.

2.3   Types of Cases

By combining the grounds mentioned above, a wide variety of actual cases may be described. According to Hart and Honoré there are five main types of cases:

Type 1: Conduct, Causation in Fact, Fault. In this case type (which exactly corresponds to Example 1) the court allocates responsibility based on the causal chain that started from the seller's faulty conduct and led to the harm. In other words, the court has to decide whether the unlawful behavior is causally related to the harm.

Type 2: Conduct, Causation in Fact. Suppose that in Example 1 the seller's conduct, despite resulting in a violation, is not faulty, because it is proven that the boy who bought the rifle showed a faked identity card and the shop keeper had no reasons to assume that this card was faked. The seller could still be responsible for the plaintiff's blinding based on strict liability *and* on the causal connection between his conduct and the harm. In other words, in this case the court may allocate responsibility to the seller, based on the causal connection between his conduct and the harm and on his strict liability as a seller of dangerous implements. Furthermore, the strict liability of the seller could be used as an argument against him even if his non faulty conduct did *not* result in a violation. The seller could be considered responsible for the harm caused to the plaintiff, simply based on his causal involvement in the case.

Type 3: Conduct, Fault. Suppose that in Example 1, no harm takes place (i.e., there is no causation involved at all). In this case a court could only allocate responsibility to the seller for his faulty conduct, i.e. his breach of the statute. This, by the way, actually happened: before the case presented in Example 1, the seller was actually convicted by a criminal court for his breach of statute.

Type 4: Conduct. Imagine a combination of types 2 and 3, where no harm takes place and the seller is not to blame because it is proven that the boy who bought the rifle did it by showing a faked identity card and the shop keeper had no reasons to assume that this card was faked. In this case a court could still allocate responsibility to the seller for his conduct, simply based on his strict liability as a seller of dangerous implements.

Type 5: No Conduct, No Causation in Fact, No Fault. This last type of case cannot be exemplified by directly considering the seller, because he has a role in the case. Clear examples of persons that could be found legally responsible for the harm, despite having no role in the case (vicarious liability), are the parents of the boy who shot (i.e. the playmate), given that there was no omission/negligence on their part.

Hart and Honoré indicate only types 1 to 5 as the most important types of cases based on empirical considerations, rather than on combinatorics. According to the authors, actual cases normally fall under one of these types. There is, though, a more profound reason why combinations such as 'no conduct-causation in fact-fault', 'no conduct-causation in fact-no fault', 'no conduct-no causation in fact-fault' find no consideration: from a legal theoretical stance, both causation in fact and fault imply (or depend on) conduct, i.e. agency.

According to the typology given above, two types of cases require the assessment of causal relations as a ground for attributing legal responsibility (case types 1 and 2). The amount of cases, for which causal reasoning is required, goes well beyond two fifths of the total cases, though. This is true for a number of reasons. Firstly, *it is very improbable that the distribution of cases over their types is even*, as most cases discussed in court deal with *actual* undesirable events, which were brought about by someone's (possibly faulty) conduct (case types 1 and 2). Secondly, even when considering case types 3 and 4, where no actual harm has happened, *courts may have to make (quite extensive) use of hypothetical causal reasoning.* The (ontological) basis of such hypothetical causal reasoning are exactly the same as the basis of reasoning about actual causes. Finally, *case type 5 generally implies a case of type 1, 2, 3 or 4.* For instance, the responsibility of a parent to pay for the damages caused by the children, can only be attributed once it is clearly established that the children actually caused the damages.

This situation imposes the formulation of clear criteria for handling problems of causation in fact when dealing with questions of responsibility. As explained in next section, legal theory has indeed dedicated a lot of attention to define such criteria.

3   Legal Theory on Causation in Fact

This section concentrates on the legal theoretical notion of causation in fact. Three main legal theoretical approaches to causation in fact are presented: causal maximalism, causal minimalism and Hart and Honoré's approach. The last approach is then chosen as our legal theoretical point of reference on matters of causation in fact.

3.1   Causal Maximalism and Minimalism

Causal maximalism allows to trace legal responsibility through causal relations solely: the person who caused the harm is responsible for it. The causal maximalist recognizes only clause 2 of Definition 2 as valid ground of responsibility attribution. Examples of maximalist criteria are:

Causal Proximity. The most general criterion provided by causal maximalists is a combination of common sense and of the principle of so called causal *proximity* to the harm. In other words, the agent that by common sense may be considered as the most proximate cause of the harm is *the* cause of the harm and should, therefore, be held responsible for it.

Beale's Criteria. These rules reformulate the notion of proximity in terms of mechanical forces, by providing a sort of Newtonian universal view on causation in fact.

Epstein's Criteria. Inspired, on the one hand, by Beale's notion of force and, on the other hand, by Hart and Honoré's analysis, which was firstly presented in the 1959 edition of [4], Epstein's criteria reformulate the notion of proximity in terms of 'paradigms': the use of force; fright; the exercise of compulsion; and the creation of a dangerous situation [4] (p.lxxiv).

Causal minimimalism [5], opposed the very possibility of distinguishing between questions of fact and questions of policy, as proposed by maximalists. The causal minimalist recognizes only clause 3 of Definition 2 as a valid ground for responsibility attribution. These should therefore receive most of the attention, because once the questions of policy of the case are solved, the remaining questions of fact may be tackled by (standard forms of) counterfactual reasoning. Examples of tests proposed by the minimalists are:

Sine qua non Test. The first and most traditional counterfactual test formulated for application to legal analysis is the *sine qua non* test. The most distinctive point of this test is that it checks for necessary conditions. In other words, according to this logical test all conditions that are recognized as necessary for the harm should be considered as causes of the harm.

But-For Test. The so called but-for test helps focusing the inquirer on the sufficient rather than on the necessary elements of the causal relation. The question that must be asked is, again, a counterfactual one, ranging on the conducts of the persons involved in the case: "Would the harm have taken place *but for* the conduct of this person?". A negative answer is equivalent to the assessment of a causal relation.

Probability Tests. There is a group of tests which detects causation in fact by testing the increased probability of the harm given the conduct of a certain person. These probabilistic approaches retain a counterfactual flavor, even though this is not always patent. In a purely probabilistic approach, an event causes another event if the occurrence of the first event is followed with high probability by the occurrence of the second event. This is very similar to the counterfactual statement that, if the first event had not occurred, the second would not have either.

Foreseeability and Risk. Two other notions that have a probabilistic flavor may play the role of additional requirements in the minimalistic causal assessment of a case: the notions of foreseeability and risk. According to foreseeability theories the defendant is liable for harm of which his conduct was a *sine qua non* condition only if the *type* of harm was objectively foreseeable. On the other hand, it may also be argues that if the defendant's conduct is a *sine qua non* condition of harm, he is responsible if the harm falls within the risks to which his conduct has exposed others.

Scope of the Rule and Equity. Other two additional requirements proposed by the minimalists as complementary to counterfactuals or probabilities are the scope of the rule violated (minimalistic tests should be applied only if it is already clear that the considered harm is within the scope of the rule violated by the person whose conduct is under scrutiny) and equity (the minimalist seeks an imposition of liability that is equitable as between parties).

3.2   Hart and Honoré's Solution

In [4] Hart and Honoré argue against causal maximalism as well as against causal minimalism. The arguments of the two scholars against the existing doctrines of legal-theoretical causation are somehow intertwined. On the one hand, Hart and Honoré see the notion of causal proximity as too vague for supporting a coherent form of legal analysis. Therefore, the definition of a clearer concept of causation in fact is needed. This should not become, though, an attempt at defining a set of rigid "rules for the determination of proximate cause", because most of these rules for handling questions of fact (e.g. Beale's) implicitly encode legal principles, i.e. answers to questions of policy. On the other hand, Hart and Honoré advocate that the correct usage of technical concepts such as foresee-ability, risk and scope of the rule is highly dependent on (the application of) a plausible notion of causation in fact; and this notion, they say, is mostly hidden by causal minimalists in the *sine qua non* test (i.e., counterfactual reasoning), which is often proposed as the necessary inferential counterpart of the technical legal notions mentioned above.

In chapters I and II of their book Hart and Honoré propose to move from the classical common sense, logical or mathematical approaches to an analytical ap-proach, which attempts at defining what it *concretely* means in legal settings for an agent to cause an event. There is some non logical knowledge of the world that must be taken into consideration when assessing causal relations. Hence, in order to find out what is such non logical generalization, the legal language of causa-tion must be studied by means of ordinary language analysis, which, at the time when Hart and Honoré wrote, was a major development in the Anglo-Saxon philosophical landscape (development which is usually attributed to the "sec-ond" Wittgenstein or Austin). Such study should refrain from both temptations of explaining everything (as in causal maximalism) and of leaving everything unexplained (as in causal minimalism). In other words, Hart and Honoré try to make explicit what both the maximalist and the minimalist leave implicit. The simplicity of the tests built around proximity or counterfactuals hides a lot of complex assumptions. These, though, are implicitly employed by the legal expert in order to make sense of those tests. Hart and Honoré notice that such freedom of application jeopardizes the consistency of the tests, especially when employed over large corpora of cases. Therefore Definition 3 is proposed as a way of mini-mizing variations of outcome in legal causal analysis, by explicitly standardizing the implicit meaning of causal proximity or of counterfactual dependence.

Definition 3 (Causation in Fact). *Agent A causes an event e, that might involve agent B, if either of the following holds:*

1. *A starts some physical process that leads to e;*
2. *A provides reasons or draws attention to reasons which influence the conduct of B, who causes e;*
3. *A provides B with opportunities to cause e.*
4. *All the important negative variants of clauses 1, 2, 3[2]*

Now, an analysis of Example 1 according to Definition 3 yields a result that is not very different from those obtained by applying any maximalist or minimalist

---

[2] An example of such negative variants is: A *does not* provide reasons or *does not* draw attention to reasons which might influence the conduct of B, who causes e.

causal criteria. Either the mother or the seller are at the beginning of the causal chain. Contrary to most classical causal tests, though, Definition 3 provides more clarity. It explicitly distinguishes the various types of causal links that connect each of the involved agents. Rather than reducing every relevant causal relation to one type (e.g. proximate cause or *sine qua non*), Definition 3 distinguishes various types of causal roles played by the persons involved in the case. For instance, the playmate (the boy who shot) has clearly started a physical process that leads to the harm (clause 1). The boy who owns the rifle has provided opportunities to the playmate for shooting. The mother of the rifle's owner has failed to provide her child with reasons for not using the rifle and this has led him to play a causal role in the harm. Finally, the seller - if he has played any causal role in the harm at all - has provided an opportunity for the harm to come about.

Hart and Honoré's effort at making things explicit is comparable under many respects to our own. Definition 3 carves a portion of causal knowledge that is very relevant to AI&Law research. In order to make it more rigorous and possibly useful to *automatic* classification and/or interpretation, Definition 3 should be reconfigured along clear ontological lines and restructured by means of a subsumption hierarchy, i.e. a so called is-a hierarchy. Which is what we do in sections 4 and 5.

4   Philosophical Preliminaries

The first and most obvious restructuring distinguishes in Definition 3 four main ontological levels, corresponding to four main types of causation, as usually described in the philosophical literature: physical causation, agent causation, interpersonal causation, negative causation[3]. *Physical causation* is described by the final part of clause 1 of Definition 3, where the definition mentions *a physical process that leads to an event*. *Agent causation* is described by the initial part of clause 1, where Definition 3 mentions *an agent starting a physical process*. The agreement around cases of agent causation is not reached as easily as in cases of physical causation. This is due to the problem of detecting the beliefs, desires and intentions of the agent that starts the physical process. Things become even more complex when considering *interpersonal causation*, described by clauses 2 and 3. One might be tempted to consider interpersonal causation just as a subcase of agent causation, where the psychological state of an agent exerts a causal influence on another agent. Things are not that simple, though. The causal influence that an agent may exercise on someone else may be physical in

---

[3] Distinguishing between varieties of causation is the pragmatic answer of the philosophy of causation to the (temporary?) lack of stable scientific theories of some fundamental phenomena. For instance, without a stable neuropsychological solution of the mind-body problem, it is impossible to choose in a principled way between a reduction of agent causation to physical causation and a reduction of physical causation to agent causation.

nature or psychological or a combination of the two. Finally, the most elusive case of causation is *negative causation*. Definition 3 refers to negative causation in clause 4 as to *all the important negative variants of the preceding clauses*. It is ontologically very difficult, almost paradoxical, to accept the general idea that something that does not exist can cause anything. For reasons of space we can not analyze the subtleties of this fascinating problem here.

In [2] definitions are given for physical and agent causation within the wider structure of CausatiOnt and some analytical material is provided on interpersonal and negative causation, which are both left as research objectives. In this paper we limit the scope of the presentation of CausatiOnt to the knowledge needed for defining physical and agent causation.

Before starting with the detailed presentation of CausatiOnt's class hierarchy, the following general philosophical biases of CausatiOnt should be highlighted:

Cognitivism. CausatiOnt is based on the assumption that causal relations are neither purely ontological nor purely epistemological. Therefore, the representation of causal knowledge cannot be limited to the ontological elements of causal relations (i.e. the entities). It must be extended to the epistemological elements (i.e. the categories) and to the phenomenological relations between them (i.e. the dimensions). This extension might seem as a non parsimonious scientific practice. But it gives us some room to explain what in causal reasoning pertains to us as observing entities and what pertains to the world as observed entity. Furthermore, by not limiting ourselves to ontology we provide a clear way of distinguishing semantically similar terms (e.g., matter, a category; mass, a dimension; object, an entity). In a similar fashion, we are able to adopt the distinction defined in [6] between causality (a category, representing *general causal principles*) and causation (a reified relation, i.e. an entity, representing *particular causal relations*).

Singularism. CausatiOnt is based on singularism, according to which physical causation relates events, i.e. particular changes of the world located in space and time [7].

Functionalism. CausatiOnt is based on functionalism [8, 9, 10], which may be seen as the continuation of singularism by other means. The main difference from singularism is that functionalism seeks sharper tools than the notion of change for detecting physical causation. The various functionalist views proposed so far try to reduce the notion of causation to physical notions, such as energy or momentum transfer between physical processes, in accordance to contemporary Physics.

Agentism. According to CausatiOnt actions are characterized in terms of the one's knowledge of one's own actions (awareness) and one's control on one's own action (governance). In turn, the notion of control is based on the notion of trying taken as the distinguishing factor between actions and mere body movements. Furthermore, CausatiOnt adopts a classical Davidsonian view [11] on reason explanations, given in terms of motives, reasons and other (so called) mental entities (e.g., intentions and believes).

Formalism. According to CausatiOnt, like according to most treatments of causal relations, physical causation has the formal properties of transitivity, asymmetry and non reflexivity, while agent causation is certainly intransitive and asymmetric and, possibly, reflexive.

5 $_{CAUSATI}\mathrm{O}^{NT}$

This section presents some parts of CausatiOnt, the parts that contain the concepts that are minimally needed for defining the relations of physical and agent causation. For conciseness we do not spend much time on matters of representation. Our ontology was implemented in Protégé-2000, a fairly liberal knowledge representation tool, based on the classical is-a relation. The figures, shown in the following, reproduce part of our is-a hierarchy. It should be noticed that such figures were automatically generated by Ontoviz, the graphic tool of Protégé-2000. For this reason they may sometimes be visually confusing, in the sense that they do not always mirror the order of presentation of our ontology in this article. We, therefore, have to ask for some patience from the reader, for the purpose of being conducted to a correct reading of the figures.

5.1 $_{CAUSATI}\mathrm{O}^{NT}$'s Top Level

We present here the contents of the four top boxes shown in figure 1: noesis, category, dimension and entity. We illustrate both the intended meaning of such terms and we briefly introduce the subsumed concepts that are relevant to the present exposition.

Noesis. The first ontological choice, to which we commit ourselves, is avoiding to make a truly ontological choice. As explained in the philosophical preliminaries, after years of struggling with the notion of causal relation (and those related to it, e.g. matter, object, process, energy, work, power, etc.) two main general properties of causal relations appeared quite clear:

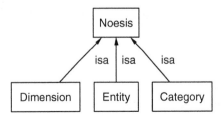

Fig. 1. $_{CAUSATI}\mathrm{O}^{NT}$'s top level

1. *Causal relations are neither purely ontological nor purely epistemological.* They are something in between.
2. *Therefore, the representation of causal knowledge cannot be limited to the ontological elements of causal relations (i.e. the entities).* It must be extended to the epistemological elements (i.e. the categories) and to the phenomenological relations between them (i.e. the dimensions).

Given 1 and 2 we define the top class of our ontology as follows.

Definition 4 (Noesis). *Noesis is the psychological counterpart of experience (i.e. perception, learning and reasoning).*

The notion of noesis has a rather long philosophical tradition, which dates back to Greek Philosophy. A number of words stemming from the root *nous-* (e.g. *noein*, thinking, *nous*, mind, *noumenon*, the object of thought) were used to indicate whatever was related to thought as a psychological activity. In the XX century, the notions of noesis and noemata were employed by the phenomenologists (e.g. Husserl) to indicate, respectively, the process and the result of perceptual and intellectual activity.

As far as we are concerned, we adopt here the notion of noesis in its broadest cognitive sense. We consider all the experiences of an individual human being to be physical phenomena. On the one hand, perceptual experiences (e.g. perceiving the color red) are the result of the interaction between the physical world (i.e. light) and an individual's sensory system (e.g. his optic nerve and other parts of his brain). On the other hand, intellectual experiences (e.g. thinking about the notion of color) occur in the brain, i.e. they too are physical phenomena. Besides their physical nature, though, both perceptual and intellectual experiences generally seem to have a psychological counterpart, i.e. a part of which the individual is aware (i.e. the color red, in the example of perceptual experiences, and the notion of color, in the example of intellectual experiences). Any such psychological counterpart of an experience is noesis.

Category. A category is that part of noesis, which cannot be (philosophically) reduced to any other parts. It must therefore be assumed as a basic intellectual element[4], which structures our perceptual experience of the world and our reasoning about the world. We define it as follows.

Definition 5 (Category). *Category is knowledge-related (i.e. epistemological) noesis.*

Categories form the intellectual *background* of our noetic experience of the world (i.e. of our perception, learning and reasoning about the world). Even though categories play a crucial role in noesis, we are hardly aware of them in our experience. When perceiving, learning or reasoning we are not fully aware of the

---

[4] The expression 'assuming a notion as *basic* intellectual element' is used here as a synonym of 'postulating a notion'. In other words, categories must be postulated.

categories that are supporting our effort. For instance, when reasoning about (i.e. having an intellectual experience of) or perceiving (i.e. having a physical experience of) an entity (e.g. an object), a number of categories (e.g. matter and quantity) make our experience possible, even though they are not immediately present to our mind and/or to our sensory system.

Categories are, therefore, here understood as in (Kantian) Epistemology: as the basic notions on which our (intellectual and perceptual) experience builds up[5]. Categories are different from sets, classes and instances. They are different from sets because they are not collections of (prototypical) individuals. Categories are different from classes because they have no properties describing them. Finally, categories are different from (prototypical) individuals because they are universal not particular.

We consider it to be important for an AI-like ontology to contain a description of the categories on which it is based. Even though categories do not play a direct role in reasoning about and/or perceiving entities, they may play two other important roles in an ontology:

1. On the one hand, as support to reasoning about knowledge at a general level.
2. On the other hand, as purely descriptive notions that clarify the intuitive meaning of the terms that are used in reasoning about entities (which we call the dimensions, see below).

Our intent is to use categories in the sense indicated at point 2 above. We therefore present a number of terms that indicate the basic epistemological structure assumed in our ontology. As shown in figure 2 we distinguish between two main groups of categories: the categories of existence and the categories of experience. The opposition between these two types of categories is the epistemological equivalent of the opposition, within noesis, between entity (or Ontology) and category (or Epistemology). In other words, just like in noesis, where we distinguish existence (the entity) from knowledge (the category), in category we distinguish between the knowledge of what exists (category of existence) from the knowledge of the modes of knowledge (category of experience). These second categories describe how we know what exists (or, rather, how we know the categories of existence). Categories of existence encompass notions such as space, matter, energy, change and others); whereas category of experience encompass notions such as quantity, quality and time.

An important subcategory of change is causality. There has been a lot of philosophical discussion concerning both the ontological and the epistemological status of causal relations. In accordance with [6] we provide here the first half of the solution proposed by us. We adopt the term 'causality' to indicate *the epistemological counterpart of an ontological dependence*. We see here causality as the epistemological counterpart of an ontological dependence between categories

---

[5] We want to avoid to use here the expression *a priori* in order to describe the status of categories. As a matter of fact, under a noetical perspective nothing is *a priori* and one may see categories as the result of evolution, both of individuals and of species.

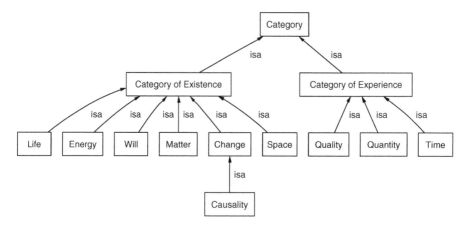

Fig. 2. $_{CAUSATI}O^{NT}$'s class Category and subclasses

of existence. In other words, from an epistemological point of view causality is an ontological constraint between the categories of existence. Such constraint fixes the possibility of existence of one category relative to another. We propose here to adopt the following ontological dependence between categories of existence as standard notion of common sense causality: will cannot exist without life, life cannot exist without energy, matter and space. In other words there is an ontological dependence between will and life, on the one hand, and energy, matter and space, on the other hand.

Dimension. From the (theoretical) background consisting of the categories the dimensions emerge, which we define as follows.

Definition 6 (Dimension). *Dimension is experience-related (i.e. phenomenological) noesis. A dimension relates two categories.*

The standard example of a dimension is mass. By experience, all physical objects have a mass, which is the quantity of matter they comprise. We never have, though, a concrete experience of either matter or quantity as such. Therefore, we must assume their existence as categories, rather than as entities, and employ them in the definition of the notion of mass. In other words, the concrete notion of mass relates the epistemological to the ontological part of our noetic experience. We experience objects (ontology) as having mass (phenomenology), which relates two categories: matter and quantity (epistemology).

In the definitions of dimensions, we associate categories to one another with the expression 'experienced by means of'. This is to underline the fact that the definition of dimensions in terms of categories is not an ontological but a phenomenological definition. We therefore say, for instance, that mass is matter *experienced by means of* quantity (rather than mass *is* a quantity of matter), where the experience of matter by means of quantity is a purely *intellectual* one, as both matter and quantity are categories, not entities.

Furthermore, it should be noticed that we use the expression 'experienced by means of' also in the definition of entities in terms of dimensions. In this case, the expression 'experienced by means of' refers to the *perceptual* (rather than the intellectual) experience of an entity (e.g. an object) through a dimension (e.g. mass).

The following dimensions have been defined: volume (space experienced by means of quantity), form (space experienced by means of quality), location (space experienced by means of time), mass (matter experienced by means of quantity), material (matter experienced by means of quality), state (matter experienced by means of time), work (energy experienced by means of quantity), energy-form (energy experienced by means of quality), power (energy experienced by means of time), direction (change experienced by means of quantity), transition (change experienced by means of quality), period (change experienced by means of time), sensitivity (life experienced by means of quantity), instinct (life experienced by means of quality), age (life experienced by means of time), intentionality (will experienced by means of quantity), representational content (will experienced by means of quality), enactment (will experienced by means of time).

Some of such dimensions are shown in figures 3 and 4, as descriptors of a class (for instance, dimension 'mass' is a descriptor of class 'object' and usually takes numeric values).

Entity. The notion of entity indicates something that exists separately from other things and has a clear identity. Entities are the subject of study of ontology. We define entity as follows.

Definition 7 (Entity). *Entity is existence-related (i.e. ontological) noesis.*

In Example 1 examples of (different types of) entities are: the event of the trigger being pulled; the boy who pulls the trigger (both his body and his mind); the process of being pulled; the trigger; the causal connection between the event of the trigger being pulled and the event of the plaintiff being hit.

5.2 $_{CAUSATI}O^{NT}$'s Causal Entities

By means of the dimensions we define here some of the entities needed for the definition of causal relations. We proceed as follows: we firstly introduce the definition of physical entity, object and process; we then define the notion of mental entity; and, finally, we define the notions of occurrence and event.

The dimensions that stem from the categories of physical existence (i.e. space, matter, energy, change) provide us with the necessary terminology for defining physical entities. We define physical entity as follows.

Definition 8 (Physical Entity). *Physical entity is an entity experienced by means of one or more of the following dimensions: volume, form, location, mass, material, state, work, energy-form, power, direction, transition, period, sensitivity, instinct, age.*

As show in figure 3, there are three main physical entities: objects, organisms (which we do not treat here) and processes. They are defined as follows.

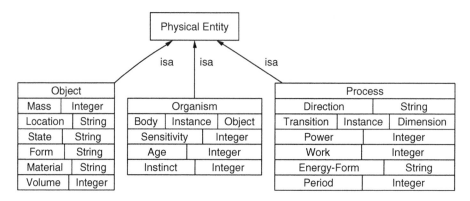

Fig. 3. $_{CAUSATI}O^{NT}$'s class Physical Entity and subclasses

Definition 9 (Object). *Object is a physical entity which is experienced by means of* all *of the following dimensions: volume, form, location, mass, material, state.*

In Example 1 an example of object is the trigger.

Definition 10 (Process). *Process is a physical entity experienced by means of* all *of the following dimensions: work, energy-form, power, direction, transition, period.*

In Example 1 an example of process is being pulled.

The dimensions that stem from the categories of psychological existence (i.e. will) provide us with the necessary terminology for defining mental entities.

Definition 11 (Mental Entity). *Mental entity is either:*

1. *An entity experienced by means of* one or more *of the following dimensions: intentionality, representational content and enactment.*
2. *Or a process that has* either *of the following dimensions as transition: intentionality, representational content and enactment.*

As shown in figure 4 there are two main mental entities: thought and mental process. Thought is often understood as the content of some cognitive state. Just as for the case of the notion of object we are able to provide here a modular definition of the notion of thought, as follows.

Definition 12 (Thought). *Thought is a mental entity which is experienced by means of* all *of the following dimensions: intentionality, representational content and enactment.*

In example 1 a thought is the boy's desire to buy the air rifle.

Mental processes form a special type of processes. On the one hand, they are described by the same dimensions as physical and biological processes (i.e. work, energy-form, power, direction, main transition, period): mental processes

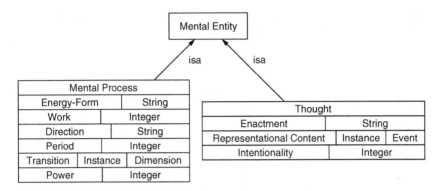

Fig. 4. $_{CAUSATI}O^{NT}$'s class Mental Entity and subclasses

actually are physical processes, in the sense that they (must) have some physical counterpart. On the other hand, though, they are also mental entities, because their transitions pertain to the dimensions of thoughts rather than of objects or organisms. In other words, mental processes unify the types of entities that are generally considered as characterizing the notion of agency: physical (in its broad sense, including biological) and mental entities.

Definition 13 (Mental Process). *Mental process is both a mental entity and a physical process which has* either *of the following dimensions as its transition: intentionality, representational content and enactment.*

In example 1 a mental process is the action of buying the air rifle.

Another type of entity, non physical but relational, must be introduced here in order to subsequently generate the notion of event.

Definition 14 (Occurrence). *Occurrence is a* reified relation *between objects, processes, thoughts and/or occurrences.*

An event is a reified relation between a process, an object, an action and an agent. We define an event as follows.

Definition 15 (Event). *Event is an occurrence of a process (the occurrence) involving an object (the subject), where the process is possibly initiated by an action (the act) of an agent (the actor).*

In Example 1 an example of event is the trigger being pulled.

Finally, the notion of causation may be defined.

Definition 16 (Causation). *Causation is an occurrence of two events, the cause and the effect.*

Two remarks are needed here. Firstly, the relation of causation introduced in Definition 16 is the counterpart, within our ontology, of the relation introduced in Definition 3 (i.e., causation in fact). It should be noticed that Definition 16 subsumes Definition 3, as the former can subsume more types of causation than those subsumed by causation in fact (which are, according to the preliminary analysis of section 4, physical, agent, interpersonal and negative causation). Definitions 17 and 18 define the first two of such types. Secondly, Definition 16 is very broad and it is needed as a definitional node in the ontology. In other words, all the clauses that provide the sufficient conditions for more restrictive (and therefore more interesting) causal relations are provided in the definitions subsumed by Definition 16. This does not mean that the relation introduced in Definition 16 is indistinguishable from simple sequencing of events. It should not be forgotten that Definition 16 introduces a *type of occurrence*. This has, of course, a rather strong implication: *by definition* all *reified* relations between events are causal relations. But, on the other hand, a niche is carved for logical (i.e. non reified) relations between events (e.g. temporal or mereological relations), which keep their non causal nature.

Physical causation is a type of causation and there are a number of conditions that must be met by any two considered events in order for physical causation to hold.

Definition 17 (Physical Causation). *Physical causation is causation between an event E_1, which is an occurrence of a physical process P_1 (the occurrence of) involving an object O_1 (the subject), and event E_2, which is an occurrence of a physical process P_2 (the occurrence of) involving an object O_2 (the subject). A relation of physical causation holds between E_1, the cause, and E_2, the effect, if the following conditions are met:*

1. *O_1 and O_2 are not the same object, according to the adopted identity criterion for objects.*
   Comment: the subjects must be truly distinguished objects.
2. *P_1 and P_2 are not the same process, according to the adopted identity criterion for processes.*
   Comment: an event cannot cause itself. By this clause we adopt the view that causation is an irreflexive relation.
3. *P_1's period precedes P_2's period.*
   Comment: the cause temporally precedes the effect. Even for processes that are temporally distributed (i.e. continuous) the causing process starts before the caused one. By this clause we adopt the view that causation is a temporally asymmetric relation.
4. *P_1's energy-form is the same as P_2's energy-form or E_2 is reducible to events $E_{2,1} \ldots E_{2,n}$ such that:*
   (a) $E_{2,1} \ldots E_{2,n}$ are occurrences of processes $P_{2,1} \ldots P_{2,n}$, which all have the same energy form of P_1.
   (b) $E_{2,1} \ldots E_{2,n}$ have as their subjects objects $O_{2,1} \ldots O_{2,n}$, which are the grains of O_2, according to the adopted structural constraints.
   In the interaction between two objects energy is transferred or transformed. In this latter case, the transformation of energy should be reducible to a transfer of energy between the cause and the events occurring to the grains of the object of the effect.

5. P_1's direction is the same as P_2's direction or P_1's power is greater or equal to P_2's power or P_1's work is greater or equal to P_2's work.
   Comment: this clause accounts for the fact that usually changes of one sign cause changes of the same sign (i.e. an increase can usually only be caused by an increase and a decrease by a decrease). If this condition cannot be tested (which might be the case when lack of information makes it impossible to establish the directions of either P_1 or P_2) or if it is not satisfied, one may want to use the principle of the dispersion of energy in order to distinguish the cause from the effect.

6. The category of existence of P_2's transition can not exist without the category of existence of P_1's transition, according to the adopted causality constraint.
   Comment: changes in O_1's dimensions can only affect those dimensions of O_2 that are ontologically dependent on the dimensions changed in O_1, according to the adopted causality.

It should be added that we take physical causation to be a *transitive* relation. In Example 1 an example of physical causation is the relation between the event of the trigger being pulled and the event of the plaintiff being hit.

As far as agent causation is concerned we take it to be a subclass of physical causation. There are a number of conditions that must be met by the two considered events in order for agent causation to hold. The most prominent of such conditions are the existence of a relation of physical causation between the first and the second event and the knowledgeability of the actor of the first event.

Definition 18 (Agent Causation). *Agent causation is causation between an event E_1, which is the occurrence of a physical process P_1, initiated by actor Ag_1 by act Ac_1, to a subject O_1 and event E_2, which is the occurrence of physical process P_2 to subject O_2. A relation of agent causation holds between E_1, the cause, and E_2, the effect, if the following conditions are met:*

1. E_2 is not initiated by any actor, say, Ag_2 performing any act, say, Ac_2.
   Comment: There is no *novus actus interveniens* between the cause and the effect.
2. There is a relation of physical causation between E_1 and E_2.
3. E_2 is the representational content of a thought with no enactment that is in Ag_1's mind.
   Comment: The actor must have in mind the result of the process (directly or indirectly initiated by his action. Such awareness can range from simple belief (i.e. foreseeability) to intent (goal).

Finally, we consider agent causation to be an intransitive relation. This property of the relation descends from clause 1 of definition 18.

6   Conclusion

Reasoning about causation in fact is an essential element of attributing legal responsibility. Therefore, the automation of the attribution of legal responsibility requires a modelling effort aimed at the following: a thorough understanding of the relation between the legal concepts of responsibility and of causation in fact; a thorough understanding of the relation between causation in fact and the common sense concept of causation; and, finally, the specification of an ontology of the concepts that are minimally required for (automatic) common sense reasoning about causation.

In this article we offered a worked out example of the indicated analysis. Such example consists of: a definition of the legal concept of responsibility (in terms of liability and accountibility); a definition of the legal concept of causation in fact (in terms of the initiation of physical processes by an agent and of the provision of reasons and/or opportunities to other agents); an AI-like ontology, called CausatiOnt, of the common sense (causal) concepts that are minimally needed for reasoning about the legal concept of causation in fact (in particular, the concepts of category, dimension, object, agent, process, event and act).

References

[1] Lehmann, J.: Causation in Artificial Intelligence and Law - A modelling approach. PhD thesis, University of Amsterdam - Faculty of Law - Department of Computer Science and Law (2003)

[2] Lehmann, J., Breuker, J., Brouwer, B.: Causation in ai&law (to appear). AI and Law (2004)

[3] Valente, A.: Legal Knowledge Engineering - A modelling approach. IOS press (1995)

[4] Hart, H., Honore, T.: Causation in the Law. Oxford University Press (1985)

[5] Green, L.: Judge and Jury. Kansas City (1930)

[6] Hulswit, M.: A semeiotic account of causation - The cement of the Universe from a Peircean perspective. PhD thesis, Katholieke Universiteit Nijmegen (1998)

[7] Ducasse, C.: On the nature and observability of the causal relation. Journal of Philosophy 23 57-68 (1926)

[8] Russell, B.: Human Knowledge. Simon and Schuster (1948)

[9] Salmon, W.: Scientific Explanation and the Causal Structure of the World. Princeton University Press: Princeton (1984)

[10] Dowe, P.: Causality and conserved quantities: A reply to salmon. Philosophy of Science 62, 321-333 (1995)

[11] Davidson, D.: Essays on actions and events. Oxford University Press (1980)

A Constructive Framework for Legal Ontologies

Aldo Gangemi *, Maria-Teresa Sagri **, and Daniela Tiscornia **

*Laboratory for Applied Ontology, ISTC-CNR,
(Institute for Cognitive Sciences and Technology
of the Italian National Research Council), Rome Italy
** ITTIG-CNR (Institute for Theory and Techniques for Legal
Information of the Italian Research Council), Florence, Italy

Abstract. The increasing development of legal ontologies seems to offer inter-esting solutions to legal knowledge formalization, which in past experiences lead to a limited exploitation of legal expert systems for practical use. The pa-per describes how a constructive approach to ontology can provide useful com-ponents to create newly designed legal decision support systems either as local or Web-based semantic services. We describe the relation of our research to AI&Law and legal philosophy, the components of our Core Legal Ontology, the JurWordNet semantic lexicon, and some examples of use of legal ontologies for both norm conformity and compatibility. Our legal ontologies are based on DOLCE+, an extension of the DOLCE foundational ontology developed in the WonderWeb and Metokis EU projects.

1 Introduction

Originating from work carried out within a joint collaboration between the Laboratory for Applied Ontology of ISTC-CNR, and ITTIG-CNR, we show how legal ontologies offer a solid support for legal information systems, as they permit to make explicit the underlying assumptions, as well as the formal definition of the components of legal knowledge. We outline how some tasks carried out in the past can be revisited in a new perspective that can scale down to lightweight Semantic Web or information extraction application, or up to large knowledge-based systems requiring complex inferences.

The Semantic Web is a preferential context for legal ontology-driven applications, e.g. in the form of dynamically integrated *semantic web services*, directed towards citizens, companies, and institutions. Legal knowledge-based applications are also facing semantic integration problems that can be partly solved by using appropriate formal ontologies. When used jointly with a computational lexicon and NLP tools, legal ontologies can enhance information extraction from semi-structured and non-structured data. For a sample of the growing literature on these applications, see the LegOnt workshops proceedings: [1][2], the WORM workshops proceedings: [3][4], and this volume [5].

We introduce the theoretical basis of a Core Legal Ontology (CLO), currently used to support the definition of domain ontologies, the definition of a juridical wordnet, and the design of legal decision support systems. CLO is a so-called *constructive* on-

V.R. Benjamins et al. (Eds.): Law and the Semantic Web, LNCS 3369, pp. 97–124, 2005.
© Springer-Verlag Berlin Heidelberg 2005

tology, since it allows to reason over the contextual constraints that can be intentionally adopted by a cognitive agent when recognizing or classifying a state of affairs.

Three kinds of legal tasks in the Civil Law countries are supposed to be supported by CLO: *conformity checking*, *legal advice*, and *norm comparison*.

Conformity checking requires the representation of social and legal situations with reference to legal norms. A simple example is shown in Sect. 4.

Legal advice is a more complex scenario of conformity checking. It requires an investigation of the relations between legal cases and common sense situations that are not easily reconducible to expected cases. In large scale applications, legal advice involves crucial problems such as causality and responsibility assessment, open-textured concepts, interpretation issues, which are still being investigated from an ontological perspective (a more complex example of conformity, related to bundles of norms, is presented in [6]).

Norm comparison is explained here in the light of normative conflict handling. The theoretical notion of conflict between norms is introduced, with special reference to the assessment of compliance between EU directives and national legislation (an example is detailed in [7]).

The paper is structured as follow:

- Sect. 2 provides links to legacy methodologies for *legal knowledge formalization*.
- Sect. 3 introduces the basic theoretical framework of the Core Legal Ontology. The DOLCE foundational ontology and its *constructive* extension, D&S, are introduced.
- Sect. 4 presents CLO, its main classes and relations, a simple example of *legal advice*, and the JurWordNet lexical ontology, compliant with CLO.
- Sect. 5 describes how CLO can be used to represent *norm comparison* by introducing the notion of *compatibility scenario*.

2 The Legacy and the Problems

Using logic in the legal domain is an established tradition, and the application is possibly one of the most controversial. Normal vs. defeasible logics, case-based reasoning, event calculus, problem-solving methods, logic of argumentation, deontic logics, etc. constitute an as wide as possible palette of legal applications of logic that cannot be reviewed – let alone evaluated – within an article. We only list here some issues raised in the past, suggesting that a paradigm-breaking, ontology-based approach should learn from successful results and failures of legacy approaches.

The 80's experiences in the field of legal knowledge formalisation were mainly dedicated (especially in continental Civil Law countries) to the choice of the best paradigm of representation (declarative versus deductive approach, rule-based, logic-based), while in the 90's most of the AI&Law community turned its attention to the features of legal reasoning and of the dialectic dimension of law (deontic modalities, defeasible reasoning, argument construction).

Though, investigation on the type of entities involved in legal knowledge has been understated, leading to a partly opaque methodology for knowledge modelling: formalising legislative knowledge used to be a subjective process, time- (and cost-) consuming, relatively unreliable from the user's perspective, and not easily re-usable by different applications. As a consequence, legal expert systems never came out of the level of prototypical applications.

Before explaining our approach in the next sections, we list a sample list of the topics that past literature has treated extensively, and have been (or will) therefore considered by us:

- *Rule-based systems* (either as logic programming or production systems) and the ways of approximating the structure of legislation in formal terms [9][10][11][12][13][14][17]
- *Top-down* and *bottom-up* knowledge: legal definition, open-textured concepts, case-based reasoning [15][16][23]
- *Normative positions* (duties, rights, etc.) and deontic logic [15][17][18][19][20]
- *Meta-norms* and representation levels [13][21]
- *Epistemology vs. ontology*, and the nature of the entities in the legal world [5][17][22][55]
- *Argument construction* [8]

The need of an extended typology of legal entities is becoming a pressure, even from traditionally "bottom-up" approaches. For example, the need to pair case-based reasoning with an ontology of first-principles is being investigated [23] in order to represent the two kinds of structures employed in reasoning: abstraction from cases, and satisfaction of constraint sets (e.g. norms).

The level of granularity is also a core issue in developing Semantic Web ontologies, specially because a decentralized architecture is emerging for ontologies as well: how to compare/integrate/transform two ontologies about a close domain, but with a different detail encoded in its vocabulary and axioms?

Our approach to first principles and granularity aims at flexibility. We concentrate on the *ontological* nature of the legal domain, be it about the *entities* of the mental, social, or properly legal world. Those entities include the *constraints* that legal norms are supposed to generate over those *worlds*. I.e., we hold that:

- *representations of entities in context* are the primary structure manipulated in reasoning
- these representations are *constructed* by following certain structural dispositions, similar to those described by phenomenology, Gestalt psychology and related theories (e.g. [24][25][26])
- the *logical form* of representations should be as neutral as possible from an ontological viewpoint, in order to be able to "reengineer" any existing formal or informal theory, in terms of ontological *descriptions* or *redescriptions* of whatever entities can be constructed by the cognitive system of an agent
- such (re)*descriptions are put in the same ontological domain as the entities represented*, thus enabling comparison and reuse of the contextual assumptions.

A first, intuitive exemplification of what happens when we formalise a logical domain so liberally stated is that we can talk of the constraints defined in a traffic norm for limiting the speed of vehicles in the same domain as the entities (cars, persons, speeds, drivings) involved in the application of that norm.

In the next sections, we introduce such an ontological framework.

3   The Foundational Framework

The basic types of entities that populate the domain of Law are assumed to be clearly identifiable and reasonably intersubjective, and, as such, they are pointed out through a minimal set of properties and relations from DOLCE [27] and some of its recent extensions, notably the "Descriptions and Situations" ontology (D&S) [25][26][28]. DOLCE extended by D&S will be referred here as "DOLCE+".

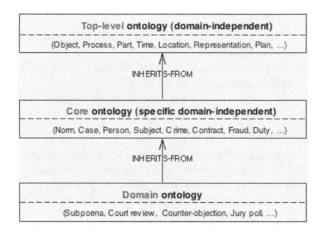

Fig. 1. Examples of classes and relations as distributed in the legal ontology library strata

DOLCE (a *a Descriptive Ontology for Linguistic and Cognitive Engineering*) is a *foundational ontology* (FO) developed originally in the EU WonderWeb project[1]. FOs are domain-independent axiomatic theories, contain a rich axiomatization of their vocabulary, and are used in order to make the rationales and alternatives underlying different ontological choices as explicit as possible.

DOLCE is essentially a top-level FO, while DOLCE+ is an extension of DOLCE containing some modules dedicated to core ontologies of contexts, time, space, plans, etc. The current implementation of DOLCE+ is DOLCE-Lite-Plus, which aims at:

- allowing the implementation of DOLCE-based ontologies in languages that are less expressive than FOL. Temporal indexing is partly supported by 'composing' originally indexed relations with temporal location relations. Even this support is not provided for description logic versions of DOLCE-Lite-Plus, like OWL-DL.
- allowing a description-logic-like naming policy for DOLCE signature. In many cases, different names are adopted for relations that have the same name but different arities in the FOL version, or for relations that have polymorphic domains
- allowing extensions of DOLCE, and modularizing them
- taking benefit of the services of certain implemented languages – specially the classification services provided by description logics – in order to support domain applications.

---

[1] http://wonderweb.semanticweb.org

DOLCE categories are conceived as *conceptual containers*: there is no "deep" metaphysical implications with respect to "true" reality, and the domain of quantification ranges on *possibilia* (possible, not only actual entities, so that we are allowed to postulate entities out of existentially quantified variables, which are not explicitly introduced in a model, cf. [27]). Basic DOLCE top-level includes the following mutually disjoint categories and relations (Fig. 2):

- **Endurant** (including Objects or Substances) and **Perdurant** (including Events, States, or Processes) are linked by the relation of *participation*.
- Endurants are *localized in* space, and get their temporal location from the perdurants they participate in. Perdurants are localized in time, and get their spatial location from the endurants participating in them.
- **Qualities** *inhere in* either Endurants (as Physical or Abstract Qualities) or in Events (as Temporal Qualities), and they correspond to "individualized properties", i.e. they inhere only in a specific entity, e.g. "the color of this court", "the velocity of this serve", etc.
- Each kind of Quality is associated to a **Quality Space** representing the space of the values that qualities can assume (e.g. a metric space).
- Different quality spaces associated to the same kind of quality are admitted.
- Quality Spaces, as all **Abstracts** (the fourth category), are neither in time nor in space.
- **Space** and **Time** are specific quality spaces.
- Different kinds of space and time are admitted (e.g. Galilean vs. Newtonian).
- Different endurants or perdurants can be spatio-temporally co-localized.
- Relations between instances of a same category are contemplated, e.g.: *part, constitution, connectedness*, etc.

This framework is partly depicted in Fig. 2. For the sake of visual clarity, we show our ontologies in UML class diagrams, assuming a description logic-like semantics [29] for them: *classes* are interpreted as *concepts* (but dashed class boxes are interpreted as *individuals*), *generalization* is interpreted as *formal subsumption*, *association* is interpreted as a binary relation with cardinality encoded for it and its inverse (where no cardinality is indicated, the default is 0..*). The ontologies mentioned here are available in various languages and formats [http://www.loa-cnr.it].

In DOLCE+, basic DOLCE is extended by means of the D&S ontology[2]. In D&S, DOLCE is taken as a *ground ontology*, i.e. an ontology that is used to represent the entities in a domain, without considering their epistemological (constructive) status [26].

For example, the entities (e.g. from social reality) constrained by norms and regulations are in the domain of the ground ontology, in this case of DOLCE. Therefore, the legal world is conceived as a *description* of social reality, an ideal view of the behaviour of a social group, according to a system of rules that are commonly accepted and acknowledged.

The current version of CLO is based on the D&S distinction between **descriptions** (in this domain *legal* descriptions, or *conceptualisations*), which encompass laws,

---

[2] Besides WonderWeb, D&S is currently refined as an ontology of plans and information objects in the EU Metokis project: http://metokis.salzburgresearch.at.

norms, regulations, crime types, etc., and **situations** (*legal facts* or *cases* in the legal domain), which encompass legal states of affairs, non-legal states of affairs that are relevant to the Law, and purely juridical states of affairs. This enables us to use such distinction to represent meta-juridical conceptualisations (*meta-norms*) as well.

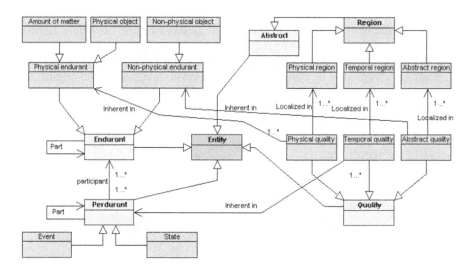

Fig. 2. A UML class diagram showing the basic classes and relations of DOLCE

D&S basic predicates and axioms are briefly sketched in the following [26][28]:

(i) a **Description** is a social object, which represents a conceptualization, hence it is generically dependent on some cognitive agent, and is communicable [26]. Like physical objects, social objects have a lifecycle, can have parts, etc. Differently from physical objects, social objects are dependent on some agentive physical object that is able to *conceive* them. Descriptions have typical components, called *concepts*. Example of descriptions are regulations, plans, laws, diagnoses, projects, plots, techniques, etc. (for an explanation of such a variety, and of respective differences, cf. [28]).

(ii) a **Situation** is an entity that appears in the domain of an ontology when there is a description whose components can "carve up" a view (*setting*) on that domain. A situation aims at representing the referent of a "cognitive disposition" towards a world, i.e. the willingness, expectation, desire, belief, etc. to carve up that world in a certain way. Consequently, a situation has to *satisfy* a description (see below). Examples of situations, related to the examples of descriptions above, are: facts, plan executions, legal cases, diagnostic cases, attempted projects, performances, technical actions, etc.

(iii) a **Concept** is also a social object, which is **defined by** a description. Once defined, a concept can be **used in** other descriptions. The **classifies** relation relates concepts and entities (then possibly even concepts). There are several kinds of concepts reified in D&S, the primary ones (**role**, **course**, and **parameter**) being distinguished by the categories of entities they classify in DOLCE:

Defines(x,y) $\rightarrow$ Description(x) $\wedge$ Concept(y)
Classifies(x,y) $\rightarrow$ Concept(x) $\wedge$ Entity(y)
Classifies(x,y) $\rightarrow$ $\exists$t. TimeInterval(t) $\wedge$ Classifies(x,y,t)[3]
Concept(x) $\rightarrow$ SocialObject(x) $\wedge$ $\exists$y. Defines(y,x) $\wedge$ Description(y)
Role(x) $=_{df}$ Concept(x) $\wedge$ $\forall$y. Classifies(x,y) $\rightarrow$ Endurant(y)
Course(x) $=_{df}$ Concept(x) $\wedge$ $\forall$y. Classifies(x,y) $\rightarrow$ Perdurant(y)
Parameter(x) $=_{df}$ Concept(x) $\wedge$ $\exists$y. Classifies(x,y) $\wedge$ $\forall$y. Classifies(x,y) $\rightarrow$ Region(y)

Examples of roles are: *manager, student, assistant, actuator, toxic agent,* etc. Examples of courses are *routes, pathways, tasks,* etc. Examples of parameters are: *speed limits, allowed colors* (e.g. for a certain book cover), *temporal constraints,* etc. Roles can be **specialized by** other roles, e.g. *president of Italian republic* specializes *president of republic*:

Specializes(x,y) $\rightarrow$ Role(x) $\wedge$ Role(y)
$\forall$xy$\exists$z. (Classifies(x,y) $\wedge$ Specializes(x,z)) $\rightarrow$ Classifies(z,y)

(iv) **Figures**, or **social individuals** (either agentive or not) are other social objects, defined by descriptions, but differently from concepts, they do not classify entities:

Figure(x) $\rightarrow$ SocialObject(x)
Figure(x) $\rightarrow$ $\exists$y. Description(y) $\wedge$ Defines(y,x)
Figure(x) $\rightarrow$ $\neg\exists$y. Classifies(x,y)

Examples of figures are organisations, political geographic objects, sacred symbols, etc.

(v) **Agentive figures** are those which are assigned (agentive) roles from a society or community; hence, they can *act* like a physical agent:

AgentiveFigure(x) $\rightarrow$ Figure(x) $\wedge$ $\exists$y,z,w. Description(y) $\wedge$ Role(z) $\wedge$ Description(w)
$\wedge$ y$\neq$w $\wedge$ Defines(y,z) $\wedge$ Defines(w,x) $\wedge$ Classifies(z,x)

Typical agentive figures are societies, organizations, and in general all socially constructed persons.

(vi) Figures are not dependent on roles defined or used in the same descriptions they are defined or used, but they can act because they **depute** some powers to some of those roles. In other words, a figure classified by some agentive role can play that role because there is someone (or something) that plays other roles in the descriptions that define or use the figure. Those roles classify endurants, which result to **act for** the figure:

DeputedBy(r,f) $\rightarrow$ Role(r) $\wedge$ Figure(f) $\wedge$ $\exists$d. Description(d) $\wedge$ Uses(d,r) $\wedge$ Uses(d,f)
DeputedBy(r,f) $\rightarrow$ $\exists$r$_1$. Role(r$_1$) $\wedge$ Classifies(r$_1$,f)
ActsFor(e,f) $\rightarrow$ $\exists$r. Role(r) $\wedge$ DeputedBy(r,f) $\wedge$ Classifies(r,e)

---

[3] For brevity, we introduce and use D&S relations without a *temporal index*. In fact, e.g. *classifies* has to understood at a time *t*. In languages like OWL-DL, some workarounds must be used in order to express temporal indexing.

In complex figures, like organizations or institutions, a *total enactment* is possible (usually limited to some actions), when an endurant plays a *delegate*, or *representative* role of the figure.

(vii) Since descriptions and concepts are (social) objects, they can also be classified by a role in another description. This recursivity can manage meta-level descriptions in D&S (e.g. a *norm* for enforcing norms will define a role that can classify the *enforced norm*). The same machinery acts when managing norm conflicts (see section 4).

(viii) The *classifies* relation is specialized by three subrelations: **played by**, **sequences**, and **valued by**, for three different categories in DOLCE (Endurant, Perdurant, and Region)[4]:

$$PlayedBy(x,y) =_{df} Role(x) \land Endurant(y) \land Classifies(x,y)$$
$$Sequences(x,y) =_{df} Course(x) \land Perdurant(y) \land Classifies(x,y)$$
$$ValuedBy(x,y) =_{df} Parameter(x) \land Region(y) \land Classifies(x,y)$$

(ix) Roles or figures, and courses are related by relations expressing the **attitudes** that (players of) roles, and figures can have **towards** a course:

$$AttitudeTowards(x,y) \rightarrow (Role(x) \lor Figure(x)) \land Course(y)$$

Attitude towards is the descriptive counterpart of the "participant-in" relation used in the ground ontology, i.e. attitudes are *participation modes*. In other words, the AttitudeTowards relation can be used to state e.g. *alethic, epistemic*, or *deontic* operators, as well as *agentivity* or *subjection* that an endurant can have with respect to an action or process.

For example, a person is usually *obliged* to drive in a way that prevents hurting other persons. Or a person can have the *right* to express her ideas. Another, more complex example: a BDI application to a certain ordered set of tasks including initial conditions (beliefs), final conditions (desires), and ways to reach goals (intentions). In other words, moving from beliefs to goals is a way of bounding one or more agent(s) to a sequence of actions. In our *plan ontology* [28] this intuition is deepened considerably.

(x) Parameters and roles, figures, or courses are related by a **requisite for** relation, expressing the kind of requisites entities that are classified by roles or courses should have:

$$RequisiteFor(x,y) \rightarrow Parameter(x) \land (Role(x) \lor Figure(x) \lor Course(y))$$

Requisites are constraints over the attributes of entities. When a situation satisfies a description that uses parameters, endurants and perdurants that constitute the situation must have attributes that range within the boundaries stated by parameters (in DOLCE terms, entities must have qualities that are mapped to certain value ranges of regions).

---

[4] Only three categories from DOLCE have been assigned a concept type at the descriptive layer, because the resulting design pattern is simpler, and no relevant knowledge seems to be lost, at least in applications developed until now.

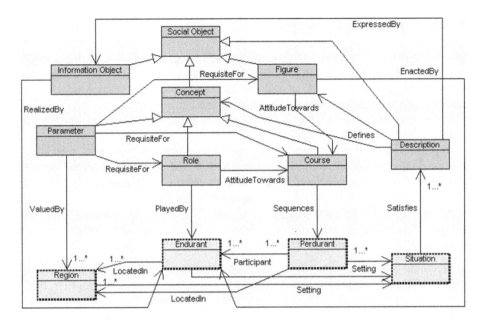

Fig. 3. The D&S Design Pattern as a UML class diagram. The lower part of the pattern is called the *ground ontology*, the higher is called the *descriptive ontology*; a situation satisfies a description if the two parts match according to specified rules

For example, a *speed limit of 50kmph* can be a requisite for a *driving task*; a satisfying situation will have any *speed* of driving (e.g. in an instance of *driving in Rome by car*) to be less or equal to *50kmph*.

(xi) Information objects are other social objects, **expressed according to** special descriptions called *combinatorial systems* (or *codes*), which are able to **express** descriptions and other social objects. Information objects are **realized by** objects whose properties match those required by the combinatorial system (cf. [28] for more details on these ideas, and [30] for a review of the relations between ontology and semiotics):

InformationObject(x) → SocialObject(x)
InformationObject(x) → ∃y. Description(y) ∧ ExpressedAccordingTo(x,y)
InformationObject(x) → ∃y. Endurant(y) ∧ RealizedBy(x,y)
Description(x) → ∃y. InformationObject(y) ∧ ExpressedBy(x,y)

(xii) The **setting** relation holds between situations and entities from the ground ontology. At least a perdurant must exist in the situation setting:

SettingFor(x,y) → Situation(x) ∧ Entity(y)
SettingFor(x,y) → ∃z. Perdurant(z) ∧ SettingFor(x,z)

We have introduced only a subset of the axioms and predicates used in DOLCE+ (see related papers), which are used to characterize the basic notions of CLO.

4 The Core Legal Ontology

The development of the Core Legal Ontology (CLO) takes into account methodologies proper of *foundational* ontologies [27], proposals in the field of legal ontologies (e.g. [31], Breuker et al. in [5]), as well as a large literature on legal knowledge representation and legal philosophy (see introduction and below).

CLO organises juridical concepts and relations on the basis of formal properties defined in DOLCE+.

In practice, a *legal description* D_T (the *content* of a norm, a regulation, a decision, etc.) is assumed to be the reification of a theory T that (potentially) formalizes the content of a norm or a bundle of norms, while a *legal case* C_S is assumed to be the reification of a state of affairs S that is a logical model of T.

When we use this distinction together with the DOLCE foundational ontology, we get typical mapping functions from the elements of T into the components of D_T, and from the elements of S into the setting of C_S. For example:

- Perdurant entities (e.g. *hearing, stabbing, driving*) in a case setting must be *sequenced by* some legal course of events (e.g. *reconstructed steps of a murder, driving constraints from a traffic norm*). There can be *optional* (or even *discarded*) actions (e.g. envisaged by a special class of courses), which – if present – must be sequenced as well.
- Endurant entities (e.g. *person, knife, car*) in a case setting must *play* some legal role (e.g. *citizen, witness, weapon, vehicle*). Optional endurants can be envisaged by special roles.
- Region entities (e.g. *in the afternoon, ≤60kmh*) in a case setting must be *values for* some legal parameter (e.g. *murder time, speed limit*). Optional regions are envisaged by special parameters.
- Legal courses, roles, and parameters are all *defined* or *used by* a legal description.
- Legal parameters are *requisites for* roles and courses (e.g. *murder time* can be a requisite for its reconstruction, *speed limit* is a requisite for a (legal) driving task).
- Legal roles have an *attitude towards* a *course* of events (e.g. citizens are *obliged to* a procedure to paying taxes).
- Legal persons are *agentive figures*.
- Legal texts are *information objects realized* by legal documents or other material representations.

Hence, a legal description defines or uses legal persons, as well as legal roles, legal courses of events, and legal parameters that classify entities that result to be bound to the setting that makes a legal case emerge. This framework enables us to build a complex, *functional* representation of the Law and of its facts. It is also clear that functions can be constructed out of different norms for the same entities; this is the reason why CLO is a *constructive ontology*.

4.1 Reified Satisfiability for Legal Descriptions

Since the *satisfaction* relation holding between legal descriptions and cases is the reified counterpart of the formal semantic *satisfiability* relation, we can specialize it in order to create a *taxonomy* of satisfiability. In fact, various kinds of semantic satisfiability can be envisaged according to the *function* a theory is supposed to describe, for example:

- The way of *executing* an obligation.
- The way of *exercizing* a power.
- The way of *realizing* a desire.
- What is *believed* to be true.
- The *suggested* way to act.
- What is *expected* to happen.
- The way of *preventing* something to happen.
- The way of *assessing* the *conformity* of a state of affairs against a rule.
- The way of *assessing* the *compatibility* of two norms.

The **satisfies** (SAT) relation holds between situations and descriptions, and implies that at least some concept in a description must classify at least some entity in the situation setting:

$$\text{SAT(x,y)} \rightarrow \text{Situation(x)} \land \text{Description(y)}$$
$$\text{SAT(x,y)} \rightarrow \exists z.\ \text{Concept(z)} \land \text{Uses(y,z)} \land \exists w.\ \text{SettingFor(x,w)} \land \text{Classifies(z,w)}$$

This constraint is quite generic and even counterintuitive from a logical viewpoint. In fact, for specialised descriptions additional constraints should be given in order to reason over the satisfaction of candidate situations. This "relaxed" semantics for satisfaction needs some explanation.

In general, D&S (and CLO) does not constrain situations to include *only* entities classified by the concepts of a description. In other words, reified satisfaction admits *redundant* models (which result to be *undecidable* from a strict semantical viewpoint).

This assumption may seem logically rough, but real world uses of D&S have shown that most situations derive from legacy situations that already have an internal structure, and depriving them under the sole purpose of getting non-redundant situations seems a bad practice. For example, a *detective report* may contain useless informations from the point of view of a certain *legal rule*, but to a certain extent, it is important to preserve the *unity* of the report, instead of "cleaning" it up to a new entity that merely satisfies the legal rule description.

Under this assumption, the same situation can satisfy different descriptions that can even be unrelated. The formal consistency is given by the fact that legacy situations already satisfy other descriptions.

Moreover, D&S admits a *qualified satisfaction*: the set of concepts that "must" classify an entity in a situation can be explicitly stated by means of a set of axioms that specialise the *satisfies* relation for a certain domain.

Summing up, reified satisfaction in D&S allows for situations that can be redundant on one hand (the respective non-reified models would be undecidable, but reified ones aren't, because they are decidable with respect to the ground ontology), and more restricted on the other hand (only certain non-reified models would be acceptable). Since reification allows a common domain for both ground and descriptive parts of an ontology, reified satisfaction does not lead to undecidability, and allows a custom design of the satisfiability conditions.

4.2 A Simple Example: Art. 142 of the Italian Traffic Code

In order to exemplify our method to formalize norms and bundles of norms, we take a norm out of the first paragraph in the Art. 142 of the Italian Traffic Code (the bold-faced words are the text of the norm we formalize):

*1. Ai fini della sicurezza della circolazione e della tutela della vita umana **la velocità massima non può superare** i 130 km/h per le autostrade, i 110 km/h per le strade extraurbane principali, i 90 km/h per le strade extraurbane secondarie e per le strade extraurbane locali, ed **i 50 km/h per le strade nei centri abitati**, ...*

The selected norm states that "in urban roads, the maximum speed limit is 50kmh" (provided possible exceptions for special vehicles and/or roads, which we ignore here for the sake of simplicity). Here we present the resulting model (Fig. 4), built according to the legal adaptation of DOLCE+.

Firstly, we introduce the entities mentioned in the norm, either explicitly ot *implicitly* (like *vehicle* and *driver*). Implicit entities reveal the actual *systemic* nature of the Law, which hardly presents itself in the form of isolated norms:

LegalNorm(UrbanSpeedLimit@Art142_ITC)
Parameter(UrbanSpeedLimit)
LegalRole(Vehicle)
LegalRole(Driver)
LegalCourse(DrivingTask)
LegalCourse(RunningTask)
SpeedValue($\leq$50kmh)

Secondly, we introduce the relations between the norm and its components, e.g. the urban speed limit *defined* in the norm, as well as the *used* concepts:

Defines(UrbanSpeedLimit@Art142_ITC, UrbanSpeedLimit)
Uses(UrbanSpeedLimit@Art142_ITC, Vehicle)
Uses(UrbanSpeedLimit@Art142_ITC, Driver)
Uses(UrbanSpeedLimit@Art142_ITC, RunningTask)
Uses(UrbanSpeedLimit@Art142_ITC, DrivingTask)

Thirdly, we provide the *articulation* of the concepts inside the norm, e.g. the relation between the parameter and its expected value, the attitudes prefigured by roles with respect to to course, the ordering of roles and tasks, etc.:

ValuedBy(UrbanSpeedLimit, $\leq$50kmh)
ObligationTowards(Driver, DrivingTask)

AnankasticDutyTowards(Vehicle, RunningTask)[5]
RequisiteFor(UrbanSpeedLimit, RunningTask)
DependsOn(Driver, Vehicle)
DirectSuccessor(ConcurrencyTask, DriverTask)
DirectSuccessor(ConcurrencyTask, RunningTask)

A simple case (involving a guy named A. Basilisco and a high-speed travel on his car) is then depicted which should be checked for conformity to the model that formalizes the norm:

LegalCase(Driving_PT_130804_#1209)
LegalPerson(A.Basilisco)
Car(TR4#PT130CC21)
SpeedValue(120kmh)
Activity(A.Basilisco's_travel_130804)
SettingFor(Driving_PT_130804_#1209, A.Basilisco)
SettingFor(Driving_PT_130804_#1209, TR4#PT130CC21)
SettingFor(Driving_PT_130804_#1209, A.Basilisco's_travel_130804)
SettingFor(Driving_PT_130804_#1209, 120kmh)
LocatedIn(A.Basilisco's_travel_130804, 120kmh)
ParticipantIn(A.Basilisco, A.Basilisco's_travel_130804)
ParticipantIn(TR4#PT130CC21, A.Basilisco's_travel_130804)

We can easily realize that the case does not conform to the norm, since although most mandatory concepts in the norm classify appropriate entities:

PlayedBy(Driver, A.Basilisco)
PlayedBy(Vehicle, TR4#PT130CC21)
Sequences(ConcurrencyTask, A.Basilisco's_travel_130804)
Sequences(RunningTask, A.Basilisco's_travel_130804)
Sequences(DrivingTask, A.Basilisco's_travel_130804)

the requisite expressed by the urban speed limit cannot classify the speed value of the car in the case:

? ValuedBy(UrbanSpeedLimit, 120kmh)

no, because:

>(120kmh, 50kmh)

and then 120kmh cannot be a part of the ≤50kmh region (i.e., an accepted value). Since the satisfaction axioms for legal norms require that *all* mandatory concepts (UrbanSpeedLimit is one of them) in a norm must classify appropriate entities, the legal

---

[5] An anakastic duty [54] is a deontic notion for required activities that must be executed by non-agentive objects, in this case any object playing the role of vehicle.

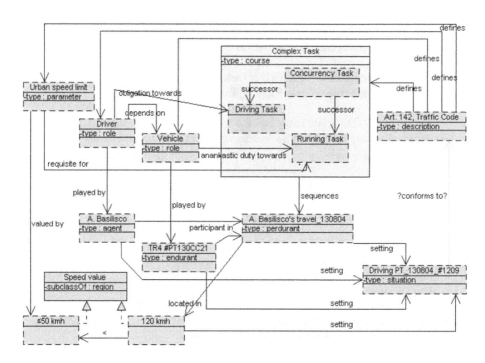

Fig. 4. *A UML class diagram showing an application of CLO to describe a simple traffic norm and a case of non-conformity (see text). Dashed boxes represent* individuals

case does not conform to the traffic norm, and the *reactive power* of the legal system can be enacted against the non-conforming driver.

The example presented may appear quite redundant compared to a traditional rule-based approach, but despite the triviality of the example, we appreciate the following advantages, involving the *legal system as a whole*:

- Both first order rules and rules containing modal operators are reified as sets of first-order assertions.
- *Patterns* of normative content can be built by specialising the predicates and axioms from a same core theory (CLO).
- The reused or implicit reference to other norms can be represented in the same domain as the one explicitly referenced in the norm.
- Constraints existing in the reference (*ground*) world (e.g. the velocity of an object) are represented in the same domain as the normative world, but they are also explicitly distinguished and interwoven.
- As shown in sections 4 and 5, conflicting norms can be compared with respect to to a meta-description, also represented in the same domain.
- Ongoing work seems to show that for norms including more than 5 or 6 descriptive entities, the resulting model seems even less complex than a corresponding one based on rule-based systems.

– Extensive reification allows for lightweight first-order theories and models, which can be represented in less expressive Semantic Web languages like OWL-DL [32] without much loss of content, then enabling also automatic classification of cases thorugh description logic reasoners.

4.3 Types of Entities in the Legal World

CLO and JurWordNet are populated by legal notions, which are represented according to the abovementioned assumptions. Here we informally discuss some of those notions and how they are represented.

Law, in the generic sense of the Latin *ius*, is *composed of* norms that include social and ethical rules, practices, and conventions. Law is a complex, autonomous entity, which includes its self-recognition rules [33], therefore it cannot be considered as a mere *sum* of norms, as shown even in the most trivial normative contexts.

Legal norm is defined in legal theory as the 'meaning of a prescriptive proposition'. In CLO, Legal Norm is a sub-class of (Social) Norm, which is *expressed by* a Normative Text, and is *realized by* a (physical, electronic, etc.) Document. Since we consider a legal norm as a collection of (reified) propositions and not as a sequence of linguistic expressions, we do not commit to a strict correspondence between a norm as conceptualised in CLO and a segment of legal text, either as partitioned by the hierarchical structure of Legislative Acts (paragraphs, sub-paragraph, etc.), or as articulated by a natural language.

Regulations. In a wider meaning, all normative propositions deductively inferred by a norm, including norms instantiated by a legal decision or stated by contract, can be considered norms [34]. In CLO the class *regulation* encompasses all entities which can be considered norms according to this wide interpretation.

Types of norms. Norms may even be *satisfied by* purely juridical Situations, as for norms that describe others norms: (e.g. amendments, law making norms, validity norms.). A legal norm *functionally depends on* Constitutive Norms and on Collective Acceptance (for a discussion of collectives and their ontological status, cf. [35] and [36]). Among norms, *constitutive* and *regulative* norms are distinguished. Approximately, Constitutive Norms introduce new entities in the ground ontology, while Regulative Norms provide constraints on existing ground entities. In particular, Constitutive Norms *define* (in the D&S sense) e.g. Legally-constructed Institutions, Legal Functions and Legal Powers. *Definition* and *power-conferring rules* are sub-classes of constitutive norms. Regulative Norms *define* Behaviour Courses, and have at least one Modal Description as a *proper part*.

For example, according to their type, norms can define:

– Legally-constructed persons (defined by constitutive norms).
– Institutional agents (defined by constitutive norms).
– Legal roles (defined by constitutive norms).
– Institutional powers (defined by power-conferring norms).
– Behaviours (defined by regulative norms).
– Incrimination acts as legal courses (defined by incriminating norms).
– Legally-relevant Cognitive courses (defined by presumptions).

Modal Descriptions are typically *proper parts* of other norms. They contain some *modal* relation (called *attitude towards* in D&S) between Legal Roles or Agents defined or used by the norm, and Legal Courses of events (descriptions of actions to be executed according to the norm). The classification of Modal Descriptions is based on the Hohfeld's *Theory of basic conception* and on the *Theory of normative positions* [37][38]. Recent revisions by legal philosophers and logicians [39][20][39] provided a formal framework and a computational transposition of it. Following Hohfeld's approach, the normative positions are mainly described throughout relations of opposition/correlation between them (see below for examples). In the DOLCE+ ontology, modalized descriptions reify epistemic, deontic or action logic statements. Non-reified theories are traditionally expressed in some deontic or action logic, as in [39], but the reified counterpart allows one to talk of partial or incomplete statements, and allows reasoning on them at first-order. Here we list some classes of legal modal descriptions.

- **Legal Rights** are a *social advantage* (Bentham), a *free choice* (Hart), or a *protected interest* (MacCormick); it justifies the imposition of duties, the entitlement of claims and privileges, the transfer of powers. In this wide sense, it includes subjective rights. In the strict sense, it is, according to the Hofheldian definition, *correlative of* Duty and better expressed by Claim, which is a subclass of Legal Right.
- Other normative positions are **Duty**, **Privilege**, (*correlative of* **Non-Right**), **Immunity**, (*correlative of* **Disability**). Disability is *opposite of* Abstract Power.
- **Abstract Powers/Capacities** are *proper parts of* constitutive rules that assert attitudes for some roles or figures to be entitled of rights/claims, or of specific powers. In Civil Law systems, Capacity to Act is a subclass of Legal Capacity. The role *legal subject* (see below) is entitled of a legal capacity, but not necessarily of a capacity to perform valid legal acts.
- **Legal Powers** are *proper parts of* power-conferring norms; the most important subclass is that of Institutional Powers.
- **Legal Empowerments** are *proper parts of* power-conferring norms, and imply, as a Prerequisite, a Potestative Right or a simple Power. Potestative Rights are the powers to create (or modify) legal states of affairs in the sphere of other legal subjects. They require, as a prerequisite, the Disability of the involved subject (e.g., Civil Law's *patria potestas* of parents towards minor children), or the Willing of the involved subject, as *expressed* by an Act of Delegation, and by a Mandate. The *opposite of* Potestative Right is Liability (not of the directed bearer of obligation, but of the involved subject).
- **Faculty/Implicit Permission:** in deontic logic an implicit permission derives from the absence of an obligation; they differ from legal powers because they don't imply the production of new legal effects. It is *opposite*, in Hohfeld's theory, to Non-Right.
- **Explicit Permissions** imply a Liability of the permitted agent towards the agent who detects the power to permit, the adoption of the permitted goal, and the empowerment of the permitted agent in relation to the permitted action. They are *proper parts of* Authorisations [39].

Legal Roles are (functional) roles *played* by either physical or social objects. Among legal roles, some of them constitute the basic entities of the legal world, such as Legal Subject and Legal Asset. Legal Subject is an *agentive* legal role, while Legal Asset is *non-agentive*. Legal subjects can be *played* either by physical agents or by legally constructed individuals. **Legal Functions** are legal roles, *played* by legal subjects. Among legal functions, so-called Primary Functions (e.g. Son, Heir, Citizen) are *defined by* constitutive norms.

Legal Agents (legally-constructed social individuals) are agentive figures *defined* by constitutive norms. A Natural Legal Person *plays* the role Legal Subject because of its only physical existence (but the property is extended temporally before and after death, as far as legal effects of her actions are still ongoing). A Legal Person needs to fit strict requirements, such as age, mental non-illness, or artificial existence. **Legally-constructed Institutions** (e.g. Ministries, Bodies, Societies, Agencies) are legal agents that perform legal acts, on behalf of powers conferred by means of power-conferring norms. They are created by constitutive norms that justify their existence and validity. An important subclass of them includes Institutional Powers.

Legal Information Objects are information objects that *express* legal descriptions according to some combinatorial code. For example, Expression of Willingness may be a Linguistic Object (an Oral Expression), as well as it can be realized through manifested actions. Legal Information Objects are in fact *realized* by some e.g. physical document. They can *specifically depend on* **Legal Documents**, in which a certain form is a requirement for the valid existence of a Legal Act (for instance: a Will, a Juridical Text).

Legal Cognitive Objects (e.g. Will, Agreements, Mistakes) are situations, which *depend on* information objects, and are settings for mental processes or states. Cognitive objects have a *specific dependence* on agentive physical objects (e.g. a natural person), and either satisfy existing social and legal norms, or are *cases* of non-conformity.

Among legal cognitive objects, (expressed) Intentionality (to do something) is subsumed by (expressed) Will (to do sth), which is subsumed by (assumed or expressed) Consciousness (of sth). *Suitas* (Free Will) grounds the distinction between fault and intentional fraud in Crime Law.

Legal Facts (including *cases*) are situations *depending on* norms (only facts relevant for legal systems are legal facts). Legal facts may include Natural Facts (e.g. a death), which are dependent on phenomena, but not on (inherently intentional) human actions. On the other hand, Human Facts depend on conscious intentional human actions. Human facts include: i) Institutional Facts, which are the legal counterpart of natural phenomena, being directly created by the application of constitutive norms, ii) Legal Acts, which depend on the will of some legal agent, iii) Legal Transactions, which depend on the intentionality of some legal agent.

Crimes are situations that *satisfy* **incriminating norms**. Incriminating norms define or use at least one *course* (the commitment to a sanctioning action) related to some action that is *forbidden* or *illegal* to some legal role or agent. *Aggravating* or *extenuating circumstances* are situations (e.g. *being an institutional representative*, or *being linked by a parenthood relation to the victim*, etc.) that are *proper parts* of a crime situation.

The notion of **responsibility** that is of crucial relevance in the legal domain is not enough defined yet, as it needs to be linked to a notion of material *causation* which is still in progress inside the DOLCE framework (cf. Lehmann, in [5], [40]).

Among **qualities** that are usually *inherent in* entities from the setting of legal transactions are: *temporal qualities* such as duration (typical *legal parameters* are: Deferment, Expiration, Term, etc) and *validity assessment qualities* (e.g. Valid, Void, Voidable).

4.3 JurWordNet: An Ontology-Driven Legal Lexicon

Semantic lexicons are means for content management. Coupled with Natural Language Processing tools, they integrate parsing of morpho-syntactic aspects with shallow meaning understanding, and are thus basic elements in many implementation areas.

JurWordNet [41] is an ontology-driven semantic lexicon, designed as an extension of the Italian version [42] of *EuroWordNet* [43].

The motivation for JurWordNet originates from the Norme In Rete₆ (NIR) project, to which JurWordNet provides a source of metadata for semantic tagging. JurWordNet can also be used as a support tool for information retrieval and extraction systems, in order to facilitate the access to heterogeneous and multilingual data₇, and a conceptual source for information extraction, automatic tagging, etc. With reference to norm comparison, JurWordNet can be considered a link between the domain ontologies and the legislative texts, since it provides a wide coverage of legal concepts and their lexical realisations.

As in the original WordNet [44], JurWordNet senses are represented by *synsets*. A synset is a set of terms (*house, home, dwelling domicile*), linked by a relation of meaning equivalence (expressing approximately the same conceptualization). Proper synsets in the legal lexicon are rare, while we found it important to create mapping relations to common language, in order to allow imprecise searches made by non-experts when using terms from common language instead of juridical terminology. Besides taxonomic (*hyponymy*) relations, the synsets of legal lexicon also have associative horizontal relations such as *meronymy* and *role*.

Consistent to WordNet projects, the developing methodology favors the use and harmonization of already existing lexicon resources. Relevant concepts have been extracted in a *bottom-up* way, from a corpus of queries made to legacy legal information systems. In particular the lists of the Italgiure/Find system, the largest Italian legal information system, developed by the Italian *Corte di Cassazione*, produced:

- the Semi database, 11,000 key words and lemmas, conceptually connected
- the list of terms that common users includes in AND, from which derives the *list of syntagms*, a group of about 13,000 two-word expressions

---

⁶ Report on *"Il progetto Norme in rete"*, Rome, www.normeinrete.it/documenti, 2000.
⁷ The Project LOIS (Legal Ontologies for Knowledge Sharing), financed within the e-Content program ,aims at creating a JurWordNet in five European languages., (English, German, Portuguese, Czech, and Italian, linked by English).

- the list of words that common users include in OR, the so-called *analogical chain*. Analogical chains are made up of synonyms, or terms that, at least in a certain amount of researches, were declared interchangeable by the majority of users
- from syntagms, the taxonomy was automatically created by using *head* and *modifier* terms, aided by a parsing of a corpus of dictionary glosses. A consolidated corpus of about 2000 synsets will be almost automatically augmented through the link with thesauri and keywords for juridical databases.

The most interesting function of wordnets is the disambiguation of **polysemy**. For instance, the Italian juridical term *canone* means both a payment in money or in kind, against a contract; or, in Canonic Law, a universal juridical norm. The Italian term *mora* is meant both as "unjustified lateness in discharging an obligation" and as "the amount of money due as a fine against the delay". The Italian term *alimento* substantially changes its meaning if considered in its singular form as "food", or plural form as "alimony". The entry *alienation* in a juridical context is a juridical act; whereas in common Italian it has several meanings, all unrelated to the legal technical meaning.

Often, sense distinctions do not only concern the history of language, but also interdependent notions used in organizing social reality. For instance, a typical **systematic polysemy** is that between an institution, a function, and a physical object: the entry *President of the Republic* can indicate a physical person, the constitutional body, or the holder of the state function. Another example, very common in Law, is the systematic polysemy involving both a normative content and a physical entity: the entry *contract* may be conceptualized as a legal transaction, as a physical document, or as an information object. The entry *appeal* can express the sense of a *petition* made to a Judge, and the *written document* of that petition. The entry *office* can express the function and the physical place where the function takes place.

Systematic polysemy shows neatly the need for detailed ontology. While semantic lexicons can represent simple polysemy, the systematic relations occurring between the different senses cannot be expressed. Rich axiomatic theories like CLO provide the needed relations to account for systematic polysemy, for example a legal transaction (e.g. the content of a contract) is *expressed* by an information object (e.g. the linguistic encoding of the content of a contract), which is *realized* by a legal document (e.g. the physical object realizing the encoding of the contract). A detailed application of a core ontology based on DOLCE+ to systematic polysemy is presented in [45] for the biomedical domain.

In the legal domain, cross-lingual correspondences between synsets cannot be established on the sole basis of meaning equivalence, since (current) legal systems adopt different principles and different configurations of the legal semantic space. In Law, we do not refer to *translations* of a legislative text but rather to *multilingual versions* of a same text. In fact, the actual lexical structure of a text across different languages will be notably different, since it has to mirror the different normative structures, not only the different linguistic rules.

As an example, the Italian entry *capacità giuridica* has no equivalent in English, since there is no general theory on legal capacity within Common Law that may be compared to the notion within the Italian legal system.

In an ontological perspective, the Civil Law theory underlying *capacità giuridica* can be represented within a core ontology that is so general to be shared also by

Common Law. The intended meaning of *capacità giuridica* can thus be reconstructed by generating a paraphrase that uses terms from Common Law. As a matter fact, this operation is usually performed by experts of International Law, but it relies exclusively on their skills (and the literature produced). As shown in Sect. 5, the problem is currently widespread due to e.g. EU directives to member states.

5   Legal Ontologies as Frameworks for Norm Comparison

The first intuitive argument for the adoption of ontologies as a formal components for logical comparison of norms is that they can provide a common (even if not neutral) language to express them, since only homogeneous entities can be compared. A further practical consideration is that most initiatives in the field of legal standard definition (LeXML, Metalex, NIR) consider legal ontologies strictly connected to the structuring of normative text. The ontology is therefore both a description model and a source of metadata for semantic tagging, providing at the same time a tool for conceptual retrieval and a model of content which maintains strict references to the text.

As illustrated in [46], norm comparison may be conceived in two ways:

- As a diachronic process, norms from the same system and regulating the same domain may be compared in order to detect differences related to changes in time, or specialisations of a situation (amendment, exception, extension).
- As a synchronic process, norms of different systems, regulating the same situation, can be compared in order to assess differences in national or local policies, in regulated behaviours, in social impacts, etc.

The first issue, dealing with the dynamic aspects of legal systems, requires, as pointed out in [46] and [47], an accurate definition of external and meta-level assumptions, defining criteria of specificity, ordering, and meta-criteria for resolving conflicting criteria. It is not completely clear, at the present state of research, how the ontology-based approach could offer new contributions to such well-known and long-time debated problem within the AI&Law Community, since a subsumption criterion does not seems effective enough in detecting specialty (exceptions) when applied to the legal domain. On the other hand, a promising technique, based on CLO, is being tested, as briefly presented in this section.

The second aspect assumes social relevance, as the setting up of methodologies for merging different regulations may have actual applications and produce useful results into the globalization process that involves regulatory environment as well.

The comparison of norms regulating the same situation in different jurisdictions requires the solution of several legal issues, e.g. the completeness of the corpus (how to asses if all the norms relevant for a certain issue have been taken into account), the detail of granularity, the degree of legal authority of the sources (e.g. the different weight of case-based norms in Common Law vs. Civil Law countries). On the other hand, the relationships between European and national legislations, which we are here proposing as a test candidate, seem to be a relatively simplified field of experimentation, where several of these issues can be partly ignored.

Two possible perspectives on comparison are:

– To check the correspondence between the Directive's policies and the regulative aims of the national lawmakers, underlining the national regulation that implements the Directive.
– To compare the national legislations adopting the same Directive in order to evaluate the level of harmonisation actually reached.

The two goals need different requirement and assumptions that we do not treat here, as our aim is to explain how CLO may actually be of practical utility. As preliminary remark, the choice of European/national legislation for testing the methodology offers advantages because of:

– The clear identification of normative sources to be compared (every national Act implementing an EC Directive can be clearly and autonomously identified).
– The explicit assertion of the normative goals and social policies in the premises, that provides explicit criteria of analysis.
– The standard structure of the text, to which an already consolidated methodology for structuring and tagging legislative acts, can be applied.
– The conceptual similarity among national and European domains: both norms regulate the same behaviours, but, while national laws consider citizens as direct addressers, the European prescriptions are mainly rules of conducts for national law-makers. The deontic structure of European norms are often commitments to permit, to forbid, to create, or to impose duties and sanctions; but sometimes convey weaker suggestion or guidelines.

On the last point, we refer to our experience in the NIR project: as all national projects aimed at providing standard DTDs for structuring legislative texts, the Italian project Norme In Rete has produced classes of metadata, containing information both on the legal issues (authority, date of enactment, identifiers, references, validity) and on the textual components (typology of normative sources, hierarchical organization of the sections). The content metadata include the definition of the normative functions of norms [48] that enable to describe a text as a collection of norms, classified according to their function.

As a first step in the comparison process, text structuring "pre-processes" the normative information, in order to identify the entities involved in the regulation (definition, constitutive norms), to enable the comparison of similar classes of norms (prescription, sanctions, administrative or financial regulations), and to exclude rules dealing with the management and updating of parts of a legal system (amendments, cross-links), which are only relevant to a national dimension.

In comparing the normative structure of EC and national texts, it is likely to assume that most EC regulations include prescriptive rules directed to the national legislative bodies of the Member States, which should be implemented, at the national level, as prescriptions, constitutive rules, and procedures. The selected sets of norms are then conceptualized in two domain ontologies, as represented in Fig. 5:

– *EC directives* and *national laws* are represented in separate ontologies, which both inherit the *Core Legal Ontology* and *Foundational Ontology* used to build the Core.
– The ontology of the *content domain* (social world) addressed by the directives is also based on the Foundational Ontology.

- The *national implementation* of directives should inherit both from EC directives and from the national laws, without being inconsistent.
- *Rules of conduct* and *codes of practice* typical of the directive's domain should inherit from (and to be consistent with) the national implementation of the directive.
- Any compliant *application ontology* will inherit from all those ontologies, besides the basic *service* and *task* ontologies addressed by the application.

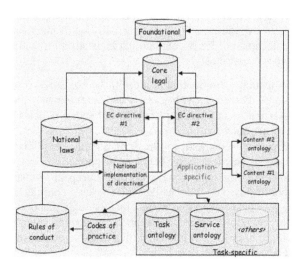

Fig. 5. An ontology library for EC Directives and applications. Arrows mean "inherits from"

5.1 Comparing Conflicting Norms: Internal and External Conflicts

According to [49], «a significant part of legal reasoning can be considered as contradiction handling».

Contradiction detection between norms can be considered as a special case of norm comparison [50][46]; antinomies can be singled out from the mere reading of the statements in texts, but more often, they arise when a case has to be decided and two norms or bundles of norms can be applied. This does not necessarily lead to norm incompatibility, since there exists an entrenchment of norms [47] that derives from the hierarchical structure of legal systems and that preserves compatibility.

In legal theory two kinds of antinomies are distinguished: *deontic* (or *logic*, or *internal conflicts*), and *teleological* (or *external conflicts*). According to A. Ross [51] three types of deontic antinomies can occur:

1. A total antinomy arises when the temporal, spatial, individual and material circumstances that the normative statements aim at entirely coincide: a norm imposes exactly what the other prohibits; one imposes exactly what the other disallows to do; or one prohibits exactly what the other allows.
2. An *antinomy* can be *partial* when the two incompatible norms have an application scope that only partially coincides.
3. A *general/exception contradiction* holds when norms have a partly identical application scope, so that one can subsume the other.

Deontic antinomies are traditionally solved by choosing between several contradictory normative statements or between normative bases suitable to justify the stating of contradictory decisions. The judge's choice, in taking into account one of these bases, must be justified by a rational reasoning process, grounded on deductively valid steps. According to McCormick [52], if two rules propose contradictory solutions, judges predetermine a selection criterion that is found *inside* the systems of rules, in order to keep the general *consistency* of the decisional reasoning process. A decision must be *consistent* with all the valid rules in the normative system.

Legal systems traditionally provide several criteria of resolution; among them the hierarchical structure of legal systems has been indicated as the main source of conflict resolution [49]. Hierarchical structure is based on:

1. Source ordering (*lex superior* prevails), based on authoritative entrenchment.
2. Specialty ordering (*lex specialis* prevails), subordinated to source ordering.
3. Chronological ordering (*lex posterior* prevails), subordinated to specialty ordering.
4. Domain ordering, where a legal domain can be superordinated to a sub domain

By the application of one of these criteria, one of the two norms is applied. In Civil Law systems, both norms maintain their validity in the system, unless the legislator explicitly eliminates it from the systems by means of an explicit norm (*abrogating* norm). In Common Law systems, due to the *stare decisis* principles, the conflicting norm, when declared by a justified decision, it is either regarded as invalid and excluded from the system, or it is maintained in the legal system but with no effect.

Internal consistency is, according to [52], just one of the requirements for justifying the correctness of the decision, as antinomies cannot in some cases be solved by traditional criteria of resolution.

When criteria are in conflict or when they appear insufficient or inefficient, a judge is unable to infer the solution of the case at hand from an existing valid rule. The selection of valid premises must be justified on the ground of the *general principles* implicit in the legal system. The legal system is at the same time composed of rules and principles. Unlike rules, which apply to a qualified set of cases, principles are not attached to specific facts. They provide objectives, general orientations of justice, equity or other ethical or moral requirements.

In grounding the choice of the normative base on the selected general principle, a judge must justify in the same way the *external coherence* of the decision, even if the solution is only related to the case at hand.

The collision of principles must be solved differently than contradictions between rules. While contradictions between rules find an ending on the ground of validity, the conflicts between principles are *teleological antinomies,* which requires a wider notion of consistency (*external consistency* or *coherence,* in the term of McCormick).

According to [53], two situations can arise: depending on the circumstances, either the interpreter estimates the total conflict so that only the exclusive application of one of the opposite principles is possible, or the conflict is partial and the principles can be reconciliated. McCormick states two parameters for solving conflicting principles: "making sense in the system" (*coherence*) and "making sense in the world" (*consequences arguments*). The decision is *coherent* when the selection of the normative basis is justified by a general criterion consistent with the general principles of the system; it is *consequent* when the judge can demonstrate that the legal consequences of the decision are socially more effective than those of a decision driven by the opposite principle.

A large part of legal theory considers judicial decisions and contracts as *individual norm*s, encompassed in a wide meaning of *norm*. In our model, we consider judicial decisions a subclass of regulations, sharing the same conceptual structure of norms.

In terms of D&S, decisions are therefore *descriptions*, which describe *ex-post* the possible setting of a state of affairs, or the conformity of a description to possible and multilayered compatibility scenarios.

5.2 Compatibility Between Entrenched Norms

In the *constructive* framework of DOLCE+ and CLO[8], norms are first-order entities, then their possible logical *inconsistency* disappears, and migrates into *disjointness* of the respective classes of situations that can result from the application of the norms. For example, if – given a certain social situation s – a norm n_1 allows exercizing a profession in the setting of s, while another norm n_2 does not allow that exercise, then n_1 and n_2 are in conflict, and not because they are logically contradictory, but because there is at least one situation s_1 that has s as a part, and cannot satisfy both norms (see [7] for a detailed example of this case type).

Once assessed that two norms are conflicting (usually because two parties make different claims), it remains to be seen if CLO can support us in the conflict resolution process. In [7] we propose the following approach: *Compatibility* is assessed as a case of *conformity* between a *compatibility scenario* and a situation including a *set of norms*. By *conformity* we mean that a case satisfies a legal description. In case of *ground* regulative norms (norms not involving other norms in their satisfying cases), like those analyzed in [50], or the example in Sect. 4, a social situation must *conform* to a norm in its legally relevant setting. In case of more abstract norms, conformity is assessed against situations that contain other norms. Compatibility assessment is one of those cases: two or more possibly incompatible norms should conform to a compatibility *meta-norm* (or a principle, an ideal, etc.).

A *compatibility scenario* is represented as a specialization of the CLO design pattern (specialized on its turn from D&S by introducing legal subclasses in the place of D&S categories). Legal Compatibility is represented as a kind of *legal description* that can be satisfied by a Legal Entrenchment *case* whose setting includes certain regulatory levels for pairs of norms, according to *superordination* parameters, *entrenchment* roles, *compatibility assessment* courses, etc. Hierarchical structuring is represented as *superordination parameters* valued by regulatory levels according to the source, specialty, time, and domain of norms. Norms play some *entrenchment role* according to their hierarchical position. The algorithm to assess compatibility is specified in a *compatibility assessment course*.

Each norm involved in legal compatibility can be exploded into other CLO patterns that represent its satisfiability conditions.

Despite the hierarchical structuring of norms, legal compatibility is not always satisfiable in legal theory (because of *norm dynamics*), as well as in jurisprudential prac-

---

[8] A preliminary constructive approach was partly presented in [50] that presents an application for detecting diachronic norm compatibility.

tice, leading also to the problem of *alternative interpretations*. The compatibility scenario can be used to assess or simply to represent those cases, making it formal the case for unsatisfiability. On the other hand, McCormick's *social effectiveness* of conflict resolution is outside of internal coherence principles and superdination, and the rational arguments adopted by judges for effectiveness possibly require customized *practice descriptions* (e.g. of local judicial departments), or mixed socio-legal interpretation spaces.

6 Conclusions

We have presented some results of a joint research between the Laboratory for Applied Ontology and ITTIG-CNR. The general methodology applied in the collaboration uses formal ontology techniques and resources to formalize legal knowledge and the Italian legal lexicon. In the paper we have introduced: the DOLCE+ foundational ontology, on which a Core Legal Ontology is being defined; the JurWordNet lexicon based on CLO, and a sketch of how to use CLO to represent judicial Acts delivered in presence of incompatible norms [7]. Applications based our results have been (or are being) built in order to perform comparison of diachronically distinct norms in the same domain [50], to detect compliance of synchronically distinct norms, to control the conformity of activities against previous agreements or contracts, to represent so-called *bundles-of-rights* [6], and to support information retrieval and extraction.

The research carried out so far is featuring interesting applications (a couple of industrial systems implementing ontology-driven semantic service have been implemented by ELSAG Banklab and Selesta Ars, two Italian software houses), and collaborations on an international basis (e.g. the EU FP5 *OntoWeb* Network's *Working Group on Legal Ontologies*, the *Action Spécifique sur les Ontologies Juridiques* started in France, and the research on regulatory ontologies at the Universidad Pompeu Fabra in Barcelona).

On the other hand, legal systems are a formidable challenge for any formalization project, and only large, multinational projects motivated by an actual interest from legislators and enactors of (inter)national legal systems could let us conceive of a future "ontological legal system".

References

[1] Winkels, R. (ed.), Second International Workshop on Legal Ontologies (LEGONT), at the Jurix Conference, http://lri.jur.uva.nl/~winkels/legont.html, 2002.
[2] Breuker, J., Gangemi, A., Tiscornia, D., Winkels, R. (eds.), ICAIL03 Wks on Legal Ontologies, Edinburgh, http://lri.jur.uva.nl/~winkels/legontICAIL2003.html, 2003.
[3] Jarrar, M., Salaun, A. (eds.), First Workshop on Regulatory Ontologies, OTM Workshops, Springer, 2003.
[4] Jarrar, M., Gangemi, A. (eds.), Second Workshop on Regulatory Ontologies, OTM Workshops, Springer, 2004.
[5] Benjamins R., Casanovas P., Breuker J., Gangemi A. Law and the Semantic Web. Berlin, Springer, 2004.

[6] Sagri M.T., Tiscornia D., Gangemi A. An Ontology-based Approach for Representing "Bundle-of-rights", Jarrar & Gangemi (eds.), Second International Workshop on Regulatory Ontologies, in OTM Workshops, Springer, 2004.

[7] Gangemi A, Prisco A, Sagri MT, Steve G, Tiscornia D, "Some ontological tools to support legal regulatory compliance, with a case study", in Jarrar M, et al. (eds.), Proceedings of the WORM03 Workshop at OTM Conference, Springer Verlag, Berlin, 2003.

[8] Alexy R. A Theory of Legal Argumentation, Oxford: Clarendon Press, 1989.

[9] Allen L.E. e Saxon C.S. Analysis of the Logical Structure of Legal Rules by a Modernized and Formalized Version of Hohfeld's Fundamental Legal Conceptions, Martino, Socci (eds.), Automated Analysis of Legal Texts, Amsterdam: North-Holland, 1986.

[10] Kowalski R. e Sergot M. The Use of Logical Models in Legal Problem Solving, in (Narayan and Bennum eds.), Law, Computer Science and Artificial Intelligence, Ablex, 1989.

[11] Sergot M. The Representation of Law in Computer Programs, in Trevor Bench Capon (ed.) Knowledge Based Systems and legal Applications, Academic Press, 1991, pp. 3-68.

[12] Antoniou G., Billington D., Governatori G., Maher M.J. Representation results for defeasible logic, ACM Transactions on Computational Logic, 2, 2, 2001.

[13] Hamfelt A. e Barklund J. Hierarchical Representation of Legal Knowledge with Metaprogramming in logic, in Proceedings of First Compulog-NetWorkshop, Imperial College, London, 1992.

[14] Bench Capon T. e Coenen F. Isomorphism and Legal Knowledge-based systems, in Artificial Intelligence and Law: An International Journal, 1(1), 1992, pp.65-86.

[15] Jones A., Sergot M. On the Characterization of Law and Computer Sustems: The Normative Systems Perspective, in Deontic Logic in Computer Science, (a cura di J. Ch. Meyer e R. J. Wieringa, Wiley (UK), 1993.

[16] Kolodner, J.L. Case-based reasoning. Morgan Kaufmann, Calif., US, 1993.

[17] Breuker, J. and N. den Haan, Separating world and regulation knowledge: where is the logic? In Sergot, M. (ed), Processing of the third internetional conference on AI and Law, New York, Association of Computing Machinery, 1991.

[18] Chisholm R.M., Contrary to duty imperative and deontic logic, in Analysis, 24, 1963.

[19] Hohfeld W. N. Some fundamental legal conceptions as applied in legal reasoning , Yale Law Journal , XXIII, n.1, pp.16-59, 1913.

[20] Jones A. and Sergot M., A Formal Characterisation of Institutional Power, Journal of IGPL, 4(3), 429-445, 1996.

[21] Bowen K.A., Kowalski R. Amalgamating Language and Metalanguage in Logic Programming, in Clark e Tarnlund (eds.), Logic Programming, London: Academic Press, pp. 153-172, 1982.

[22] Moore, M., Legal Reality: A Naturalist Approach to Legal Ontology, Law and Philosophy, 21, 619-705, 2002.

[23] Forbus, K., Mostek. T., Ferguson, R., An analogy ontology for integrating analogical processing and first-principles reasoning, in Proceedings of AAAI02, 2002.

[24] Karmiloff-Smith, A. Beyond Modularity: A Developmental Perspective on Cognitive Science. Cambridge, MA.: MIT Press, 1992.

[25] Gangemi A., Mika P. Understanding the Semantic Web through Descriptions and Situation, Meersman R, et al. (eds.), Proceedings of ODBASE03, Springer, Berlin, 2003.

[26] Masolo C., Vieu L., Bottazzi E., Catenacci C., Ferrario R., Gangemi A., Guarino N. So-
      cial Roles and their Descriptions, Welty & Dubois (eds.), Proceedings of the Interna-
      tional Conference on Principles of Knowledge Representation and Reasoning (KR),
      2004.
[27] Masolo C., Borgo S., Gangemi A, Guarino N, Oltramari A. The WonderWeb Library of
      Foundational   Ontologies",   IST   2001-33052   Wonder   Web.
      http://wonderweb.semanticweb.org/deliverables/documents/D18.pdf, 2003.
[28] Gangemi A., Catenacci C., Lehmann J., Borgo S. Task taxonomies for knowledge con-
      tent, EU 6FP METOKIS Project, D07, http://metokis.salzburgresearch.at, 2004.
[29] Baader F., Calvanese D., McGuinness D., Nardi D., Patel-Schneider P. (eds.) Description
      logic handbook, Cambridge: Cambridge UP, 2002.
[30] Eco, U., Kant e l'ornitorinco, Milano, Bompiani, 1997.
[31] Visser P., T. Bench Capon, Ontologies in the Design of Legal Knowledge Systems, to-
      wards a Library of Legal Domain Ontologies, in Proceedings of Jurix 99, Leuven, Bel-
      gique.
[32] Dean, M., Schreiber, G.: Owl web ontology language reference, W3c candidaterecom-
      mendation, World Wide Web Consortium (August 2003).
[33] Hart, H.L.A. The Concept of Law, Oxford (UK), Clarendon Press, 1961.
[34] Alchourrón C. E., Buligyn E. Normative System, Springer Verlag, Wien, 1971.
[35] Searle J., The Construction of Social Reality, Free Press: N.Y., 1995.
[36] Gangemi A., Bottazzi E., Catenacci C., Lehmann J. From Collective Intentionality to In-
      tentional Collectives: An Ontological Perspective, C. Castelfranchi, L. Tummolini (eds.),
      International Conference on Collective Intentionality, to appear, 2004.
[37] Lindhal L., Position and Change. A study in Law and Logic, Reidel, 1977.
[38] Kanger S., Law and Logic, Theoria, 38, 105-132, 1972.
[39] Jones A, A logical Framework, in J.Pitt (ed.), Open Agents Societies: Normative
      Specifications in Multi-Agent Systems, Wiley and S., 2003.
[40] Pörn, I., Action Theory and Social Science, Some Formal Models, Reidel, 1977.
[41] Lehmann, J, Borgo, S., Masolo, C., Gangemi, A. Causality and Causation in DOLCE,
      Vieu & Varzi (eds.), Third International Conference on Formal Ontology and Informa-
      tion Systems (FOIS04), IOS Press, 2004.
[42] Sagri M.T. Progetto per lo sviluppo di una rete lessicale giuridica on line attraverso la
      specializzazione di ItalWordnet, in Informatica e Diritto, ESI, Napoli, 2003.
[43] Roventini A., Alonge A., Bertagna F., Calzolari N., et al., ItalWordNet: Building a Large
      Semantic Database for the Automatic Treatment of Italian, in "Linguistica Computazion-
      ale", Istituti Editoriali e Poligrafici Internazionali, Pisa-Roma, ISSN, 2000.
[44] Vossen P. (ed.). EuroWordNet A Multilingual Database with Lexical Semantic Net-
      works, Kluwer Academic publishers, 1998.
[45] Fellbaum C. (editor), WordNet: An electronic lexical database, MIT Press, 1998.
[46] Gangemi A., Battaglia, M., Catenacci, C. The Inflammation Ontology Design Pattern, in
      Pisanelli (ed.), Biomedical Ontologies, IOS Press, 2004.
[47] Boer A., van Engers T. and Winkels R., Using Ontologies for Comparing and Harmoniz-
      ing Legislation, in Proceedings of the 9th ICAIL Conference, Edinburgh, 2003.
[48] Gärdenfors P, "The Dynamics of Normative Systems", 1989.
[49] Biagioli C., An XML editor for Legislative drafting, JURIX wks on E-Government,
      2002.
[50] Sartor G., "Legal Reasoning and Normative Conflicts", in Reasoning with Inconsistency,
      1991.

[51] Gangemi A., Pisanelli DM., Steve G. A Formal Ontology Framework to represent Norm Dynamics. Proc. of Second International Workshop on Legal Ontologies, Amsterdam, 2001.

[52] Ross A. Directives and Norms. London, 1968.

[53] McCormick N., Legal Reasoning and Legal Theory, Oxford University Press, 1978

[54] Dworkin R. Taking Rights Seriously, 2nd ed., London: Duckworth, 1978.

[55] von Wright G.E. Norm and Action, London, Routledge, 1963.

[56] Valente A. e Breuker J. A Functional Ontology of Law, in Preatti del Convegno del Venticinquennale IDG, Firenze, 1993, pp.3-6

On the Ontological Status of Norms

Guido Boella, Leonardo Lesmo, and Rossana Damiano

Dipartimento di Informatica – Centro per l'Ontologia Teorica e Applicata,
Università di Torino
{guido, lesmo, rossana}@di.unito.it

Abstract. This article describes an ontological model of norms. The basic assumption is that a substantial part of a legal system is grounded on the concept of *agency*. Since a legal system aims at regulating a society, then its goal can be achieved only by affecting the behavior of the members of the society. We assume that a society is made up of *agents* (which can be individuals, institutions, software programs, etc.), that agents have beliefs, goals and preferences, and that they commit to intentions in order to choose a line of behavior. The role of norms, within a legal system, is to specify how and when the chosen behavior agrees with the basic principles of the legal system. In this article, we show how a model based on plans can be the basis for the ontological representation of norms, linking them to the upper level of a philosophically well-founded ontology (DOLCE); in this way, the model is set in a wider perspective, which opens the way to further developments.

1   Introduction

The goal of this article is to describe a proposal concerning the proper place of legal rules in a well founded ontological framework. Since the role of ontologies in computer science is to support knowledge sharing both among computer systems and between computers and humans, it is important that it represent the world as it is conceived by sentient beings (so that epistemology is possibly a term that is more suitable to the matter at hand [8]).

In this article, we do not aim at covering the ontological status of all types of rules. For instance, in a legal system, there are rules concerning the definition of concepts (e.g. Non Governative Organization) with which we are not concerned (we assume they are given in advance). But we are (at least partially) concerned with institutional roles and their attributions, since institutional roles, as authorities, are a (predefined) category of people, and their attributions define what they can and cannot do. Also, we are not concerned with the way a Court gives a verdict, which is a very complex process, but we are concerned with the presence, in the ontology, of all the concepts required to describe the facts and the evidence available to the court. In other words, this paper faces a

V.R. Benjamins et al. (Eds.): Law and the Semantic Web, LNCS 3369, pp. 125–141, 2005.

small but relevant fraction of legal knowledge[1]: it covers the norms of conduct, i.e. the norms that specify what a legal actor can and cannot do. The claim is that these rules express constraints on actions, and their relevance stands on the view that a legal system aims at organizing a society in such a way that the rights and duties of individuals and organizations are properly balanced, on the basis of superior principles.

We also aim at showing how norms affect behaviour. The formalization of prescriptive rules is assumed to be available to an agent that must do things, and that must choose what to do: this agent uses the rules to decide what he will do next; in principle, he will choose a line of action that complies with the existing rules, but in some cases he may decide that a rule is not worth being respected, either because it is in conflict with other norms, or because the risk of being sanctioned is low. Beyond moral concerns, this is the way many rational agents choose to act: it must be properly modelled, since it explicitly includes the concept of sanction, and, implicitly, guides the legislator to properly choose the sanction associated with a given rule.

The paper is organized as follows: the next section presents the upper-level of the ontology (DOLCE), and our formalization of plans; in the third section, the representation of norms is described; the fourth section shows how power and authorities fit our approach; in Section 5, we present a case study addressing the legal concept of 'goods'; then, we compare our approach with other ontological models of the legal systems; the conclusions close the paper.

2   The Upper-Level of DOLCE, and the Plans

We chose DOLCE because of the clear philosophical foundation of its basic categories [9]: they have been selected as the result of a research effort that has lasted for some years, and the motivations for the final choices can be found in the referenced papers [10,11,29]. Most of the structures addressed in the paper are based on the KIF implementation reported in [19].

Without any details, we report here some brief comments on the top-level of DOLCE, which seem necessary in order to explain the connections to plans and norms. Some of the concepts defined in DOLCE are depicted in fig.1.

The upper-level categories are *Abstract, Quality, Situation, Endurant*, and *Perdurant*. The assumption about the existence of abstract entities and qualities is rather common (with the known philosophical intricacies). The distinction between *Endurants*[2] and *Perdurants* can be specified by citing the authors: "Endurants are wholly present (i.e. all their proper parts are present) at any time they are present. Perdurants, on the other hand, just extend in time by accumulating different temporal parts, so that, at any time they are present, they are

---

[1] *"Since the norm is the most salient construct of the legal domain, we have selected it as the point of departure for our intermediate representation"* [17], p.1128.

[2] In the text, we sometime use the category names in the plural. Although this is imprecise, we believe it makes the reading more fluent.

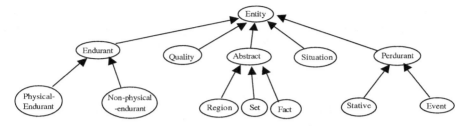

Fig. 1. A portion of the upper level of DOLCE (from [19])

only partially present, in the sense that some of their proper temporal parts (...) may be not present" [9], §2.1.

Situations "satisfy" *S-Descriptions* (situation description), a subcategory of *Descriptions*; the latter, are a subcategory of *Non-Physical-Endurants* (see fig.1). So, a situation is the 'actual' counterpart of a representation (description).

Descriptions are particularly important in this article, since, in DOLCE, plans are *S-Descriptions*. So, *Plans* are particular descriptions of situations. This placement reflects a view where plans describe something; although we would rather take a plan as the situation which is described, in order to maintain the compatibility with DOLCE, we focus in this article on the description(s) which an agent is reasoning about while he is trying to decide what to do (one or more partially specified *plan schemas*), rather than to the *execution of a plan*, i.e. the actual, real-world, events that the agent carries out. From this point of view, a plan can be imagined as a tree-like structure, where some decisions have been already taken, while others are suspended. For example, I may know about plans for travelling to far cities. And I may have the goal of being in Rome tomorrow. So I can examine the plans "go to a far city by train" and "go to a far city by plane" (two different plan schemas). If I have chosen the second schema, then I have certainly fixed the 'airport of arrival' and the 'airport of departure' (i.e. two of the participants in the plan), but, possibly, the departure time is just given as 'some time in the morning of tomorrow before 8.00 a.m.' (i.e. underspecified).

We assume that for each *Plan*, a set of *p-preconditions* and a set of *p-effects* are defined; their range is *S-Description*. This is different from DOLCE, where *precondition* is a relation between *S-Descriptions* and *situations*. We believe that is more homogeneous to maintain a relation between *S-Descriptions*; of course, the *S-Description* which acts as *p-precondition* will be *satisfied-by* DOLCE's *precondition*. For example, the plan of going Rome by plane is executable if the *S-Description* "The Rome Airport is open" is satisfied by the current *Situation*. Furthermore, we assume that each *Plan* has some *s-participant*. They are the entities involved in the plan, but need not be completely specified (I will take *a taxi*, I will take *a yellow taxi with an old, experienced driver*).[3]

Plans are the objects managed in the process of planning. The idea is that there is a *Perdurant* called *Thinking,* which has as participants the descriptions

---

[3] Of course, many features of the plan ontology have been left out, but the goal of this paper is just to address the role of plans in the representation of norms.

embodied in the brain. In particular, *Planning* is that type of *Thinking* that works upon the mental representation of plans. It produces new *Plans* by considering[4] known *Plans* (going to Rome by bus), by specializing existing *Plans* (the taxy company has been chosen), or by discarding *Plans*. The final outcome of this process is that a plan has become an *Intention*. No *Intention* concept is currently defined in DOLCE, but *has-BDI-on* is a *modality-target* relation holding between an *Agent-role* and a *Course* (of events). specific type of *Course*, we call *Intention* the role assumed by the sequence of *Tasks* which the planning agent has chosen. Correspondingly, we call *has-intention-on* the subrelation of *has-BDI-on* which refers to intentions (wrt. beliefs and desires).

But what is the role of *Intention*? Agents always act: if the current time is t_i, then agent A is doing something at t_i and will try to do something at t_{i+1}; that something is specified by A's current intention. Since, during planning, an agent considers many *Plans*, but just one of them becomes his *Intention*, he needs some way to decide which *Plan* is the best. In our model, we assume that:

- The choice is based on the agent's *preferences*;
- The preferences are applied to states that can be originated (either directly or indirectly) by the execution of the plan;
- From a computational point of view, applying the preferences to a state amounts to evaluating the *utility* of that state;

In our view, these criteria characterize the *rationality* of agents. The use of utilities in the planning activity has been described elsewhere [5]. Here, some comments are needed on the second point. In fact, the reason why preferences are not necessarily applied to (i.e. the utility is not necessarily evaluated on) the state directly resulting from the execution of the plan, is one if the key features of our approach to norms.

In general, the execution of a plan has certain effects on the environment (*p-effects*). But this new situation can also produce further foreseeable changes. This is especially true in case the world is populated by other agents, who may interact with the planning agent. So, the agent must try to imagine how the world would be after some sequence of reactions from the environment. So, the utility of a plan is evaluated on the basis of the state that obtains after the execution of the plan, and after some re-actions of the environment to the resulting state (we assume here a two-level lookahead: plan execution + reaction). The major point is that the environment is assumed to be able to react to the breach of norms; so, in order to model the behaviour of an agent, we need a way to specify how the environment reacts to such a situation. Note that we have used the very general term 'environment'; this leaves unspecified which are the relevant components of such an environment. Currently, we assume the existence of a *Normative-Agent-Role*, who has to enforce the respect of law (he can be a single individual, as a policeman, or a social body). Note that the presence of normative

---

[4] By 'considering', we mean here the process of moving around (e.g. from LTM to STM) pieces of descriptions.

agents does not exclude that the respect of a norm is a value 'per se' (embodied in preferences of the agent).

3   Norms

In DOLCE, *Norm* is a subcategory of *Regulation*: *Norms* have the function of constraining *Perdurants*. In order to explain our approach to norms, let us introduce an example. As we have seen, a *Plan* has *p-preconditions* and *p-effects*. The *p-preconditions* of a plan schema pose some constraints on the applicability of the plan. The *p-preconditions* for cooking spaghetti with garlic, oil, and chili pepper (GO&CP), is to have spaghetti, oil, chili pepper, water, a pan, and some fire (a very easy recipe). As usual, *p-preconditions* are (physical or practical) conditions that prevent the action from being executable. But it could happen that the King of ThatKingdom has prohibited this recipe. Or, perhaps, this prohibition applies just to dinners with more than 7 participants, or to dinners served after midnight, and so on. Also, in some situations (here and now) garlic could not be a nice ingredient (because of its side-effects on your breath); or you know that one of your guests does not like chili pepper. All of these are not *p-preconditions*: if you have all the things you need, you can cook them in all situations described above. Anyway, these rules constrain your freedom to cook spaghetti GO&CP; you can pay for that: the King may imprison you, or your guests may decide that they will never accept another invitation from you.

The "norms" we have exemplified above are not *p-preconditions*, but constraints on plans. We stress that in all of these examples, the utility of that recipe is reduced by the presence of the norm, so, it is possible that in absence of the norms, your intention for tonight dinner is to cook spaghetti GO&CP, but in presence of one or more of these norms, your intention is to prepare rice

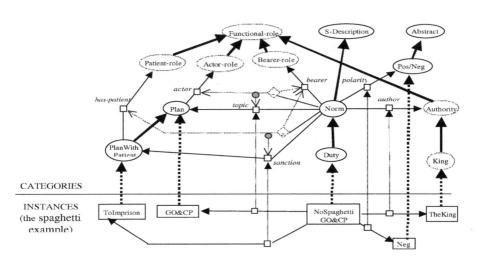

Fig. 2. Norms and Plans: an example

with mushrooms: you have chosen a different plan, whose utility is lower than the plan of spaghetti without norms, but is higher than the plan of spaghetti with norms (since the violation of the norm reduces the utility). The problem, now, is how to express the norms.

Let us consider the case of the King's prohibition in its basic form (independent of the number of participants and of daytime). The rule involves three or four elements: the involved plan, the authority who posed the norm, and the agent who is taken as responsible for the execution of the action; the fourth element is not strictly required, but it is very common: it is the sanction[5] the agent will undergo in case he does not respect the rule. So, a norm is not a plan, but 'refers' to a plan, in the sense that it (as a description) includes (is related to) a description of the action (i.e. the plan) which is forbidden (or permitted).

In fig.2, we introduce the basic notions related to norms, and apply them to our spaghetti example. In the figure, it is stated that

1. *Norms* are a subcategory of *S-Description* (thick arrow).
2. *Norms* have a *topic*[6], the *Plan* the norm is about (thin arrows with squares are relations).
3. *Norms* have a *polarity*. Its range is the abstract set composed of the two elements *pos* and *neg*. If the value is *pos*, then the norm refers to something an agent must do, otherwise it refers to something he must not do.
4. Every *Norm* has a *bearer*. More precisely, it has a set of bearers: usually, norms apply to categories of agents, and not to single individuals.
5. Every *Plan* has an *actor*, who is the 'main character' of the plan. Although the *actor* of the plan is conceptually distinct from the planning agent, currently we assume that the two roles are played by the same individual.
6. The *actor* of a plan, if that plan happens to be the *topic* of the *Norm*, and if that *actor* is of the right category, becomes an (individual) *bearer* of the rule (dotted diamonds are constraints on relations; here, it is said that the *actor* of the *topic* of the *Norm* is equal to the *bearer* of the *Norm*).
7. Every *Norm* is associated with a *sanction*[7], which is a *PlanWithPatient* (the subclass of *Plan* which is in some *has-patient* relation with an individual playing a *Patient-Role*).
8. There is a specific subcategory of *Norm* called *Duty* (see [2,4,15]).
9. The *bearer* of the *Norm* is the *has-patient* of its *sanction*. Of course, this does not take into account the notion of *responsibility*, but we assume that being an agent who freely chose a given line of behavior is the basis for further elaborations of this concept.
10. The *author* of a *norm* is an *Authority* (see Section 6).
11. *ToImprison*, *Go&CP*, *NoSpaghettiGO&CP*, are individual instances of *PlanWithPatient*, *Plan*, and *Norm*, respectively (boxes are instances linked to their class via dotted arrows).

---

[5] For different positions on the role of sanctions in law, see [13,16].

[6] The term *topic* is inspired to Ross [22]'s "theme".

[7] We are dealing here with 'normative' rules. In other cases, the sanction may be replaced by a reward.

4   Authorities

Traditionally, legal scholars like [13] distinguish between primary laws, whose purpose is to direct the behavior of citizens, and secondary laws, which serve, among other functions, to the maintenance and dynamic management of the normative system. These rules form a "subsystem of rules for change": rules which have legal effects and which are instrumental to the primary system, in that they regulate the regulation (e.g., art. 2 of Italian Civil Code: "the creation of laws [...] is regulated by constitutional laws (Cost. 70)"). This subsystem, according to Hart, does not include only the rules of change which specify how new laws are introduced or old ones removed, but it also includes rules about "powers for the private citizen".

It seems reasonable to consider all these rules, which correspond to what Hohfeld calls *Power* as somewhat akin to a *Privilege*. Since *Privileges* are assumed to be a special kind of *Norms*, also *Powers* are seen as particular subcategories of *Norm*. In particular, we introduce *JurPlans* and *LawPlans*[8]: *JurPlans* establish new *IndividualConstraintsOnBehavior*, while *LawPlans* establish new *Norms*. An example of *JurPlan* is 'renting a car', where, if the plan is executed correctly and by a person who can do it (according to an existing *BasicPower* norm), new *IndividualConstraintsOn Behavior* are set up, regulating the behavior of the two parties (duties and privileges of the renter and of the client). On the contrary, the introduction of a new norm stating that only people older than 20 may rent a car is the execution of a *LawPlan*.

Of course, not every agent may execute *JurPlans* or *LawPlans*. An agent who can do that is said to have *Power*. For example, the owner of a car rental agency has the *Power* to rent a car, and, according to the hypothetical rule mentioned above, anybody older than 20 (with a driving license) has the *Power* to hire a car. Both of these *Powers* are *BasicPowers*, since they enable the execution of plans that establish individual duties. On the contrary, only people (or institutions) having some *LawPower* can modify the minimal age for renting a car, since this implies a modification of the legal system. The result of this conceptual analysis is depicted in fig.3.

In principle, *Power* does not tell us very much: there is some action that an agent can perform that has some effect concerning Legal Relations. But, apart from the final qualification about the type of effect, this is true for every action: this is the very definition of an action (or a plan, if the action is complex). So, it is sufficient that such an action be defined, in order to obtain *Power*: if the action does not exist, then no *Power* exists; if the action does exist, then there is the *Power*; but provided that the preconditions are satisfied! And the origin of *Power* seems to be in the preconditions. Usually, they express factual constraints: if there is no lamp, you cannot turn the light on. But in this case, preconditions are 'conventional', in the sense that even if they do not hold, the

---

[8] This is consistent with [13], p.33, who characterizes power-conferring norms as recipes for creating duties.

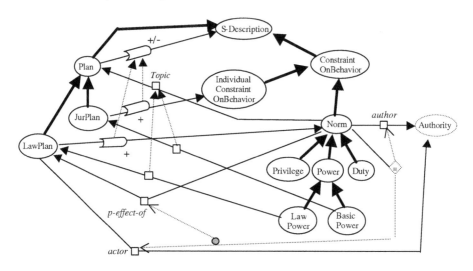

Fig. 3. *Norms* and *Power*

action appears to be executable. So, if a judge looks at a person while walking in the street, and tells him: "I condemn you to two years", the 'condemn' action seems to have been executed, but, of course, this is not so. But where do these further constraints come from? The answer is that there needs to be some *Norm* (or a set of norms) that defines the action.

We must remark that what is in order here is not the introduction of a *Norm* (an action which always require an *Authority*), but the introduction of a *Plan*, as, for instance, the 'selling and buying' plan. But according to the previous discussion, there is no way to define this plan, other than having a (set of) norm introducing it, i.e. no *JurPlan* or *LawPlan* can exist, unless it is the topic of some *Norm*. In other words, an agent cannot 'invent' the plan 'selling and buying', as he could 'invent' a new plan for organizing a party: the latter can be invented, because its effects are factual effects (if the party ends up being a nice party, the plan is good) but the former cannot be invented, since it will never have any effect at all, unless some authority establishes which are these effects, and under which conditions they are achieved (see fig.6).[9]

In fig.3, we also show the placement of *Authority* in the ontology. Note that *Authority* is a material role, since individuals or groups can become or cease to be authorities. Fig.3 shows that the *Author* of a *Norm* is the *Actor* of the *LawPlan* whose effect is that *Norm*.

---

[9] Some rules exist independently on any *Power*. They are the rules of tradition (not to be confused with the rules coming from written religious texts). Their origin is unclear: they are rules to which everybody in a society usually conforms, just because they exist, and because who does not respect them is not respected by other people. This situation does not seem to pose any special problems for the ontological framework we are proposing.

5   A Case Study: Fruits

In this section, we report the result of a preliminary study on a legal concept, i.e. fruits (see Italian Civil Code, art. 820). A *Fruit* is something that is obtained by somebody as the result of his ownership of something else. For instance, you obtain the apples if you own an apple tree, you obtain some money if you own a house and you rent it out. Notice that the presence of fruits does not affect the ownership of the thing.

5.1   Goods

Goods are defined as a subcategory of *Endurants*[10]. We partition the goods in two subcategories: those goods that may undergo a property relation (*Subject-ToProperty*), and those which cannot (*NotSubjectToProperty*). The individuals of the first category can play two roles: goods that, at some time, are owned by somebody (*Asset*), and goods which are temporarily not owned by anybody (*ResNullius*). The *PropertyRel* relation involves a *Legally-Constructed-Person* (the *owner*) and a *SubjectToProperty* good (the owned thing: *ownee*). An *Asset* is the *object* of a *SubjectToProperty* good, for which there is a *PropertyRel* relation. On the contrary, a *ResNullius* is not involved in any *PropertyRel*.

5.2   Fruits

Fruits are *Goods*. There are two types of *Fruits*: *NaturalFruits* and *CivilFruits*. *NaturalFruits* are goods that are "detachable" parts of some "original" good, and which originated out of the original good via some natural process (e.g. the growth of apples, peaches, etc. – the birth of a lamb out of its mother, etc.). In this paper, we will not discuss natural fruits any more.

On the contrary, *CivilFruits* are *Assets*, which have changed their *owner*. The general idea is that some agent *A1* owns (and possesses) some *Good G1*; then, he can decide to exchange the possession (maintaining the ownership) against some *Good G2*, usually for a limited period of time. A second agent *A2* gets the possession of *G1* and gives *G2* to the first agent. In this situation, *G2* is a *CivilFruit* of *G1*. The simplest example is that of (house) rental, where *G1* is the rented house, *A1* is the owner of the house, *A2* is the tenant and *G2* (the *CivilFruit*) is the amount paid for the rent. All of this is ruled by some *JurPlan* (as a *Contract*), which must be executed by the involved parties (*A1* and *A2*). As seen before, in order to be authorized to execute a *JurPlan*, an agent must have some *JurPower*. In the example of house rental, this power has been given to the owner *A1* by the original act of buying the house. On the contrary, the power exercised by *A2* is due just to his being a *Legally-Constructed-Person*,

---

[10] As one referee pointed to us, the specification of what may constitute a *Good* from a legal point of view requires a more careful analysis. Since the focus of this example is on *Fruits*, and, at least in principle, any *Good* can produce *Fruits*, we leave open the problem of a better characterization of *Goods*.

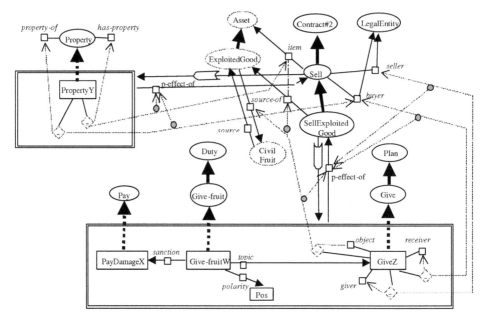

Fig. 4. Fruits

and to his power over the money he pays for the rental. Of course, all of this produces new legal relations, in particular, new *Privileges* for *A2*; these are the *Privileges* associated with the *Possession* relation, which has been created as an effect of the execution of the *Rent* contract.

In fig.4, we have depicted some of the concepts discussed above. In particular, it has been made explicit that:

1. *CivilFruit*, since it is an *Asset*, has a *owner* (linked to it via the *PropertyRel* concept).
2. *CivilFruits* come from some other *Good*, which we have called *ExploitedGood*.
3. The *owner* of the *ExploitedGood* is the same as the *owner* of the *CivilFruit*.
4. There exists a special type of *Contract* involving exactly two contractors (*Contract#2*).
5. A subtype of type of *Contract#2* is *FruitProducingContract*. The two contractors are called the *giver* and the *receiver*.
6. *FruitProducingContract* involves two *Goods*, called the *primary* and the *secondary*.
7. A first *effect* of a *FruitProducingContract* is that a new instance of the *Possess* relation is created (*PossessX* in the figure).
8. A second *effect* of a *FruitProducingContract* is that a new instance of *PropertyRel* (*PropertyY*) is established.
9. The *owner* of *PropertyY* is the *giver* of the *FruitProducingContract* which produced the creation of *PropertyY*, while the *ownee* of *PropertyY* is the *secondary* of *FruitProducingContract*.

10. The *primary* of *FruitProducingContract*, which is an *Asset*, as an effect of an execution of *FruitProducingContract* takes the material role of *ExploitedGood*, as well as the *secondary* takes the role of *CivilFruit*.

This is just a simple example, but it makes explicit that there is no *CivilFruit* without an *ExploitedGood* (item 2), and it specifies how *CivilFruits* come into being (item 10). What can easily be made is to introduce *specializations* of *FruitProducingContract*. So, we can have *ApartmentRental*, *LandRental*, *BankDeposit*, etc. all of which inherit the general features of *FruitProducingContract*. In particular, all of them share the effect that some *Asset* becomes a *CivilFruit*.

5.3   A Norm on Fruits

As an example of norms concerning fruits, we consider part of the article 1477 of the Italian Civil Code: the seller must give the buyer the possible fruits produced by the sold asset (the *ExploitedGood*). More precisely, if the *owner* of a *Good*, which is currently playing the role of *ExploitedGood* sells that *Good*, then also the associated *Fruits* must be given to the buyer.

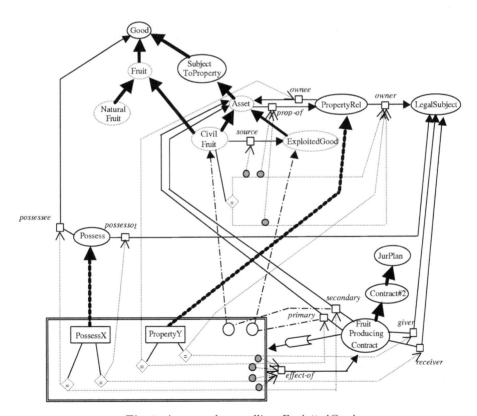

Fig. 5. A norm about selling *ExploitedGoods*

Fig.5 shows the relevant part of the representation. The focus of the example is the *Norm* instance *Give-FruitW*, which is a *Duty* that comes into being as an effect of the execution of *SellExploitedGood*, which is a *JurPlan*. This instance is analogous to the instance of *Property* that refers to the fact that the buyer is now the owner of the sold item, in the sense that both of them are effects of a selling action. Note also that the *Norm* mentioned in the previous paragraph is not represented explicitly, since it is actually part of the definition of the *Power* associated with the definition of *SellExploitedGood*. In fact, as stated in Section 4, the issuer of the Italian c.c. article 1477 had the power to (implicitly) define the *SellExploitedGood* action (although no name was given to it). Within this definition, the effect of creating the *Duty* of transferring the *CivilFruits* was included, and this is what is depicted in the figure.

1. *Selling* is a specific type of *Contract#2* (and hence a *JurPlan*).
2. Among the effects produced by *Selling* there is a change of *Property*: a new instance of *Property* is established (shown in the figure) while a previous property is cancelled (not shown in the figure).
3. When the sold *item* is an *ExploitedGood*, a specific subcategory of *Sell* is defined: *SellExploitedGood*.
4. Beyond the (inherited) effects produced by *Sell*, *SellExploitedGood* produces a further *effect*: a new *Duty* (*Give-fruitW*). The *bearer* is the same legal subject who plays the role of *seller* of the *Selling* action; this does not need to be specified explicitly, since it is inferred from the general rule that the *bearer* is the *has-agent* of the *topic* of the *Norm* (i.e. the *giver*).
5. On the contrary, it is explicitly stated that the *giver* of the *Civil-Fruit* is the same as the *seller* of the *ExploitedGood*.
6. The *Assets* which must be given by the *seller* to the *buyer* are the *CivilFruits* produced by the asset which has been sold.
7. According to the Italian civil code, when a duty created by an obligation is violated by an agent, he must refund the damages created to the beneficiary: the sanction associated to the *Give-fruit* duty is thus to repay the buyer for the damage due to not giving the fruits of the sold assets.

6   Ontological Models of the Legal System

Classical formalizations of legal reasoning are based on deontic logic, as [1,21,27,28], to quote just a few examples. More recently, ontologies have been adopted as a means to shape the legal domain, beyond the basic deontic primitives. Ontologies have been used in a wide range of applications, from legal advice (see the application of the CLIME ontology to Maritime Law [6,30], the representation of cadastral data and norms ruling the Real Property Transactions [23] and to the access to legal information ([24,31]). Various studies aimed at proposing ontological primitives [20] or at comparing and evaluating different approaches to legal ontologies [3,26]. In this section, we overview three models, which seem more relevant for setting the context of the present work.

In various papers, Breuker, Valente and Winkels (BVW) have described a 'functional model' of legal systems [7,25].

Their perspective is much wider than ours, but BVW's view of model-based reasoning is relevant in this context. Their approach moves away from pure heuristic reasoning towards a full representation of the principles and contents of legal knowledge. However, they claim that full model-based reasoning is not adequate for the task at hand, so that "weaker versions of model-based reasoning that do not require full envisioning" [25], p.1082 are preferable. It cannot be denied that full-blown model based reasoning is hardly feasible in a domain as complex as legal reasoning. However, it seems that some further steps towards this end can be useful to meet the goal of linking legal concepts to world knowledge.

Our view is that many of the concepts which are related to the notion of agency (i.e. behavior, intention, knowledge/belief) are relevant in legal modelling, but they still lack an adequate formalization in terms of ontological primitives. We claim that BDI models, together with their involvement of desires and intentions, are one of the essential bricks required to expand and extend BVW's analysis. In fact, in assessing a case, it is not only necessary to decide if one or more norms have been broken, but also to understand why an agent did break them. And this cannot be done, unless one has a view of the reasoning mechanism that led the agent to choose that specific line of behavior (see also the description of *Agent causation* in [18]). The present article tries to specify which is the link between an agent's intentions, his behavior and the norms that affect them. In this sense, it can be seen as an extension of BVW's model, although our focus is more on the reasoning of the agent than on the reasoning of the legal system.

Similar comments apply to the system described in [17], where the "conceptual frame-based ontology" includes three types of frames: norm frames, act frames, and concept-description frames. The norm frames include five slots, which describe the subject of the norm, the legal modality of the norm (duty-imposing, permission or power-conferring), the action to which the norm refers to (What must be done or forborne?), and some extra conditions of application (place and time). As we have seen, we assume that a sixth slot is required, i.e. the sanction. In our view, this is essential in the task of explaining how the existence of a norm affects the behavior of agents. Actually, the act frame includes three slots that are related to agent behaviour: *cause, aim,* and *intentionality,* but it is not clear if they have any impact on the actual model. In any case, the glosses reveal that these terms are used in a rather different way than we do (see Section 4).

A third model which is relevant here is that presented in [12]. It is based on three conceptual primitives, i.e. *states of affairs, events* and *rules.* States of affairs concern any type of piece of reality (as 'John is a thief', or 'A minor cannot make a valid will'), and are changed by events (as 'John taking away the car of Gerald' or 'An international treaty being ratified'). There are subcategories of events:

"*A special kind of events are acts: events that consist of the intentional behaviour of an individual. A special category of acts are the so-called juristic acts*" [12], p.1049.

In our view, one of the most important features of Hage & Verheij proposal is the parallel existing between the pair <event,causality> and the pair <rule,constitution>. The events change the state of affair 'obtaining' (i.e holding) before the event into a new state of affair obtaining after the event. And this new state of affairs is causally related (via its 'effects') to the event. On the contrary, two state of affairs (that occur simultaneously) are related via a constitution relation (called supervenience) if there is a rule establishing the existence of this relation. For instance, the event 'signing of a contract' is causally related to the state of affair 'the contract is signed', and 'the two contractors are under a contractual bond' supervenes to the latter. In case of supervenience, there are conventional conditions for the existence of the relation: it is not different to have the contract signed and to have two individuals under a contractual bond, provided that there is a rule stating the correspondence; so, it is mainly a problem of description of a state of affairs which actually is a single one.

According to the previous discussion, we claim that actions, the way people use their knowledge about actions, and the way people decide which goal(s) to pursue via their actions, have a basic role in defining a legal ontology.

7   Conclusions

In this article, we have presented an ontological model of norms, based on the behaviour of agents. We have shown that norms can be characterized as *constraints on behaviour*, i.e. as statements specifying what an agent can and cannot do, and what happens when a norm is broken. The basic idea is that agents choose a line of behaviour according to the utility they may gain; and usually the breach of a norm produces a decrease in the estimated utility, because of the risk of being sanctioned. In order to include in the ontology knowledge about behaviour, we have provided a sketch of an ontological representation of plans, showing how a *Norm* can affect the planning process: the presence of a *Norm* can urge an agent to adopt a given line of behaviour (complying with the norm) instead of another (breaching the norm). This is obtained by introducing the notion of utility and by letting the agent determine his intention according to the expected utility.

Although the article has mainly addressed primary norms, it has also shown that the proposed model covers *authorities* in a legal system, and the way they are created. Finally, we have shown how the model applies to a specific case study (*Goods* and *Fruits*).

Two final comments concern the degree of coverage of the article with respect to the various components of a legal system and the complexity of the representation. As we have stated in the introduction, the goal of this paper is not to develop a general model of a legal system (see the models described in Section 6), but only to give an ontological characterization of a specific aspect, i.e. the role of primary norms. In principle, norms are just a small portion, although crucial, of such a model (see Section 2). Representing norms in an ontologically plausible way is the first step towards the implementation of a general model; this can be grounded on the behaviour of agents; agents are the entities which populate the societies that are regulated by legal systems. We believe that adopting them as the foundation for the representation is, in our view, the main contribution of this work. Of course, other agents do exist, most noticeably the judges; also judges (as all agents) are subject to norms, but they also have the role of assessing cases; this is a particular activity, that is not addressed in this paper, but that can be arguably assimilated to a kind of diagnostic reasoning: given some evidence (symptoms), classify the situation according to the categories appearing in the system. Since, in doing that, the court must respect some norms, it seems reasonable to assume that the model applies to it equally well, provided that a suitable representation is associated with the process of assessing the case.

Finally, the complexity of the representation. We have argued in favor of a language including some constructs that makes the language computationally hard. Although this is not the focus of the paper, we must stress that this appears to be unavoidable, unless one is able to show that the same concepts can be represented with simpler constructs, or that the knowledge expressed by these concepts can be left out of the ontology without loss of information. We believe that neither is the case, so that we hope that suitable heuristics can help a reasoner to obtain results within acceptable time limits.

References

1. C. Alchourron: Philosophical foundations of deontic logic and the logic of defeasible conditionals. In Meyer, J.-J., and Wieringa, R. (eds): *Deontic Logic in Computer Science: Normative System Specification*, pages 43-84. John Wiley & Sons, 1993,.

2. L.E. Allen and C.S. Saxon: Better Language, Better Thought, Better Communication: The A-Hohfeld Language for Legal Analysis. *Proc. of 5th Int. Conf. on Artificial Intelligence and Law*, ACM Press, 1995.

3. T.J.M. Bench-Capon: Task Neutral Ontologies, Common Sense Ontologies and Legal Information Systems. *Proc. 2nd Workshop on Legal Ontologies at Jurix*, pages 15-19, 2001.

4. G. Boella, L. Lesmo, L. Favali: The Definition of Legal Relations in a BDI Multiagent Framework, *Proc. of AI*IA 01*, pages 225-236, Springer Verlag, Berlin, 2001.

5. G. Boella, L. Lesmo: A game theoretic approach to norms. *Cognitive Science Quarterly 2*, 2(3-4), pages 492-512, 2002.

6. A. Boer, R. Hoekstra, R. Winkels: The CLIME Ontology. *Proc. 2nd Workshop on Legal Ontologies at Jurix*, pages 37-47, 2001.

7. J. Breuker, A. Valente and R. Winkels: Legal Ontologies: A Functional View. *Proc. of the First Workshop on Legal Ontologies*, pages 23-36, 1997.
8. J. Breuker, R. Winkels: Use and Reuse of Legal Ontologies in Knowledge Engineering and Information Management. *AI & Law, In press.*
9. A. Gangemi, N. Guarino, C. Masolo, A. Oltramari, L. Schneider: Sweetening Ontologies with DOLCE. *Proc. EKAW 2002*, Siguenza, Spain, 2002.
10. N. Guarino: Some ontological principles for designing upper level lexical resources. In *Proc. First Int. Conf. on Language Resources and Evaluation (LREC 1998)*, Granada, 1998.
11. N. Guarino, C. Welty: Evaluating Ontological Decisions with OntoClean. *Communications of the ACM 45*, pages 61-65, 2002.
12. J. Hage, B. Verheij: The Law as a Dynamic Interconnected System of States of Affairs: a Legal Top Ontology. *Int. J. Human-Computer Studies 54*, pages 1043-1077, 1999.
13. H. Hart: *The Concept of Law.* Clarendon Press, Oxford, 1961.
14. H. Herrestad, C. Krogh: Obligations directed from bearers to counterparties. *Proc. of 5th Int.l Conf. on Artificial Intelligence and Law*, ACM Press, 1995.
15. W.N. Hohfeld: *Fundamental Legal Conceptions as Applied in Judicial Reasoning and Other Legal Essays*, Yale Univ. Press, New Haven, Conn., 1919.
16. H. Kelsen: *General Theory of Law and State* (Wedberg trans.), New York, Russell & Russell, 1945.
17. R.W. van Kralingen, P.R.S. Visser, T.J.R. Bench Capon, H.J. van den Herik: A principled approach to developing legal knowledge systems. *Int. J. Human-Computer Studies 54*, pages 1127-1154, 1999.
18. J. Lehmann, J. Breuker, B. Brouwer: Causation in AI & Law. *ICAIL 2003 Workshop on Legal Ontologies & Web Based Legal Information Management*, pages 1-34, Edinburgh, 2003.
19. C. Masolo, S. Borgo, A. Gangemi, N. Guarino, A. Oltramari: *WonderWeb Deliverable D18. Ontology Library.* Final Report (ver. 1.0, 31-12-2003).
20. L. Mommers: A knowledge-based ontology of the legal domain. *Proc. 2nd Workshop on Legal Ontologies at Jurix 2001*, pages 1-7, 2001.
21. H. Prakken, M. Sergot: Dyadic deontic logic and contrary-to-duty obligations. In Nute, D. ed., *Defeasible Deontic Logic*, pages 223-262, Kluwer, 1997.
22. A. Ross: *Directives and norms.* Humanities Press, New York, 1968.
23. H. Stuckenschmidt, E. Stubkjaer, C. Schlieder: Modeling Land Transactions: Legal Ontologies in Context. *2nd Workshop on Legal Ontologies at Jurix 2001*, pages 58-66, 2001.
24. D. Tiscornia: Ontology-driven Access to Legal Information, *DEXA 2001- Workshop LISA, Legal Information Systems and Application*, Munich, 2001.
25. A. Valente, J. Breuker, B. Brouwer : Legal modelling and automated reasoning with ON-LINE. *Int. J. Human-Computer Studies 54*, pages 1079-1125, 1999.
26. P.R.S. Visser, T.J.M. Bench-Capon: A comparison of Four Ontologies for the Design of Legal Knowledge Systems. *Artificial Intelligence and Law 6*, pages 27-57, 1998.
27. L. van der Torre, Y. Tan: Cancelling and overshadowing: two types of defeasibility in defeasible deontic logic. *Proc. 14th Int. Joint Conference on Artificial Intelligence (IJCAI' 95)*, 1525-1532, Morgan Kaufmann, 1995.
28. G.H. von Wright: Deontic logic. *Mind 60*, pages 1-15, 1951.

29. C. Welty, N. Guarino: Supporting Ontological Analysis of Taxonomic Relationships. *Data and Knowledge Engineering 39*, pages 51-74, 2001.
30. R. Winkels, D.J.B. Bosscher, A. Boer, J. Breuker: Generating exception structures for legal information serving. *Proc. ICAIL 99*, pages 182-189, New York, 1999.
31. R. Winkels, D.J.B. Bosscher, A. Boer, R. Hoekstra: Extended Conceptual Retrieval. In J.A. Breuker et al. (eds): *Legal Knowledge and Information Systems 2000*, pages 85-98, IOS Press, Amsterdam, 2000.

Building Legal Ontologies with METHONTOLOGY and WebODE

Oscar Corcho[1], Mariano Fernández-López, Asunción Gómez-Pérez,
and Angel López-Cima

Facultad de Informática. Universidad Politécnica de Madrid,
Campus de Montegancedo, s/n. 28660 Boadilla del Monte. Madrid, Spain
{ocorcho, mfernandez, asun, alopez}@fi.upm.es

Abstract. This paper presents how to build an ontology in the legal domain following the ontology development methodology METHONTOLOGY and using the ontology engineering workbench WebODE. Both of them have been widely used to develop ontologies in many other domains. The ontology used to illustrate this paper has been extracted from an existing class taxonomy proposed by Breuker, and adapted to the Spanish legal domain.

1 Introduction

When the application of the technology in a specific area attains some degree of maturity, it stops being an art and becomes an engineering. A characteristic of an engineering is that it provides methods, methodologies and tools to perform the tasks required in such area. Methodologies state "what", "who" and "when" a given activity should be performed [7], and tools give support to such activities. Ontological Engineering refers to the set of activities that concern the ontology development process, the ontology life cycle, the methods and methodologies for building ontologies, and the tool suites and languages that support them [12].

Some outstanding works on how to develop ontologies methodologically are the following: Uschold and King's [24], Grüninger and Fox's [14], METHONTOLOGY [9, 10], and On-To-Knowledge [20], among others. Concerning software platforms that aid in ontology development, we can mention Protégé-2000 [18], OntoEdit [21], KAON [17], and WebODE [1], among others.

In this paper we present how to develop a legal entity ontology following METHONTOLOGY and using WebODE (the methodology and software platform proposed by the Ontological Engineering Group at UPM). With them we have built ontologies in different domains, like Chemistry, Science, knowledge management, e-commerce, etc.

This paper is addressed to experts in Law who want to build ontologies in that domain. We present how we have adapted a class taxonomy proposed by Breuker[2], to build a legal entity ontology in the context of the Spanish legal domain. We have used

---

[1] Now at Intelligent Software Components (ocorcho@isoco.com)
[2] http://zeus.ics.forth.gr/forth/ics/isl/projects/ontoweb/notes/legal-ontol-ontoweb-sard-2002.ppt

V.R. Benjamins et al. (Eds.): Law and the Semantic Web, LNCS 3369, pp. 142–157, 2005.

METHONTOLOGY (section 2) and WebODE (section 3) as our methodological and technological frameworks. Section 4 describes briefly other methods and methodologies, and tools. Finally, section 5 presents conclusions to this work.

2   Building a Legal Entity Ontology According to METHONTOLOGY

2.1   METHONTOLOGY in a Nutshell

METHONTOLOGY [9, 10] was developed within the Ontological Engineering group at Universidad Politécnica de Madrid. This methodology enables the construction of ontologies at the knowledge level, and has its roots in the main activities identified by the IEEE software development process [15] and in other knowledge engineering methodologies [13].

ODE and WebODE [1] were built to give technological support to METHONTOLOGY. Other ontology tools and tool suites can also be used to build ontologies following this methodology, for example the ones mentioned in the introduction: Protégé-2000 [18], OntoEdit [21], KAON [17], etc. METHONTOLOGY has been proposed[3] for ontology construction by the Foundation for Intelligent Physical Agents (FIPA), which promotes inter-operability across agent-based applications.METHONTOLOGY guides in how to carry out the whole ontology development through the specification, the conceptualization, the formalization, the implementation and the maintenance of the ontology (see figure 1). We now describe briefly what each activity consists in:

- The *specification* activity states why the ontology is being built, what its intended uses are and who the end-users are.
- The *conceptualization* activity in METHONTOLOGY organizes and converts an informally perceived view of a domain into a semi-formal specification using a set of intermediate representations (IRs) based on tabular and graph notations that can be understood by domain experts and ontology developers. The result of the conceptualization activity is the ontology conceptual model. The *formalization* activity transforms the conceptual model into a formal or semi-computable model. The *implementation* activity builds computable models in an ontology language (Ontolingua [8], RDF Schema [4], OWL [5], etc.). Tools implement automatically conceptual models in varied ontology languages. For example, WebODE imports and exports ontologies from and to the following languages: XML, RDF(S), OIL, DAML+OIL, OWL, CARIN, FLogic, Jess, and Prolog.
- The *maintenance* activity updates and corrects the ontology if needed.

METHONTOLOGY also identifies management activities (schedule, control, and quality assurance), and support activities (knowledge acquisition, integration, evaluation, documentation, and configuration management).

---

[3]   http://www.fipa.org/specs/fipa00086/

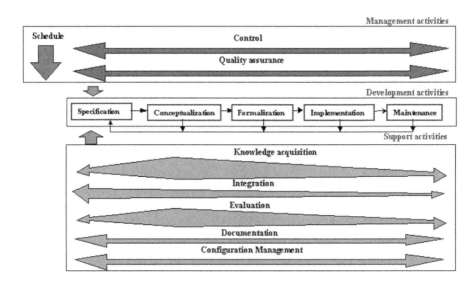

Fig. 1. Activities in the ontology development proposed by METHONTOLOGY

In the next sections we show the process followed to conceptualize an ontology about legal entities (juridical persons, organizations, etc.) in the Spanish legal domain. As already commented above, we have adapted a class taxonomy of legal entities proposed by Breuker for the Spanish legal domain. The definitions provided for some of the legal terms of this ontology are adapted from the LEGAMedia lexicon[4].

2.2 Main Ontology Modelling Components

METHONTOLOGY proposes to conceptualize ontologies with a set of tabular and graphical IRs. Such IRs allow modeling the components described in this section.

Concepts are taken in a broad sense. For instance, in the legal domain, concepts are: `juridical person`, `court`, `juvenile`, etc. Concepts in the ontology are usually organized in taxonomies through which inheritance mechanisms can be applied. For instance, we can represent a taxonomy of legal entities (which distinguishes persons and organizations), where a `juridical person` is a subclass of a `person`, a `company` is a subclass of a `juridical person`, a `private company` is a subclass of `company`, etc.

Relations represent a type of association between concepts of the domain. If the relation links two concepts, for example, `hears`, which links `court` to `lawsuit`, it is called binary relation. An important binary relation is *Subclass-Of*, which is used for building the class taxonomy, as shown above. Each binary relation may have an inverse relation that links the concepts in the opposite direction. For example, the relation `is heard` is the inverse of `hears`.

---

[4] http://www.legamedia.net/lx/lx.php

Instances are used to represent elements or individuals in an ontology. An example of instance of the concept Court is Albacete Provincial Court or Constitutional Court. Relations can be also instantiated. For example, we can express that Albacete Provicial Court hears 127/2004 lawsuit as follows: hears (Albacete Provincial Court, 127/2004 lawsuit), using a first order logic notation.

Constants are numeric values that do not change during much time. For example, adult age in Spain.

Attributes describe properties of instances and of concepts. We can distinguish two types of attributes: instance and class attributes. *Instance attributes* describe concept instances, where they take their values. These attributes are defined in a concept and inherited by its subconcepts and instances. For example, the first name of a physical person is proper to each instance. *Class attributes* describe concepts and take their values in the concept where they are defined. Class attributes are neither inherited by the subclasses nor by the instances. An example is the attribute type of control of the concept company, which can be used to determine the type of control of a private company, a public company, and a shared control company. Ontology development tools usually provide predefined domain-independent class attributes for all the concepts, such as the concept documentation, synonyms, acronyms, etc. Besides, other user-defined domain-dependent class attributes can be usually created.

Formal axioms are logical expressions that are always true and are normally used to specify constraints in the ontology. An example of axiom is that a person cannot be the defendant and the plaintiff in the same lawsuit.

Rules are generally used to infer knowledge in the ontology, such as attribute values, relation instances, etc. An example of rule is that lawsuits where juveniles up 14 years old are the defendants are heard by a juvenile court.

2.3   Conceptualization of a Legal Entity Ontology

When building ontologies, ontologists should not be anarchic in the use of the above modeling components during the ontology conceptualization. They should not define, for instance, a relation if the linked concepts are not precisely defined in the ontology. METHONTOLOGY includes in the conceptualization activity the set of structuring knowledge tasks shown in figure 2.

The figure emphasizes the ontology components (concepts, attributes, relations, constants, formal axioms, rules, and instances) built inside each task, and illustrates the order proposed to create such components during the conceptualization activity. This modeling process is not sequential, though some order must be followed to ensure the consistency and completeness of the knowledge represented. If new vocabulary is introduced, the ontologist can return to any previous task.

Task 1: To build the glossary of terms. First, the ontologist builds a glossary of terms that includes all the relevant terms of the domain (concepts, instances, attributes, relations between concepts, etc.), their natural language descriptions, and

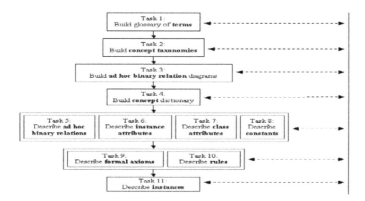

Fig. 2. Tasks of the conceptualization activity according to METHONTOLOGY

Table 1. An excerpt of the Glossary of Terms of the legal entity ontology

Name	Synonyms	Acronyms	Description	Type
adult age in Spain	--	--	The adult age in Spain is 18	Constant
Court	juridical tribunal	--	Although 'court' can be understood as a physical place or as a judge, we assume (in this ontology) that a court is a judicial tribunal	Concept
birth day	--	--	The day when a person was born	Instance Attribute
is defendant(*person, lawsuit*)	--	--	It is the lawsuit of a defendant	Relation

their synonyms and acronyms. Table 1 illustrates a section of the glossary of terms of the legal entity ontology. It is important to mention that on the initial stages of the ontology conceptualization the glossary of terms might contain several terms that refer to the same compoment. Then the ontologist should detect that they appear as synonyms.

Task 2: To build concept taxonomies. When the glossary of terms contains a sizable number of terms, the ontologist builds concept taxonomies to define the concept hierarchy.

To build concept taxonomies, the ontologist selects terms that are concepts from the glossary of terms. METHONTOLOGY proposes to use the four taxonomic relations defined in the Frame Ontology [8] and the OKBC Ontology [5]: *Subclass-Of*, *Disjoint-Decomposition*, *Exhaustive-Decomposition*, and *Partition*.

A concept C_1 is a *Subclass-Of* another concept C_2 if and only if every instance of C_1 is also an instance of C_2. For example, as Fig. 3 illustrates, `physical person` is a subclass of `person`, since every physical person is a person. A concept can be a subclass of more than one concept in the taxonomy. For instance, the concept `shared control company` is a subclass of the concepts `private company` and `public company`, since a shared control company is controlled by private and public entities.

A *Disjoint-Decomposition* of a concept C is a set of subclasses of C that do not have common instances and do not cover C, that is, there can be instances of the concept C that are not instances of any of the concepts in the decomposition. For example (see Fig. 3), the concepts `ministry` and `court` make up a disjoint decomposition of the concept `organization` because no organization can be simultaneously a ministry, and a court. Besides, there may be instances of the concept `organization` that are not instances of any of the two classes.

An *Exhaustive-Decomposition* of a concept C is a set of subclasses of C that cover C and may have common instances and subclasses, that is, there cannot be instances of the concept C that are not instances of at least one of the concepts in the decomposition. For example (see Fig. 3), the concepts `private company` and `public company` make up an exhaustive decomposition of the concept `company` because there are no companies that are not instances of at least one of those concepts, and those concepts can have common instances. For example, a `shared control company` is a `public company` and a `private company`.

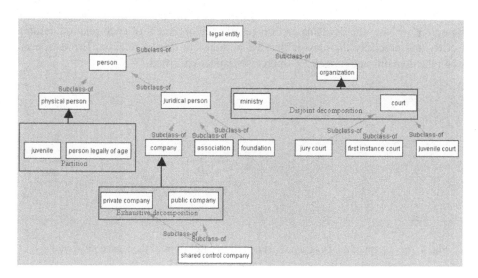

Fig. 3. An excerpt of the Concept Taxonomy of the legal entity ontology

A *Partition* of a concept C is a set of subclasses of C that do not share common instances and that cover C, that is, there are not instances of C that are not instances of one of the concepts in the partition. For example, Fig. 3 shows that the concepts `juvenile` and `person legally of age` make up a partition of the concept `physical person` because every physical is either juvenile or person legally of age.

Once the ontologist has structured the concepts in the concept taxonomy, and before going ahead with the specification of new knowledge, s(he) should examine that the taxonomies contain no errors [11]. For example, it should be checked that an element is not simultaneously instance of two classes of a disjoint decomposition, that there are not loops in the concept taxonomy, that several terms do not refer to the same concept, etc.

Task 3: To build ad hoc binary relation diagrams. Once the taxonomy has been built and evaluated, the conceptualization activity proposes to build ad hoc binary relation diagrams. The goal of this diagram is to establish ad hoc relationships between concepts of the same (or different) concept taxonomy. Figure 4 presents a fragment of the ad hoc binary relation diagram of our legal entity ontology, with the relations is plaintiff, is defendant and hears, and their inverses has plaintiff, has defendant and is heard. Such relations connect the root concepts (person and lawsuit, and court and lawsuit) of the concept taxonomies of legal entities and lawsuits. From an ontology integration perspective, such ad hoc relations express that the legal entity ontology will include the lawsuit ontology and vice versa.

Before going ahead with the specification of new knowledge, the ontologist should check that the ad hoc binary diagrams have no errors. The ontologist should figure out whether the domains and ranges of each argument of each relation delimit exactly and precisely the classes that are appropriate for the relation. Errors appear when the domains and ranges are imprecise or over-specified.

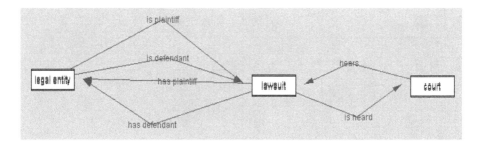

Fig. 4. An excerpt of the Diagram of ad hoc Binary Relations of the legal entity ontology

Task 4: To build the concept dictionary. Once the concept taxonomies and ad hoc binary relation diagrams have been generated, the ontologist must specify which are the properties and relations that describe each concept of the taxonomy in a concept dictionary, and, optionally, their instances.

A concept dictionary contains all the domain concepts, their relations, their instances, and their class and instance attributes. The relations specified for each concept are those whose domain is the concept. For example, the concept person has two relations: is plaintiff and is defendant. Relations, instance attributes and class attributes are local to concepts, which means that their names can be repeated in different concepts. Table 2 shows a small section of the concept dictionary of the legal entity ontology.

Table 2. An excerpt of the Concept Dictionary of the legal entity ontology

Concept name	Instances	Class attributes	Instance attributes	Relations
Court	Constitutional Court National Court Supreme Court Albacete Provincial Court	--	number of members seat territorial jurisdiction	hears
Company	--	type of control	name	--
Lawsuit	--	--	--	has defendant has plaintiff is heard
Person	--	--	--	is defendant is plaintiff
physical person	--	--	age birth day death day first family name first name nationality second family name	is mother of has father has mother is father of

As we said before, once the concept dictionary has been built, the ontologist must describe in detail each of the ad hoc binary relations, class attributes, and instance attributes appearing in it. In addition, the ontologist must describe accurately each of the constants that appear in the glossary of terms. Though METHONTOLOGY does all these tasks, it does not propose a specific order to perform them.

Task 5: To define ad hoc binary relations in detail. The goal of this task is to describe in detail all the ad hoc binary relations included in the concept dictionary, and to produce the ad hoc binary relation table. For each ad hoc binary relation, the ontologist must specify its name, the names of the source and target concepts, its cardinality, and its inverse relation. Table 3 shows a section of the ad hoc binary relation table of the legal entity ontology, which contains the definition of the relations is defendant, is plaintiff, etc.

Table 3. An excerpt of the ad hoc Binary Relation Table of the legal entity ontology

Relation name	Source concept	Source cardinality (Max)	Target concept	Inverse relation
is defendant	Person	N	lawsuit	has defendant
is plaintiff	Person	N	lawsuit	has plaintiff
Hears	Court	N	lawsuit	is heard
has defendant	Lawsuit	N	person	is defendant
has plaintiff	Lawsuit	N	person	is plaintiff
is heard	Lawsuit	N	court	hears

Task 6: To define instance attributes in detail. The aim of this task is to describe in detail all the instance attributes already included in the concept dictionary by means of an instance attribute table. Each row of the instance attribute table contains the detailed description of an instance attribute. Instance attributes are those attributes

that describe the instances of the concept and whose value(s) may be different for each instance of the concept. For each instance attribute, the ontologist must specify the following fields: its name; the concept it belongs to (attributes are local to concepts); its value type; and range of values (in the case of numerical values); minimum and maximum cardinality; instance attributes, class attributes and constants used to infer values of the attribute; attributes that can be inferred using values of this attribute; formulae or rules that allow inferring values of the attribute; and references used to define the attribute. Table 4 shows a fragment of the instance attribute table of the legal entity ontology. Some of the previous fields are not shown for the sake of space. This table contains some of the instance attributes of the concept `court`: `number of members`, `seat`, and `territorial jurisdiction`.

The use of measurement units in numerical attributes causes the integration of the *Standard Units* ontology. This is an example of how METHONTOLOGY proposes to integrate ontologies during the conceptualization activity, and not to postpone the integration to the ontology implementation activity.

Table 4. An excerpt of the Instance Attribute Table of the legal entity ontology

Instance attribute name	Concept name	Value type	Value Range	Cardinality
number of members	court	Integer	1 ..	(1, 1)
seat	court	String	--	(1, 1)
territorial jurisdiction	court	String	--	(1, 1)

Task 7: To define class attributes in detail. The aim of this task is to describe in detail all the class attributes already included in the concept dictionary by means of a class attribute table. Each row of the class attribute table contains a detailed description of the class attribute. For each class attribute, the ontologist should fill the following information: name; the name of the concept where the attribute is defined; value type; value(s); cardinality; the instance attributes whose values can be inferred with the value of this class attribute; etc. For example, the class attribute type of control would be defined for the concepts private company and public company as presented in Table 5.

Table 5. An excerpt of the Class Attribute Table of the legal entity ontology

Class attribute name	Defined concept	Value type	Cardinality	Values
type of control	private company	[private,public]	(1,2)	private
type of control	public company	[private,public]	(1,2)	public

Task 8: To define constants in detail. The aim of this task is to describe in detail each of the constants defined in the glossary of terms. Each row of the constant table contains a detailed description of a constant. For each constant, the ontologist must specify the following: name, value type (a number, a mass, etc.), value, the measurement unit for numerical constants, and the attributes that can be inferred using

the constant. Table 6 shows a fragment of the constant table of our legal entity ontology, where the constant `adult age in Spain` is defined. The attributes that can be inferred with the constant are omitted.

Table 6. An excerpt of the Constant Table of the legal entity ontology

Name	Value type	Value	Measurement unit
adult age in Spain	Cardinal	18	year

METHONTOLOGY proposes to describe formal axioms and rules in parallel once concepts and their taxonomies, ad hoc relations, attributes, and constants have been defined.

Task 9: To define formal axioms. To perform this task, the ontologist must identify the formal axioms needed in the ontology and describe them precisely. For each formal axiom definition, METHONTOLOGY proposes to specify the following information: name, NL description, the logical expression that formally describes the axiom using first order logic, the concepts, attributes and ad hoc relations to which the axiom refers, and the variables used.

Table 7. An excerpt of the Formal Axiom Table of the lawsuit ontology

Axiom name	Description	Expression	Referred concepts	Referred relations	Variables
incompatibility plaintiff defendant	A person cannot be plaintiff and defendant in the same lawsuit	not (exists(?X,?Y) (person(?X) and lawsuit(?Y) and [is plaintiff](?X,?Y) and [is defendant](?X,?Y)))	person lawsuit	is plaintiff is defendant	?X ?Y

As we have already commented, METHONTOLOGY proposes to express formal axioms in first order logic. Table 7 shows a formal axiom in our legal entity ontology that states that "A person cannot be plaintiff and defendant in the same lawsuit". The columns that correspond to the referred concepts and relations contain the concepts and relations that are used inside the formal axiom. The variables used are ?X for `person`, and ?Y for the `lawsuit`.

We must note that the definition of the logical expression may be difficult for an expert with no experience in first order logic.

Task 10: To define rules. Similarly to the previous task, the ontologist must identify first which rules are needed in the ontology, and then describe them in the rule table. For each rule definition, METHONTOLOGY proposes to include the following information: name, NL description, the expression that formally describes the rule, the concepts, attributes and relations to which the rule refers, and the variables used in the expression.

METHONTOLOGY proposes to specify rule expressions using the template *if* *<conditions> then <consequent>*. The left-hand side of the rule consists of conjunctions of atoms, while the right-hand side of the rule is a single atom.

Table 8 shows a rule that states and establishes that "Lawsuits where juveniles up 14 years old are defendants are heard by a juvenile court". This rule would let us infer the type of court for juveniles. As shown in the table, the rule refers to the concepts `juvenile`, `lawsuit` and `court`, to the attribute `age`, and to the relations `is defendant` and `hears`. The variables used are ?X for the `juvenile`, ?Y for the `integer`, `lawsuit` for ?Z and ?Z for `court`.

As in the case of formal axioms, the definition of the rule expression may be difficult for experts who have little experience in first order logic.

Table 8. An excerpt of the Rule Table of the legal entity ontology

Rule name	Description	Expression	Concepts	Referred attributes	Referred relations	Variables
juvenile courts for juveniles	Lawsuits where juveniles up 14 years old are defendants are heard by a juvenile court	If juvenile(?X) and lawsuit(?Z) and court(?W) and age(?X, ?Y) and ?Y > 14 and [is defendant](?X, ?Z) and hears(?W, ?Z) then [juvenile court](?W)]	juvenile lawsuit court	age	is defendant Hears	?X ?Z ?W

Task 11: To define instances. Once the conceptual model of the ontology has been created the ontologist might define relevant instances that appear in the concept dictionary inside an instance table. For each instance, the ontologist should define: its name, the name of the concept it belongs to, and its attribute values, if known. Table 9 presents some instances of the instance table of our legal entity ontology: `National Court`, `Supreme Court` and `Constitutional Court`). All of them are instances of the concept `court`, as defined in the concept dictionary, and they have some attribute and relation values specified, for: `seat`, `territorial jurisdiction`, and `number of members`. These instances could have more than one value for the attributes whose maximum cardinality is higher than one.

Table 9. An excerpt of the Instance Table of the legal entity ontology

Instance name	Concept name	Attribute	Values
National Court	court	seat	Madrid
		territorial jurisdiction	Spain
Supreme Court	court	territorial jurisdiction	Spain
Constitutional Court	court	number of members	12
		territorial jurisdiction	Spain

METHONTOLOGY has been used by different groups to build ontologies on Chemistry, Science, knowledge management, e-commerce, etc. A detailed description of this ontology building methodology can be found in [12].

3   Building a Legal Ontology with WebODE

WebODE[5] [1] is an ontological engineering workbench developed by the Ontological Engineering group at Universidad Politécnica de Madrid (UPM). The current version is 2.0. WebODE is the offspring of the ontology design environment ODE, a standalone ontology tool based on tables and graphs, which allowed users to customize the knowledge model used for conceptualizing their ontologies according to their KR needs. Both ODE and WebODE give support to the ontology building methodology METHONTOLOGY, described in the previous section.

Currently, WebODE contains an ontology editor, which integrates most of the ontology services offered by the workbench, an ontology-based knowledge management system (ODEKM), an automatic Semantic Web portal generator (ODESeW), a Web resources annotation tool (ODEAnnotate), and a Semantic Web services editing tool (ODESWS). A detailed description of all of them can be found in [12].

Let us start describing the WebODE ontology editor. The editor is a Web application built on top of the ontology access service (ODE API), which integrates several ontology building services from the workbench: ontology edition, navigation, documentation, merge, reasoning, etc.

Three user interfaces are combined in this ontology editor: an HTML form-based editor for editing all ontology terms except axioms and rules; a graphical user interface, called ODEDesigner, for editing concept taxonomies and relations graphically; and WAB (WebODE Axiom Builder), for editing formal axioms and rules. We now describe them and highlight their most important features.

Figure 5 shows a screenshot of the HTML interface for editing instance attributes of the concept physical person of our legal entity ontology. The main areas of this interface are:

- The browsing area. To navigate through the whole ontology and to create new elements and modify or delete the existing ones.
- The clipboard. To easily copy and paste information between forms, so that similar ontology components can be created easily.
- The edition area. To insert, delete and update ontology terms (concepts, attributes, relations, etc.) with HTML forms, and tables with knowledge about existing terms. Figure 5 shows the attributes defined for the concept physical person: age, birthday, deathday, first family name, etc.

ODEDesigner eases the construction of concept taxonomies and ad hoc binary relations between concepts, and allows defining views to highlight or customize the visualization of fragments of the ontology for different users.

Concept taxonomies are created with the following set of predefined relations: *Subclass-Of*, *Disjoint-Decomposition*, *Exhaustive-Decomposition*, *Partition*, *Transitive-Part-Of* and *Intransitive-Part-Of*. Figures 3 and 4 show different views of our legal entity ontology in ODEDesigner.

---

[5] http://webode.dia.fi.upm.es/

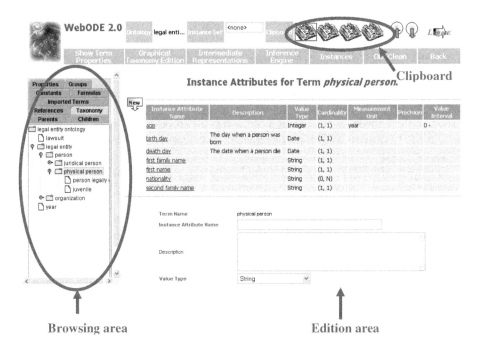

Browsing area   Edition area

Fig. 5. Edition of an instance attribute with the WebODE ontology editor

The WebODE Axiom Builder (WAB) is a graphical editor for creating formal axioms and rules, like the ones presented in table 7 and table 8. This editor aims at facilitating the creation of such components by domain experts who have not much experience with modelling in first order logic.

We now describe other ontology building services integrated in the ontology editor: the documentation service, ODEMerge, and the evaluation service. There are many other WebODE services (e.g. the OKBC-based Prolog inference engine, ODEClean, the ontology translation services, etc.) that will not be presented, since we think that they will not be specially useful for the readers for whom this paper is focused on.

The WebODE ontology documentation service generates WebODE ontologies in different formats that can be used to provide their documentation: HTML tables representing the METHONTOLOGY's intermediate representations described in section 2 and HTML concept taxonomies. In fact, the figures presented in such a section are part of WebODE screenshots.

The WebODE merge service (ODEMerge) performs a supervised merge of concepts, attributes, and ad hoc binary relations from two ontologies built for the same domain. It uses natural language resources to find the mappings between the components of both ontologies so as to generate the resulting merged ontology.

Finally, the WebODE workbench also provides the following ontology evaluation functions: the ontology consistency service and the RDF(S), DAML+OIL, and OWL evaluation services.

The ontology consistency service provides constraint checking capabilities for the WebODE ontologies and is used by the ontology editor during the ontology building process. It checks type constraints, numerical values constraints, and cardinality constraints, and verifies concept taxonomies (i.e., external instances of an exhaustive decomposition, loops, etc.).

The RDF(S), DAML+OIL, and OWL evaluation services evaluate ontologies according to the evaluation criteria identified by Gómez-Pérez [11]. They detect errors in ontologies implemented in these languages and provide suggestions about better design criteria for them.

4   Other Methods and Tools for Ontology Development

Basically, a series of methods and methodologies for developing ontologies have been reported in literature. In 1990, Lenat and Guha [16] published some general steps and some interesting points about the Cyc development. Some years later, in 1995, on the basis of the experience gathered in developing the Enterprise Ontology [23] and the TOVE (TOronto Virtual Enterprise) project ontology [14] both in the domain of enterprise modeling, the first guidelines were proposed and later refined in [23].

At the 12th European Conference for Artificial Intelligence (ECAI'96), Bernaras and colleagues [3] presented a method to build an ontology in the domain of electrical networks as part of the Esprit KACTUS project. The METHONTOLOGY methodology appeared simultaneously and was extended in further papers [9, 10]. In 1997, a new method was proposed for building ontologies based on the SENSUS ontology [22]. Then some years later, the On-To-Knowledge methodology appeared within the project with the same name [20].

Concerning ontology tools' technology, it has improved enormously since the creation of the first environments. If we take into consideration the evolution of ontology development tools since they appeared in the mid-1990s, we can distinguish two groups[6]:

- Tools whose knowledge model maps directly to an ontology language. These tools were developed as ontology editors for a specific language. In this group we include: the Ontolingua Server [8], which supports ontology construction with Ontolingua and KIF; OntoSaurus [22] with Loom; and OilEd [2] with OIL first, later with DAML+OIL, and now with OWL.
- Integrated tool suites whose main characteristic is that they have an extensible architecture, and whose knowledge model is usually independent of an ontology language. These tools provide a core set of ontology related services and are easily extended with other modules to provide more functions. In this group we can include Protégé-2000 [18], WebODE [1], OntoEdit [21], and KAON [17].

---

[6] In each group, we have followed a chronological order of appearance.

5 Conclusions

In this paper, we have shown how experts on the legal domain can develop their own ontologies following the ontology building methodology METHONTOLOGY and using the ontology engineering workbench WebODE. This methodology and tool have been successfully used by different groups for the development of ontologies in diverse domains. To illustrate how to use them, we have provided an example of how to develop an ontology about legal entities in Spain, adapting a taxonomy of legal entities elaborated by Breuker.

The main conclusion that we can transmit to the reader is that the broad experience on knowledge representation is not a necessary condition to build an ontology. Experts on the legal domain can have the initiative in the development of ontologies of their field with punctual help of experts on knowledge engineering. METHONTOLOGY allows modelling ontologies through graphical and tabular intermediate representations that can be understood by experts in one domain who are not deeply involved in the ontology field. Moreover, WebODE is a software platform that provides support to METHONTOLOGY, although it does not force to follow such methodology.

Finally, in section 4 we have presented other methods and tools so that readers can have the possibility of working according to other proposals.

Acknowledgments

This work has been supported by the project Esperonto (IST-2001-34373).

References

1. Arpírez JC, Corcho O, Fernández-López M, Gómez-Pérez A (2003) *WebODE in a nutshell.* AI Magazine, 24(3)-37-47
2. Bechhofer S, Horrocks I, Goble C, Stevens R (2001) *OilEd: a reasonable ontology editor for the Semantic Web.* In: Baader F, Brewka G, Eiter T (eds) Joint German/Austrian conference on Artificial Intelligence (KI'01). Vienna, Austria. (Lecture Notes in Artificial Intelligence LNAI 2174) Springer-Verlag, Berlin, Germany, pp 396–408
3. Bernaras A, Laresgoiti I, Corera J (1996) *Building and reusing ontologies for electrical network applications.* In: Wahlster W (ed) European Conference on Artificial Intelligence (ECAI'96). Budapest, Hungary. John Wiley and Sons, Chichester, United Kingdom, pp 298–302
4. Brickley D, Guha RV (2004) *RDF Vocabulary Description Language 1.0: RDF Schema.* W3C Recommendation. *http://www.w3.org/TR/PR-rdf-schema*
5. Chaudhri VK, Farquhar A, Fikes R, Karp PD, Rice JP (1998) *Open Knowledge Base Connectivity 2.0.3.* Technical Report. *http://www.ai.sri.com/~okbc/okbc-2-0-3.pdf*
6. Dean M, Schreiber G (2004) *OWL Web Ontology Language Reference.* W3C Recommendation. *http://www.w3.org/TR/owl-ref/*

7. de Hoog R (1998) *Methodologies for Building Knowledge Based Systems: Achievements and Prospects*. In: Liebowitz J (ed) Handbook of Expert Systems. CRC Press Chapter 1, Boca Raton, Florida
8. Farquhar A, Fikes R, Rice J (1997) *The Ontolingua Server: A Tool for Collaborative Ontology Construction*. International Journal of Human Computer Studies 46(6):707–727
9. Fernández-López M, Gómez-Pérez A, Juristo N (1997) *METHONTOLOGY: From Ontological Art Towards Ontological Engineering*. Spring Symposium on Ontological Engineering of AAAI. Stanford University, California, pp 33–40
10. Fernández-López M, Gómez-Pérez A, Pazos A, Pazos J (1999) *Building a Chemical Ontology Using Methontology and the Ontology Design Environment*. IEEE Intelligent Systems & their applications 4(1):37–46
11. Gómez-Pérez A (2001) *Evaluation of Ontologies*. International Journal of Intelligent Systems 16(3):391–409
12. Gómez-Pérez A, Fernández-López M, Corcho O (2003) *Ontological Engineering: with examples from the areas of knowledge management, e-commerce and the Semantic Web*, Springer-Verlag, New York.
13. Gómez-Pérez A, Juristo N, Montes C, Pazos J (1997) *Ingeniería del Conocimiento: Diseño y Construcción de Sistemas Expertos*. Ceura, Madrid, Spain
14. Grüninger M, Fox MS (1995) *Methodology for the design and evaluation of ontologies* In Skuce D (ed) IJCAI95 Workshop on Basic Ontological Issues in Knowledge Sharing, pp 6.1–6.10
15. IEEE (1996) *IEEE Standard for Developing Software Life Cycle Processes*. IEEE Computer Society. New York. IEEE Std 1074-1995
16. Lenat DB, Guha RV (1990) *Building Large Knowledge-based Systems: Representation and Inference in the Cyc Project*. Addison-Wesley, Boston, Massachusetts
17. Maedche A, Motik B, Stojanovic L, Studer R, Volz R (2003) *Ontologies for Enterprise Knowledge Management*. IEEE Intelligent Systems 18(2):26–33
18. Noy NF, Fergerson RW, Musen MA (2000) *The knowledge model of Protege-2000: Combining interoperability and flexibility*. In: Dieng R, Corby O (eds) 12th International Conference in Knowledge Engineering and Knowledge Management (EKAW'00). Juan-Les-Pins, France. (Lecture Notes in Artificial Intelligence LNAI 1937) Springer-Verlag, Berlin, Germany, pp 17–32
19. Noy NF, Musen MA (2000) *PROMPT: Algorithm and Tool for Automated Ontology Merging and Alignment*. In: Rosenbloom P, Kautz HA, Porter B, Dechter R, Sutton R, Mittal V (eds) 17th National Conference on Artificial Intelligence (AAAI'00). Austin, Texas, pp 450–455
20. Staab S, Schnurr HP, Studer R, Sure Y (2001) *Knowledge Processes and Ontologies*. IEEE Intelligent Systems 16(1):26–34
21. Sure Y, Erdmann M, Angele J, Staab S, Studer R, Wenke D (2002) *OntoEdit: Collaborative Ontology Engineering for the Semantic Web*. In: Horrocks I, Hendler JA (eds) First International Semantic Web Conference (ISWC'02). Sardinia, Italy. (Lecture Notes in Computer Science LNCS 2342) Springer-Verlag, Berlin, Germany, pp 221–235
22. Swartout B, Ramesh P, Knight K, Russ T (1997) *Toward Distributed Use of Large-Scale Ontologies*. In: Farquhar A, Gruninger M, Gómez-Pérez A, Uschold M, van der Vet P (eds) AAAI'97 Spring Symposium on Ontological Engineering. Stanford University, California, pp 138–148
23. Uschold M, Grüninger M (1996) *Ontologies: Principles, Methods and Applications*. Knowledge Engineering Review 11(2):93–155
24. Uschold M, King M (1995) *Towards a Methodology for Building Ontologies*. In: Skuce D (eds) IJCAI'95 Workshop on Basic Ontological Issues in Knowledge Sharing. Montreal, Canada, pp 6.1–6.10

Institutional Pragmatics and Legal Ontology Limits of the Descriptive Approach of Texts

Danièle Bourcier

CNRS-Paris
bourcier@msh-paris.fr

« To language then - to language alone - it is that
fictitious entities owe their existence- their impossible,
yet indispensable existence », J. Bentham, *Of ontology*,
CII, 23

Abstract. Pragmatics concerns itself with discourse as an illocutory act in a
dynamic context. Building an ontology means that you describe a state of the
world at a certain moment and in a certain form. How is it possible to take into
account the dynamic and implicit dimension of legal discourse in the building
of an ontology? This article mainly explores the new research area of
institutional pragmatics and will conclude with some contradictory perspectives
on pragmatics and ontology.

1 Introduction: Evolution of Pragmatic Objects

Institutional pragmatics is based on the idea that an illocutory act can only be
interpreted with regard to the conditions of validity defined by institutional
procedures and rules. In the legal context, most of these conditions are explicit. Some
of them are implicit and part of the 'common knowledge' of an institutional
community. Other conditions belong to the discretionary power of a player. The point,
however, is that these conditions cannot be properly assessed within the traditional
framework of studies on legal discourse.

We will first present the recent evolution of French research in legal language and
discourse analysis relating to pragmatics.Institutional pragmatics will then be defined
and illustrated by some examples of research on illocutory connectives.

Finally, we will conclude by proposing the notion of discretionary act as a
particular speech act of common knowledge, interacting between rule-makers and
decision-makers and will propose some reflections about the limits of ontologies
based on a symbolic, explicit and static dimension of texts.

The term 'pragmatics' belongs to a rich and ambiguous semantic network. The
adjective 'pragmatic' in English means 'dealing with acts and real effects'. In French,
the same word characterizes what is 'concrete, adapted to reality'. Many other
meanings can also be found in social sciences.

Pragmatics refers primarily to the research conducted in the many disciplines (such
as linguistics, social psychology, research on learning and semiotics) that are involved
in the description of the activity of communication using symbols of any kind :

V.R. Benjamins et al. (Eds.): Law and the Semantic Web, LNCS 3369, pp. 158–168, 2005.

natural language, computerized symbol systems, gesture, and situated cognition [1]. This approach, however, could also be valuable for scholars in disciplines which deal with institutional behaviours implied in normative activity, as for example political and legal sciences. First, legal language is not « formal » : the main activity of lawyers is to defeat or to re-build reasoning about the meaning of concept [2]. Second, human cognition is different from deliberate reasoning even in the field of law where explicit argumentation is presented as a part of decision making process. Some connectionist (sub-symbolic) models are currently better than human judge to explain chains of arguments [3]. Because of the limits of the descriptive model, research on generative processes and indirect speech acts will concern more and more the building of ontologies for legal knowledge engineering.

Pragmatics thus lay at the intersection of numerous disciplines. At first glance, the unity and boundaries of the field seem very difficult to pinpoint.

Language can be considered as a means to handle many interactional situations where actors, actions and intentions are entangled. Many markers allow for acting by speech and positions. As we know, it is impossible to describe the full meaning of a specific discourse out of its context. An ontology by definition escapes the context and does not take care of the conditions of production of Bruylant, meaning. On the contrary, the purpose of pragmatics is to explore the relationship between the use of symbols and social actors ("performers") in a given situation.

Let us examine the main topics of research in pragmatics.

First, scholars in pragmatics are interested in the social use of language dealing with the adaptation of symbolic expressions to situational contexts (interpersonal, institutional, etc...). 'Context' is thus central to the field. Is there something "out of language" in social activity? Analyses focus on discursive markers in language, testifying the prior pragmatic vocation of language. This is particularly so in the pragmatics of ordinary language. Another specificity of the "pragmatician community" is the various steps followed by its researchers. It grew out of the necessity to go further in a discipline, to explore out the niche and to integrate new facts. Conversely, to become a conscious pragmatician requires that one engages into a profound reflection on its own discipline with the help of new technical and intellectual tools. The performance of specific cognitive operations has to be described. Finally, empirism provides a sense of unity to the field, but stresses the necessity of listing methods, concepts, models and procedures through various observable and scientific objects.

I will now look at the evolution of pragmatics in legal language for the last decades in France. I will then suggest the path between linguistic pragmatics and institutional pragmatics. Legal pragmatics comes from legal rhetoricians and from the linguistic investigation into argumentation and analysis of discourse. Finally we will see that legal pragmaticians need cognitive science in order to go further in the implementation of "cognitive acts" and to integrate into the machine the interactive process using language as both knowledge procedure and interface. More specifically, the interaction between institutional actors, orders and rules produces acts which are entangled in networks of accountability. We will examine by proposing the notion of discretionary act as a peculiar illocutionary act implied in institutional common sense. Discretionary act cannot be described in a symbolic form but on the contrary can make implicit deformations in an existing ontological structure.

2 From Legal Logics to Legal Argumentation

In philosophy of law, a debate between logicians and dialecticians took place in the middle of the 1960s. It led to an important rediscovery of dialectical reasoning and dialogism. In this respect, Ch. Perelman and his seminal *Traité de l'Argumentation* [4], exerted a major influence on numerous academics and philosophers.

Traditionnally, argumentation was bound to rhetorics. Style was considered as a property of language. Rhetorics and stylistics are the 'two ways of persuading by appealing to our sensibility'... Both these disciplines held that speech figures could be assessed according to their efficiency vis à vis an auditory or vis à vis the judgment of the observer. Perelman set himself to create a rhetorics different from existing ones, and particularly from Aristotelian rhetorics. The novelty of his approach can be summarized as follows:

- argumentation is no longer limited to the art of persuasive public speeches: it can apply to texts.
- argumentation should complement the logician's theory of demonstration.
- argumentation should include an analysis of the means of proof in humanities, law and philosophy. He thereby rejected the experimental methods (linguistics) used by laboratories.

The problem was that Perelman proposed an unclear classification of figures. His description was not systematic and the main concept which could be re-used in pragmatics was that of "universal audience".

He views argumentation as a discrepancy vis à vis a norm. Argumentative strategy is thus considered to be out of language as a supplementary 'mark'. We are then supposed to have at our disposal a degree zero of use of language. It is also the case for many legal knowledge researchers.

According to his opinion, law would then be supposed to be a descriptive message a priori and arguments would be added in order to underline the effects. There would be a level of linguistics and a level of legal grammar. This double level is not operative as far as analysis is concerned: on what elements of the first level would the effects of argumentation of the second level be set up?

From another point of view, the return of argumentation provoked a dubious debate around deontic logic. The debate was articulated as follows: either logic governs discursive thought, or reasoning uses argument. Research on natural logic proved that the choice of a reasoning depends on the objects of thought (concepts) on which one works. The demonstration on the main role of logics - with the aim of disqualifying legal argumentation- was the following: the text can be interpreted from one point of view, and 'the one who reasons deductively disappears behind his speech and speaks from an universal perspective'. The speaker of a logical proposition does not exist as a speaker and all the relations between signs are conventional and explicit.

The new rhetorics of Perelman and the work of Toulmin stood in stark contrast with the formalist and symbolic mainstream. For these two thinkers, argumentation is an operative technique, which escapes from the investigation of a theory of demonstration. This technique is considered as individual and bound to the temporality of the discourse: argumentative statements would be the token statements, as opposed to the type statements of rules of law.

As previously pointed out, despite numerous works, legal argumentation has never been the object of a general theory based on a systematic approach. In fact, some authors have gone, as far as to argue that this lack of theory is to be explained by the fact that argumentation should escape from any kind of normativity.

The *Traité* of Perelman has been criticized mainly for the status of theory itself and its methodology [5]. Other mainstreams, such as the school of rational discourse and the philosophy of language of the first Wittgenstein, have sought to re-formalize some concepts like audience or value.

In law, significant research was conducted in the field of procedural theory of rational discourse: for example, a dialogue between speaker A and speaker B must fullfill general conditions of rationality. Among these rules, one can find rules of consistency, of effectivity, of sincerity, of generalisation (see 'universal audience'), of reinforcement, and of justification.

Participants must share a common knowledge (as we will see in our hypothesis about institutional common sense) and refer to the same values. For Aarnio [6], rationality is bound to acceptability : 'arguing means making one's decision as acceptable as possible'. For the first time, argumentation is related to legal pragmatics. These above approaches converge on their implication: the act of thinking has to do with understanding, and the act of speech is purely utilitarian and even "pragmatic". Argumentation, considered as a process that is external to language, is not based on linguistic criteria: it is possible to change willingly the meaning of words by a rational position (see Perelman). That perspective is very debatable from our linguistic perspective.

Let us consider the route through logics, rhetorics, the theory of rationality and the analysis of discourse.

3   From Philosophy of Language to Linguistic Pragmatics

The pragmatic linguistics under consideration here finds its origins in the mainstream philosophy of language where legal examples were prototypical.

Acts of language were picked in legal institutions (promise, declaration...). In 1962, Austin established the difference between performative and constative verbs [7]. But no linguistic clue was able to show that his theory was related to facts (legal reality). Performativity was set in opposition to a descriptivist view. All statements became "acts". It is impossible to say only something, or to describe. Following on from the same approach, Bouveresse [8] considered that legal statements are not peculiar speech acts: the theory of illocutionary acts cannot explain where obligations originate from. It is why, in 1979, Searle [9] proposed external criteria to characterize speech acts. Among the list of criteria, one may find the status of interlocutors and the extralinguistic situation allowing to accomplish the speech act. A crucial constraint appeared as essential: "institutional conditions ".

From a different perspective, Oswald Ducrot (1980) [10] and Anscombre & Ducrot (1983) [11] put forward another theory in pragmatics: the theory of semantic argumentation. This theory implies that we have no choice to use a non-marked language. Even if we want, pragmatic intention cannot be eliminated. This also signifies that discourse (like conversation) follows various maxims such as:

- there always exists a speaker, an addressee and several embedded discourses that include other speakers and discourses: various aims can coexist.
- discourse is polyphonic. This is particularly so in the case of an institutional discourse where the "I" and the "you" coexist with the "we" or, in French, the "on" (doxa) which introduces a lot of topoi (not discussed).

So the Saussurian view can be questioned: language is not a tool used for transmitting information or a chain of terms for giving a objective description of a pre-existing world as knowledge engineering could suggest. Language establishes subjective relationships between interlocutors. To Ducrot, it is the concretization of the illocutory value stressed by Austin. Any speech addressed to an interlocutor creates an obligatory relationship, assigns roles that nobody can cancel even if one does not answer. Meaning is the result of an interlocution. Ducrot goes beyond Austin and Searle by including implication as a speech act, instaured immediately by *taking the floor*. The *presupposé* and the *posé* recall the pre-existence of elements presented as obvious and so, are able to escape from the stakes of the conversation and argumentation.

The implication introduces a coup de force. There are many other coups de force in language games. The internal structure of the statement gives roles to the various parts of the discourse. The Ducrot's analysis of puisque (since) shows that several instances of enunciation can coexist: 'P parce que (because) Q' is assumed by the speaker but 'Q since P' is not. O. Ducrot has founded an 'integrated pragmatics' converging to a semantic 'working' inside the statement.

4   Foundations for a Legal Pragmatics

Ducrot's theory has been used to explain some modes of argumentation based on some connectors in the text (plays, political speech,...). The same analysis has been applied to legal discourses. The main aim is not only to confirm some results of the general theory of pragmatics but also to highlight its limits in validating some of its hypotheses.

Several types of morphems have been studied by a group of linguists and law researchers: d'ailleurs (besides), notamment (notably), and c'est-à-dire (in other words, or that is to say) These connectives are considered as triggering illocutionary acts in legal discourse. They can play a new role in hermeneutic method.

For each of them, we have established a scheme enabling to describe the functioning of argumentative moves.

Besides [12] can be considered as an unnecessary argument. In the formula:

> r: P *besides* Q

P, alone, could led to r, and Q is presented as unnecessary for the conclusion r.

Examine the following example:

'Considering it is not denied that the current expenses have been met by their mother (P) whom the custody of the children was *besides* entrusted to (Q)...'

r: the mother can deduce from her taxes the financial charges of her children (judgment).

But is the argument behind *besides* pragmatically useful in the discourse? To prove it, we will enumerate several functions following this contextual use:

besides enables to hierarchize the argument P and the argument Q.

besides enables to make the argument P unquestionable.

besides enables to give the same orientation to heterogeneous arguments (law versus fact for example).

besides leads the judge to address (tacitly) P and Q to different addressees.

The connector *besides* is the mark of the speaker who classifies his arguments.

Another connector is *notably* [13]. *Notably* is the opening marker of interpretative power. '*Are considered as 'oeuvres de l'esprit' (protected by "copyright") (A)... books, brochures and other literary artistic and scientific writings, sermons (B)...*' [French Intellectual property law (1957)]

If the article 2 of the law mentions as 'works of the mind' only works perceptible 'by sight' or 'by audition', the presence of 'notably' does not allow to rule out a priori those, which possibly could be perceived by the other senses' (r).

A *notably* B (B1, B2, B3...Bn) for r

notably B presupposes the existence of B1, B2, Bn belonging to the set A

Then *notably* allows for:

- the creation of the class B by affectation of emergent properties.
- the affectation of properties to B3.
- the inclusion of B3 in the class B.

Other connectors highlight the construction of the meaning that results from the utterance's sequences. A semantic analysis of judicial argumentation has been applied to 're-phrasing' phenomena in the decisions of Supreme Courts by means of *that is to say* (c'est-à-dire) [14]. By describing their various uses and their contextual setting, we show how the judge takes advantage of the pragmatics function of argumentative rephrasing to carry out a strategy of justification relying upon the dialectic move between the same (the alleged equivalence between two entities: A=B) and the different (the institutional leap towards the conclusion: B → r).

Let us take this example:

"*considering that if the national company AIR FRANCE is a joint stock company (A1) that is to say private company (A2) ...* "

r: the jurisdiction will be private law court

A2 = A1 (first move)

A2 → B (second move)

It would be impossible to leap from A1 to B

So, the connective that is to say allows for:

- an operation of inclusion or of belonging.
- a topicalisation by excluding an other possibility.

Which conclusions can we draw from these works on *illocutionary connectives*?

First, we can confirm that there exists an *oriented structure* of speech. Arguments cannot be moved inside a text without changing the general orientation of the discourse and the singular meaning of terms (ontology).

Second, the method puts the emphasis on the analysis of texts. It is no longer necessary to retrieve what the author intended to mean, or to draw one single meaning out of a text (the legal fiction of the "rationnal legislator"). The only possibility is to *justify metalinguistically* the meaning, which the receiver of a text is *able* to build.

Third, the speech figures (metaphors, comparisons for example) are considered as indirect speech acts. That is to say that the meaning overcomes the statement and rests on particular tacit conventions or on a contract with the addressee. Interpretation is thus not an uncontrolled process.

Fourth, legal discourse is a superb example of the theatricality of any text, especially the judicial text (Courts). A *double enunciation* can be noticed: the judge produces several perlocutory effects vis à vis several types of receivers in a network of addressees. The connective *besides* is the best example of this type of entangleness.

From a methodological point of view, the examination of these connectives in a discourse enables to segment the utterrances into arguments, to describe the relationships between these arguments and selected terms, to infer the resulting argumentative scope, and to discover rules of judicial statements.

But legal pragmatics needs more that an internal view on legal discourse. The inner strength of language is not sufficient to explain the meaning of a text:

- some explanations can be validated only if the conditions of production of the text are mentioned.
- the status of the speakers and receivers has always to be elucidated.
- conditions of felicity are also conditions of legality: they have to be assessed from that point of view.

It means that a declarative act, as well as any illocutionary act, must follow some rules of jurisdiction or of procedure to be registered as legal speech acts. Searle calls these rules 'constitutive rules', as opposed to 'normative rules'.

Bourdieu summarizes these limits in the following quotation: 'La question des énoncés performatifs s'éclaire si l'on y voit un cas particulier des effets de domination symbolique dont tout échange linguistique est le lieu... L'efficacité de ces actes d'institution est inséparable de l'existence d'une institution définissant les conditions qui doivent être remplies... Ces conditions de félicité doivent être des conditions sociales'.

This implies, as Austin had argued some decades ago, that a sociological approach is necessary to improve the theory of speech acts in the case of numerous legal interactions.

5 Towards the Modelization of Institutional Pragmatics

Two major events occurred in the field of legal pragmatics in the last decade: the arrival of activity support systems and the development of technological means of 'communication'. Building legal ontology becomes a part of this stake.

5.1 How to Perform Speech Acts in Activity Support Systems?

Process and activities in organizations are performed through the interaction of social agents, which are individual groups and organizations. In the legal domain, their actions are more formal, more structured and procedurally determined [15]. 'Legal engineers' and cognitive scientists are increasingly investigating such activities in order to create formal models to support managing, decision-making, and the performance of various legal activities. Set of rules have been translated into actions and procedures handled by computers. For example, situations of legal exchange and actions have to be designed and assessed in Electronic Data Interchange technology or more recently in *télé-procédures*. The judiciary network is intending to connect not only man to machine but a machines' network, which will simulate chains of procedures.

Unlike traditional approaches in which the organizational activity is considered as a place of information consumption, legal pragmaticians emphasize the content of activity, the agents who perform actions, and their effects on the institutional environment. Their objective is to represent the meanings of legal actions in legally created "reality". Representation of relevant knowledge modelling activity support systems requires a description of the way linguistic actions are communicated among agents including their performative content. An activity may be relevant with respect to the fulfillment of condition-action requirements, sequences, the agents involved, and their authorization for doing discretionary actions. However, the norms that govern the behaviour of organizational members are not always explicit. There are other ways of understanding orders and norms such as unwritten standards, and assumed rights and obligations. Debates about ontology emerge at this stage. The meaning and intention of a term have to be shared by all the agents that belong to the same institution, such as a court, a municipal body, and so on. Furthermore a growth in communication levels among individuals who perform an act also influences the creative effectiveness and the modelization in an *activity support system* [16].

The writing of institutional texts as an active and reactive process has to be assessed and, on the other hand, linguistic engineers are faced with the uncomputability of many processes. How can discourses of alterity be represented in a machine? How can we ensure that one formula introduces two or more meanings in a computer if we do not take into account the context? What about the translation of knowledge implied in the relationship of governance and domination? Bourdieu's concepts are questioned. How to constrain through language without linguistic markers?

5.2 How to Represent Institutional Discretion in a Decision-Making System?

To complete this panorama of research about institutional markers, I would like to present a work in progress on specific normative statements and terms in legal pragmatics: orders and rules. This research originates from two basic observations. First, deontic markers ('obligation,' 'permission' and 'right') are scarcely noticable in the legal natural language. Many institutional situations are interpreted in terms of obligations and permissions without making a reference to an illocutory modal mark. Second, it is impossible to interpret the meaning of an order or a rule without refering to the status and the jurisdiction of the speakers. The concept of *normative density* [17] can bring a new perspective on 'institutional constrains'.

Let us take several sequences:

Imagine that you have to give an order to a taxi driver driving guests to a conference from Arlanda Airport:

(1) Take them to the Stockholm University from the Airport at 1 pm.

It is possible to express this order from different viewpoints. The statement (1) means that it is an order but the taxi driver 'has the right' to choose the route.

Conversely, you (as a decision-maker) can give him the general rules:

(2) To reach the University take the first exit from the E4. Next go along Gotavagan and go to the Shell service station. Then, go through the forest and turn left towards the port. Finally turn right along the next avenue.

(3) If it is raining, go by the shortest route.

(4) If the weather is nice and you have time, you could go by the 'corniche'.

There are several kinds of rules and conditions in (2), (3), (4) which imply various types of terms. Every rule can be organized according to:

1) the strength of the implication (4)
2) the openness of the qualification in the conditions (4) What is "nice" weather?
3) the number of conditions (4)
4) the openness of the qualification in the conclusion (3). What is the shortest route?

5.3   The 'AI Turn' and Institutional Pragmatics

Since the late 1970s, the AI turn [18] governs important part of linguistics, philosophy of mind, psychology. This 'shift' concerns semiotics but also pragmatics: ' all semiotic activities consist of some modular cognitive process which can be described in terms of symbolic or informational structure- that is to say a kind of semiotic system made of rules and representation of its own'. IA as the new Pandora's box can pull out all sorts of rules and beliefs for discussion in our research on modelization of institutional pragmatics.

In order to develop this type of research, we need a cognitive analysis of the speakers' decision process. Let us consider the field of information retrieval system where traditional databases are indexed on the content of the database. The central problem is that the query must be interpreted by taking into consideration two ontological systems: the user's one and the information system's one. This type of system also has to use a model of the world that is simple enough to be intuitively conceivable by the user without reducing the possible complexity of the relations between the entities of the model: plain keyword list and a "boolean" syntax.

Numerous technological means exist in artificial intelligence (AI) for the use of legal knowledge in intelligent information systems. Expert systems provide for the possibility of effective explanation of reasoning, but they need a prior formalisation in the form of inference rules. Neural networks avoid the phase of formalisation, but they do require a learning phase and, moreover, they lack explanation abilities. Categorizations could be activated directly in line since they are neural structures and not a stored memory.

An intermediate solution, between AI systems and boolean retrieval systems, is the use of an architecture of interface based on legal expertise. The idea is very simple: the expertise is not in the modelling of the knowledge of the database, but in the use of an index representing the tasks of the domain and the institutional relationship between human and artificial actors.

But what are the tasks of the legal practitioner? To reason about acts and rules by means of an argumentation and a dialog. So the model of dialog is a representation of the structure of the argumentation. There are various cases of appeal in front of the administrative judge in French law called "appeal for abuse of power". The grounds of this appeal are, for instance, insufficient or contradictory motivations, default of legal grounds, and default of jurisdiction. Another trend could be: to recognize some pragmatic connectors in the legal text, such as but or besides or that is to say or can be considered, in which pragmatic theory identifies indicators of argumentative moves. The interpretation of an act cannot be validated by linguistic tests.

In an institutional context, we need to validate the social behaviour, the action and the decision of the decision maker as well as that of the addressee of such illocutary statement. For example, if we have to understand and model some sets of rules, we have to know about the discretionary power and the margin of appreciation given to the receiver (through the text and the context) in order to interpret the normative density of the speech and the relevant legal behaviour of this particular receiver. It has something to do with the concept of responsibility and accountability. If something fails, judge has to have a representation of the whole cognitive process followed by the decision maker and the common knowledge shared by the institution.

Moreover, the EDI and télé-procedures has to deal with the relationship of a group of speakers. The modelization of procedural acts can be very fruitful to imitate a community of machines. In this respect, we have to use psychology and formalism.

As we can see, the field of legal pragmatics can be considered as a two-way trip between the reality of legal life as a corpus of 'powering' text, and multiple potentialities of language as a means of action.

6 Conclusion: Descriptive Versus Pragmatic Ontology

We have seen legal pragmatics is concerned by the interactive function of argumentation and the emerging understanding often called 'situated cognition' (Clancey). What should be the relationship between pragmatics and ontology?

More and more, on the web, legal knowledge (official texts, other documents legally binding, non official texts) will be stored and indexed into explicit ontologies coming from various legal systems and sources. These legal ontologies describe the technical language employed by the legislators, administrative authorities, the Courts and the members of the legal professions. But discourse is not a structure of technical terms: it exhibits a number of special stylistic, idiomatic, cognitive and pragmatic features. The institutional context of the key words and all generative processes of tacit knowledge are lost although the meaning itself is at the core of the debate.

The recognition of figures (Perelman's research) in a text also ignores the cognitive and dialogic dimension of institutional discourse. To use some words such as 'reasonable and proper', 'fair use', "equity" means that a legal actor firstly delegates a part of his legal jurisdiction (or of his pragmatic competence) to an other legal actor, and secondly accepts this interpretation with regard to the (shared) institutional knowledge.

This paper argues that legal pragmaticians need to identify virtual markers of argumentative process (such as connectors but also standards or open structured concept) to describe the semantic network of institutional constraints performed through indirect speech acts. First, the controversial question of institution as a system of action, a 'space where are fixed models of behaviour' (Luhmann), could greatly benefit from this new approach. Second, the legal information retrieval could be enriched by the modelisation of text understanding in terms of generative processes.

References

1. Clancey, W.J.: Situated Cognition: On Human Knowledge and Computer Representations. Cambridge University Press, New York (1997)
2. Verheij, B.: Artificial argument assistants for defeasible argumentation. Artificial Intelligence 150 (2004) 291-324
3. Borges, F., Borges, R., Bourcier, D.: A connectionist model to justify the reasoning of the judge. In: JURIX 2003, IOS Press (2003)
4. Perelman, Ch. : Traité de l'Argumentation. PUF, Paris (1958)
5. Thiry, P. : Du fondement de l'argumentation. In : Thomasset, C, Bourcier, D. (eds.): Interpréter le droit: le sens, l'interprète, la machine, LGDJ, Paris (1997)
6. Aarnio, A. : Le rationnel comme raisonnable. La justification en droit. LGDJ, Paris (1992)
7. Austin, J.L. : Quand dire c'est faire. Translation and Presentation by G.Lane, Editions du Seuil, Paris (1979)
8. Bouveresse, J. : Propos introductifs. In: Amselek, P. (ed.): Théorie des actes de langage, éthique et droit, PUF, Paris (1986)
9. Searle, J.R. : Indirect speech acts. In: Cole, P., Morgan J.L. (eds.): Speech acts: syntax and semantics, New York, Morgan (1975)
10. Ducrot, O. et alii. : Les mots du discours. Minuit, Paris, (1980)
11. Anscombre, C. , Ducrot, O. : L'argumentation dans la langue. Mardaga, Bruxelles (1983)
12. Bourcier, D., Bruxelles, S. : D'ailleurs, un argument non necessaire ? Ses fonctions dans le discours du juge. In : Le droit en procès, CURAPP, PUF, Paris (1984) 125-145
13. Bourcier, D. , Bruxelles, S. : Discours juridique, interprétation et réprésentation des connaissances : les connecteurs d'inclusion, Semiotica 77 1-3 (1989) 253-269
14. Bourcier, Bruxelles, S. Une approche sémantique de l'argumentation juridique, Dire, c'est à dire 45, PUF, Paris (1995)
15. Dewitz, S.D., Lee, R.M. : Legal procedures as formal conversations. Contracting on a performative network. In: DeGross, J.I., Henderson, J.C., Kosynski, B.R. (eds.): Proceedings of the 10th International conference on Information Systems (1989)
16. Cekez-Kecmanovic, D.: Activity support systems, Proceedings IFORS, Bruges (1991) 24-29
17. Morand, A.: L'évaluation legislative ou l'irrésistible ascension d'un quatrième pouvoir. In : Contrôle parlementaire et évaluation, Actes du Colloque, 7 avril 1994, La Documentation Française, Paris (1995)
18. Ouellet, P. . Introduction : the AI turn and language sciences, Semiotica, 77-1/3 (1989) 1-3

Using NLP Techniques to Identify Legal Ontology Components: Concepts and Relations

Guiraude Lame

Centre de Recherche en Informatique, Ecole des mines de Paris, 35 rue Saint-Honoré,
77305 Fontainebleau, France
lame@cri.ensmp.fr
http://www.cri.ensmp.fr

Abstract. A method to identify ontology components is presented in this article. The method relies on Natural Language Processing (NLP) techniques to extract concepts and relations among these concepts. This method is applied in the
legal field to build an ontology dedicated to information retrieval. Legal texts
on which the method is performed are carefully chosen as describing and conceptualizing the legal domain. We suggest that this method can help legal ontology designers and may be used while building ontologies dedicated to other
tasks than information retrieval

1 Introduction

If the semantic Web is more than a vision but the future of the Web and if the semantic Web is to rely on ontologies, these ontologies cannot be entirely built by hand.
Many methods of ontology design have been suggested (see [10], [19], [7], [12],
[11]). Most of them include these different steps:

- a preliminary step to determine the reasons why an ontology is needed ;
- the precise definition of the domain of the ontology ;
- the specification of the task to which the ontology is dedicated ;
- the identification of the domain concepts and relations among them ;
- the collection of the concepts and relations in an ontology formalized in an appropriate language to become machine readable ;
- the integration of the ontology in a system.

We focus on the step consisting in identifying concepts and relations among them.
We claim that this step can be improved if ontology designers use Natural Language
Processing (NLP) techniques.

Ontologies are composed of concepts and relations among them, structuring an
overview of entities [16]. We assume that concepts are embodied in terms and that
semantic links among concepts are embedded in syntactical relations among these
terms.

Legal concepts are known as being open textured concepts meaning that their definition may vary depending on many factors (context, source etc). Many ontologies of
law may be defined, their components depending mainly upon the task for which
these ontologies are built for [2].

V.R. Benjamins et al. (Eds.): Law and the Semantic Web, LNCS 3369, pp. 169–184, 2005.

In this article, we present a general method for identifying legal concepts and semantic relations among them using NLP techniques. All these elements are the structuring blocks of an ontology. This method is inspired by the one defined in [1]. A similar approach is taken in [8]. In our context, the ontology is an ontology of French law and is dedicated to information retrieval. Our method relies on the principle that legal concepts are often[1] defined and conceptualized by the legislator himself. We propose to use the legal norms that are the Codes in French law to infer legal concepts and semantic relations among them. We claim that such an ontology is useful in information retrieval contexts such as interactive query expansion systems or didactical access to legal texts bases.

2 The Codes: A Previously Existing Conceptualization of the Law

We assume that the legislator, while making the law, conceptualizes the legal field. The legislator himself performs another conceptualization task when he decides to rationalize the legal field by compiling norms into Codes.

In French law, two different types of Codes may be distinguished. The first ones are those initially created. These Codes are known as the Codes Napoléon: the Civil Code or the Penal Code for example. The second ones are those created more recently, resulting on thematic compilations of previously existing norms. In French law, this process is called codification [5]; many codes have been created since the beginning of the 1990's. Independently of their types, all Codes can be viewed as conceptualizations of legal fields. First of all, their structure is logically defined: one division for one theme, from the more generic to the more specific (See Table 1). Second, the concepts are one by one defined. These definitions may be more or less explicit. For example, the definition of a *record of birth for persons born abroad* (C. civ., art. 98) is explicit. We know under which conditions a birth record may be established; we also know what the elements composing such a birth record are: "*A record taking the place of a record of birth shall be drawn up for any person born abroad who acquires or recovers the French nationality unless the record drawn up at his birth was already entered on a register kept by a French authority. That record shall state the name, first names and sex of the party concerned and indicate the place and date of his birth, his parentage, his residence at the date of his acquiring French nationality*".[2] The definition of the concept of *divorce* is less explicit (C. civ., art. 227), referring to breach of marriage: "*A marriage is dissolved 1° by the death of one of the spouses; 2° by lawfully pronounced divorce*".[3]

If the task to which the ontology is dedicated relies on inferences, i.e. on reasoning, one would need to define a *record birth for persons born abroad* with its components,

---

[1] In the case of a legal system based on texts.

[2] « Un acte tenant lieu d'acte de naissance est dressé pour toute personne née à l'étranger qui acquiert ou recouvre la nationalité française à moins que l'acte dressé à sa naissance n'ait déjà été porté sur un registre conservé par une autorité française. Cet acte énonce les nom, prénoms et sexe de l'intéressé et indique le lieu et la date de sa naissance, sa filiation, sa résidence à la date de l'acquisition de la nationalité française » (C. civ, art. 98).

[3] « Le mariage se dissout : 1° par la mort de l'un des époux ; 2° par le divorce légalement prononcé » (C. civ., art. 227).

and the conditions of its drawing. Then, the concept of *abroad* must be defined, relying on a precise definition of the countries [2]. The concept of *time* may also have to be defined, to establish the value of the concept of *residence at the date of his acquiring French nationality*. In our context of information retrieval, we claim that the only elements we need are the concepts of *birth record for people born abroad* linked to all its components (*name, first names, sex, place of the birth, date of the birth, parentage, residence*) related to the more general concept of *birth record*. With the same logic, we claim that in our ontology, we only need to define *divorce* as *breach of marriage*.

Table 1. Some Sections and Subsections of the Civil Code

Civil Code
BOOK I OF PERSONS
TITLE ONE OF CIVIL RIGHTS
TITLE ONE bis OF FRENCH NATIONALITY
Chapter I - General Provisions
Chapter II - Of French Nationality by Birth
Section I - Of French Persons by Parentage
Section II - Of French Persons by Birth in France
Section III - Common Provisions
Chapter III - Of the Acquisition of French Nationality
Section I - Of the Modes of Acquiring French Nationality
…
TITLE TWO OF RECORDS OF CIVIL STATUS
Chapter I - General Provisions
Chapter II - Of Records of Birth
Section I - Of Declarations of Birth
Section II - Of Changes of First Names and Name
Section III - Of Record of Acknowledgement of an Illegitimate Child
Chapter III - Of Records of Marriage
BOOK II OF PROPERTY AND OF THE VARIOUS MODIFICATIONS OF OWNERSHIP
TITLE ONE OF THE VARIOUS KINDS OF PROPERTY
Chapter I - Of Immovable
Chapter II - Of Movables
Chapter III - Of Property in its Relations with Those Who own it
TITLE TWO OF OWNERSHIP
Chapter I - Of the Right of Accession to what is Produced by a Thing
Chapter II - Of the Right of Accession to What Unites or Incorporates Itself with a Thing
TITLE THREE OF USUFRUCT, OF USE AND OF HABITATION
Chapter I - Of Usufruct
…
BOOK III OF THE VARIOUS WAYS OWNERSHIP IS ACQUIRED
…

3 Legal Terms and Legal Concepts

3.1 Definitions

Concepts are labeled with terms. For example, *breach of contract* or *liability* are terms that label legal concepts.

Law, tending to regulate human activities, conceptualizes the world. As a consequence, the legal domain deals with various domains such as medicine or science. Consequently, many terms, general or specific to given domains, may be assimilated to legal terms since they label objects or artifacts apprehended by law. We assume that as law regulates things, conceptualizing them, these things turn out to become legal things and legal concepts.

We define legal terms as terms labeling specific legal concepts such as *contract* or *liability* but also labeling general or specific concepts such as *passenger, doctor,* or *weapon*: all world objects or artifacts apprehended by law. Legal terms are defined as terms labeling world objects apprehended by law and artifacts created by law.

3.2 Seeking Legal Terms

To identify legal terms labeling concepts, the future components of our ontology, we have performed Natural Language Processing (hereafter NLP) techniques on the French Codes. The experiment took place on the 57 Codes available on the governmental web site for French law: Légifrance[4]. All these Codes compose our corpus of experiments. We have used a syntactical analyzer of texts called Syntex [3]. This tool performs syntactical analysis on texts, identifying nouns, verbs, adjectives and adverbs and syntactical dependencies among them (subject of verb, object of verb etc...). On these bases, applying a set of syntactical rules, the tool is able to identify complex terms such as noun phrases, verb phrases, adjective phrases etc...

Table 2. Terms extracted from the Codes

Terms
budgetary
eventually
Hauts-de-Seine
decision
elaborated
designed for disabled persons
breach of contract
notified of the decision
to acquire French nationality
to state

[4] http://www.legifrance.gouv.fr

Used on our corpus of experiment, the tool has extracted more than 500 000 terms. This list gathers terms from all syntactical categories: verbs, adverbs, nouns, noun phrases etc. Table 2 gives an example of these outputs, translated in English.

Our experiment then consisted on trying to identify among this list of more than 500 000 terms those that could be qualified as legal terms (complying with the definition given above) and those that could not.

3.2.1 Statistical Indices to Seek Legal Terms

The first step of the method removes some classes of terms from the initial list. First of all, we have decided to only consider terms belonging to just one syntactical category: the nouns and noun phrases. This choice relies on the idea that most concepts are embedded in nouns. Legal concepts that are labeled as adjectives or adverbs are then not included in our ontology.

Secondly, terms with non-alphabetical characters are removed from the initial list. Most of such terms in our list are internal or external references to texts such as *article 1382*, or values of various rates. As our ontology is dedicated to information retrieval and not to reasoning, we assume that the useful term in our ontology is, for example, the term *taxation rate* and not *taxation rate of 19.6%*.

Applying these two principles on the initial list, we obtain a list of about 300 000 terms.

The second step of our method to identify legal terms uses statistical methods classically used to weigh index terms. The idea was to weigh the terms of our list and, on the basis of these weights, determine which are legal and which are not. Various statistical indices have been used to weigh our 300 000 terms.

1. Term frequency (tf):

Term frequency (tf) corresponds to the number of times a given term occurs in all the Codes. Term frequency characteristics in our corpus of experiments are as listed in Table 3.

Table 3. Term frequency characteristics

Term frequency	
Minimum	1
1st quartile	1
Median	1
Mean	16.6
3rd quartile	2
maximum	106 386

Among 300 000, 188 158 terms (63%) appear only once. Manually analyzing some of these terms, we have concluded that they could not all be assumed as non-legal terms. Figure 3 lists important legal terms that have a frequency rate of 1.

The term presenting the maximum frequency rate is *article*. This result is not a surprise, knowing that our corpus is composed of Codes, each code being divided in various numbers of articles ; every article starts with its own reference, for example *article 1382*.

Table 4. Important legal terms that have a frequency rate of 1

Terms
chargeable activities
agricultural activities
drug forwarding
potential vendee
risk completion

That way, high frequency rates (more than 50 000) can be used to identify empty terms that can not be assumed as legal terms such as *chapter*, *code*, or *provision*. Unfortunately, manual analysis allowed us to state that terms presenting high frequency rates include legal terms such as *decree* or *law*.

This manual analysis led us to the conclusion that fixing thresholds under or above which terms may be valuably assumed as legal terms is not possible. Such a result would require complex heuristics that probably could not be applied in other contexts and experiments.

We have concluded that the frequency rate is useless in trying to distinguish legal terms from non-legal ones.

2. Inverse document frequency (idf):
Idf ([17], [15]) establishes term distribution among a corpus, relying on the principle that term importance is inversely proportional to the number of documents from the corpus in which the given term occurs (See Equation 1). Documents are defined as articles of Codes. Our corpus gathers a total of 59 275 documents. Inverse document frequencies for terms in our corpus are as listed in Table 5.

$$idf_i = \log \frac{N}{n_i} \tag{1}$$

Where N = total number of documents in the corpus,
And n_i = number of documents of the corpus in which term i occurs

Table 5. Inverse document frequency characteristics

idf	
Minimum	0.6932
1st quartile	4.2767
Median	4.7049
Mean	5.0690
3rd quartile	5.0690
maximum	7.8136

Firm is the term presenting the lowest idf, *application to the Préfecture* is the one presenting the highest idf. Traditionally, terms presenting a low rate of idf are not considered interesting because occurring in most of the documents of the corpus. Inversely, terms presenting a high level of idf are supposed to be interesting.

We have manually analyzed terms and their idf weights. It appears that legal terms may have high (superior to 7.7) as well as low idf weights (inferior to 2.5). Table 6 lists some terms with high and low idf rates that are legal terms.

Table 6. Legal terms with high and low idf rates

Idf < 2.5	Idf > 7.7
moral aid	*application to the Préfecture*
judicial guarantee	*notification through bill sticking*
educational obligation	*bond subscription*
Minister	*period for candidature registration*
Firm	*quantity of voting paper*

As for frequency rates, fixing thresholds on idf weights would require long and complex heuristics that probably could not be applied in others contexts. We then conclude that idf cannot be used to distinguish legal terms from non-legal terms.

3. Tf.idf

Combining tf with idf, the idea is to distinguish terms that, although appearing in a few numbers of documents of the corpus, present at the same time a high frequency rate in the corpus [17].

The same conclusion is drawn with tf.idf ; manual analysis allowed us to conclude that legal terms may present various rates of tf.idf, high or low. Fixing thresholds of tf.idf under or above which terms could be assumed legal terms would require long and complex heuristics.

4. Entropy

Entropy is used to measure disorder. We have computed the entropy of the distribution of terms in the corpus. A term largely distributed in a corpus, say occurring in a large number of documents of the corpus, will present a high level of entropy, meaning that this term adds little information to the general distribution of terms in the documents of the corpus. Distribution *r* of term *i* on document *x* is as described in Equation (2). Entropy is as described in Equation (3). Entropy rates for terms in our corpus are as listed in Table 7.

$$r(i)_x = \frac{tf_i(x)}{TF_i} \tag{2}$$

Where $tf_i(x)$ is the frequency of term i in document x,
And TF_i is the total frequency of term i in the corpus

$$S = -\sum_{i,x} r(i)_x \log r(i)_x \tag{3}$$

Table 7. Entropy chracteristics

Entropy	
Minimum	0.0000
1st quartile	0.0000
Median	0.0000
Mean	0.6103
3rd quartile	0.3466
maximum	60.2408

Part is the term presenting the highest rate of entropy. As for all indices, a manual analysis of entropy weights of terms did not allow us to identify thresholds on which relying to distinguish legal terms from non-legal terms.

3.2.2 Irrelevance of Statistical Indices in Seeking Legal Terms

The experiments described above suggest that statistical indices, classically used to identify index terms cannot be used to distinguish legal terms from non-legal terms and, more generally, domain terms from non-domain terms. This conclusion is indeed confirmed by a second experiment here detailed.

In the first step of this second experiment, we identified, among our list of 300 000 terms, a sub-list of terms that are surely legal terms. To obtain a sub-list of terms known to be legal terms, we have used French legal dictionaries available on the Internet. Browsing these dictionaries, we collected 1 490 terms defined in these dictionaries. Using a pattern matching procedure, we extracted from the initial list of 300 000 terms a sub-list of 111 202 (hereafter "legal terms") assumed to be legal terms as they exactly match or include a term known as being a legal term. The rest of the list (185 478) is called "other terms".

In the second step of the experiment, "legal terms" have been compared with the "other terms" on the basis of statistical indices above presented. For each of these indices (tf, idf, tf.idf, entropy), "legal terms" and "other terms" appear to exhibit exactly the same behavior in our corpus. The linear correlation coefficient between "legal terms" and "other terms" is 0.9998 for frequency, 0.9979 for idf, 0.9997 for tf.idf and 0.9999 for entropy.

As an example, Figure 1 shows the number of "legal terms" (in red, or grey) and "other terms" (in black), depending on tf.idf values. To build this graph, we considered terms presenting a tf.idf between 2 and 60, which represent more 97% of our 300 000 terms. Numbers of terms have been computed for each value of tf.idf from 2 to 60 with a step of 2.

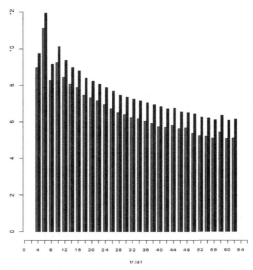

Fig. 1. Number of legal terms and non legal terms depending on tf.idf values

The general conclusion drawn from these two experiments is that statistical indices usually used to identify index terms are useless in domain term identification. This general conclusion can be derived into several statements:

1. Statistical indices such as those used in our experiments can at least be useful in identifying what we call "empty terms". As described in our experiment, high level of tf, tf.idf or entropy allowed us to detect terms inherent to our corpus such as *article*, *chapter* or *title*. We have chosen to use frequency to elaborate a list of 22 empty terms that we manually validated (see Table 8). All the terms of the initial list of 300 000 exactly matching or including one of these 22 empty terms have been removed; we then obtain a list of 118 000 terms.

Table 8. Empty terms

"Empty" term	Frequency
Title	111
chapter	107
Book	91
general provisions	87
common provisions	80

2. Domain terms such as legal terms cannot be assimilated to index terms. Index terms are usually considered as descriptors for document contents. Statistical indices used to detect them tend to single out terms that are discriminating within a given corpus of documents. Domain terms are different from discriminating terms;

a given domain term may occur in most of the documents of the corpus. For example, *contract* in the French Codes is a domain term but cannot be a good index term as it occurs in most of the documents of the corpus.

3. In such a method to identify domain terms, the choice of an appropriate corpus is fundamental. The main result of our experiment is that legal terms and other terms have the same behavior in our corpus. Another statement may be inferred from this: assuming that "other terms" are in fact "legal terms". This statement could be enforced by the fact that we have worked on a carefully chosen corpus: the Codes. This corpus has the particularity to be specific to the legal domain and to have been rationally elaborated (no repetition for example).

4. We have finally decided, on the basis of these statements, to consider our list of 118 000 terms as legal terms. Figure 9 lists a few examples of these 118 000 terms. Meanwhile, a sub-list of this 118 000 terms list has been elaborated and used in the process of detecting relations among terms (see Section 4 below). This list is called "fundamental legal terms". This list has been elaborated using discourse structures [15]. The principle of using discourse structure is to exhibit terms used by the author in specific parts of the text: titles, summary etc… Terms from our list of 118 000 occurring in the titles of Codes structures are considered as "fundamental legal terms". Our list of fundamental legal terms gathers a total of 16 681 terms.

Table 9. Examples of legal terms

Terms
chargeable activities
agricultural activities
updating scientific data
drug forwarding
potential vendee
risk completion

Legal terms have been identified, being assumed that they label legal concepts. These concepts will be one of the components of our ontology.

In the second step of our method, we identify the relations that exist among these legal terms that label legal concepts.

4 Relations Among Terms and Concepts

Semantic relations exist among concepts such as the one linking *divorce* with *marriage* or *damages* with *obligation*. These semantic relations are expressed in texts through syntactic forms such as "*a marriage is dissolved by lawfully pronounced divorce*" or "*the damages result from the non-performance of an obligation*". We then look for syntactic relations among terms to identify semantic relations.

4.1 Texts Analysis Methods

The text analysis we perform on Codes blends syntactical analysis with statistical analysis. We use different methods: syntactical analysis combined with statistical methods, simple syntactical analysis, and purely statistical analysis.

4.1.1 Syntactical Analysis

We used a tool called Syntex [2] to identify terms in our documents (see Section 3.2).

Based on syntactical analysis, Syntex also establishes syntactical dependencies among terms, determining for example that a given noun phrase is subject or object of a given verb. For example, in Article 98 of the Civil Code given above (see Section 2), the tool outputs that *French nationality* is object of *acquire* and *recover*. Contexts are then defined, merging terms with syntactical roles. In our example, the contexts of *French nationality* are [to acquire, OBJECT] and [to recover, OBJECT]. With these results, comparisons of terms with the syntactic contexts they share can be performed, allowing validating semantic relations among terms. For example, *child* and *minor* share contexts such as [guardianship, OBJECT] or [to endanger, SUBJECT].

4.1.2 Analysis of the Coordination Relations

In this methods, documents are parsed and terms that are separated with the conjunctive phrase *and* or *or* [13] are identified. This method relies on the previously established list of legal terms ("fundamental legal terms"). Given this list, a program parses the documents, identifying these terms and checking whether two of them are separated by *and* or *or*. To narrow the results of such a method, it has been applied on the titles of sections and subsections of all the Codes, not on all the texts of the Codes. In the example given above (see Section 2) of the sections and subsections of the Civil Code, such a program outputs that *first names* and *name* may be related, as are *property* and *various modifications of ownership* and *use* and *habitation*. These outputs have to be manually checked to validate which relations are semantically relevant, and which are not.

4.1.3 Statistical Analysis

A statistical method has been performed on the Codes using the previously defined list of legal terms to identify relations among them. The method relies on the idea that two semantically related terms often occur in similar contexts. In this method, contexts are words surrounding a given term, independently of their syntactic roles. Context words may be defined as a given number of words occurring before and after a given term. In our case, context words are defined as all words surrounding a given term occurrence in an article of a Code. In the example presented above (see Section 2), if *French nationality* is the given term, its context words will be *record*, *place*, *birth* etc. Previously defined terms are called target words [9] and the words surrounding these terms are called context words. Each context word is weighted with a mutual information measure which quantifies the dependency existing in texts among the context word and a given target word [9] (see Equation 4).

$$MI_{(cw)} = \log\left(\frac{f_{cw}}{f_c f_w} + 1\right) \qquad (4)$$

Where MI = mutual information,
c = context words,
w = target words,
f_{cw} = joint frequency for c and w,
f_c, f_w = individual frequencies of c and w.

A vector linking each context word to its weight is associated to each target word. These vectors are compared two by two with the cosine measure [9] (see Equation 5).

$$Sim_{a,b} = \frac{\sum_{ab} p_a p_b}{\sqrt{\sum_a p_a^2 \sum_b p_b^2}} \qquad (5)$$

Where $Sim_{a,b}$ = cosine similarity measure for terms a and b,
p_a = weight of context words for term a,
p_b = weight of context words for term b,
ab = number of context words shared by term a and term b.

Consequently, each tuple of target words is associated to a similarity score. A threshold has to be defined, above which tuples are considered valid. A manual validation may also be performed on these results.

4.1.4 Pattern Matching
This method relies on a previously defined list of terms. It consists in linking terms with the ones that include them. As an example, with this method, *contract* will be related *to breach of contract, contract of deposit* etc. A program parses the list of legal terms and identifies, with a pattern matching function, those that need to be linked together. This method is coarse but, applied to a list of well-identified legal terms, can give good results, especially in our context of an ontology dedicated to information retrieval.

4.2 Results

All the methods presented above have been applied on the 57 Codes available on the governmental site publishing French law on the Internet[5]: the Penal Code, the Civil Code, the Intellectual Property Code etc… Each Code being divided in articles, the 57 Codes represent more than 59 000 articles, gathering a total of more than 6 millions words. Fundamental legal terms, such as defined above (Section 3.2.2), have been used as a previously established list of terms.

On the basis of the list of legal terms, applying the methods above presented, we have identified relations among terms. Most of the methods used to identify relations among terms need manual validation or experimental threshold determination.

The analysis of the coordination relations needs human validation of the outputs of the program parsing the Codes. Applied on the titles of sections and subsections of the Codes, we obtain a list of more than 5 000 sequences of text. Validating these results took us 15 hours to identify 2 580 relevant relations established among 3 762 different terms.

---

[5] http://www.legifrance.gouv.fr

The statistical analysis based on the outputs of Syntex requires thresholds determination. As stated above, terms are compared on the basis of the syntactic contexts they share. Comparison is quantified with various indices[6]: number of shared contexts, terms and contexts' productivity (number of contexts and terms they respectively occur with) etc. Each of these indices needs a threshold above which it is assumed that results are good. Determining these thresholds requires empirical approximations and tests, comparing the relevance of results for each value of the indices. These experiments have been done, fully described in [4] and in [14].

The statistical analysis that compares terms on the basis of the words they co-occur with also needs a threshold. Contexts are compared with the cosine similarity measure. We have fixed a threshold of 0.8, meaning that two terms are supposed to be related when they share more than 80% of their contexts.

Gathering all the results of these methods, we obtain a list of 103 994 terms, each being related at least once to another term. Among them, 17 688 are related to more than one term. Typical results of all these methods are as described in Table 10.

Table 10. Related terms

Term 1	Term 2	Method
teaching	*Research*	Coordination relation
offence	*Crime*	Syntactical analysis
offence	*Infringement*	Syntactical analysis
minor	*Child*	Syntactical analysis
usufructuary	*exercise of undivided rights*	Statistical analysis
birth	*record of birth*	Pattern matching
contract	*breach of contract*	Pattern matching

5   Toward a Legal Ontology

Legal terms, assumed to label legal concepts, and relations, assumed to match semantic relations among these terms, have been identified. Terms and relations among them put together constitute a graph that we call "ontological resource". This graph can be seen as a description of the legal domain, but an ontology is more than that. An ontology is constituted of concepts and semantic relations among them. In an ontology, concepts are defined by the semantics of the relations established between each concept and others.

The next step of our method is then to infer semantic relations from relations more or less automatically identified. To reach that goal, we have first identified a list of semantic relations labeling ontological relations.

First of all, there is the relation of subsumption is_a. We distinguish two relations of subsumption, a legal one and a general one. The legal one is established between a concept and a legal qualification of its concept, and the general one is established

---

[6] All these indices are described in [4] and in [14].

between a concept and a general sort of this concept. For example, *universal legacies*, *legacies by universal title* or *specific legacies* are legal sorts of *legacies* defined in French law while *legacy of movables* is a general sort of *legacy*. This means that a given *legacy of movables* may be a *universal legacy*, a *legacy by universal title*, or a *specific legacy*. Depending on this legal qualification, different sets of legal rules may be applied to the given *legacy of movable*. We believe that this distinction made between two kinds of relations of subsumption is specific to the legal domain. The main reason being that the legal is_a relation infers legal qualification and, thus, application of specific sets of legal rules. The second type of relations is the one linking a concept and its components. As an example, the relation between *price of a sale* and *sale*. The third type of relations is the one linking a concept to a related one. For example, the relation existing between *legacy* and *gift*. The last type of relation is the one allowing identifying another sense of the one assumed for the initial concept. For example, if the concept *exchange* is defined as follows: *international exchange* is a legal *exchange*, *multilateral exchange* is a legal *exchange* and *parties of the exchange* is a component of *exchange*; it is clear that *exchange of glances* doesn't have the same meaning. *Exchange of glances* will then be related to exchange with the relation "is another sense of".

All these relations are listed in Table 11.

Table 11. Relations

Relations
Is_a_legal_sort_of
Is_a_general_sort_of
Is_a_component_of
Is_related_to
Is_another_sense_of

We assume that attributing semantic relations to legal terms labeling legal concepts amounts to conceptualization operation, in the sense that these concepts are then defined. This enables us to infer an ontology from our "ontological resource", derived from texts analysis.

Our ontology is integrated in a legal information system that offers interactive request expansion and didactical access to legal documents. This system is available on the Internet: http://ontologie.w3sites.net.

6   Conclusion

In this article, we present a general method relying on text-based NLP techniques to identify components (concepts and relations among them) of an ontology dedicated to information retrieval (IR). Text analysis is performed on particular legal documents: the Codes. These documents have been chosen for their characteristics: the Codes are logically structured and each legal concept is defined. We assume that a conceptualization of the legal field is expressed in these Codes.

This method mainly relies on automatic techniques and tools such as syntactical analyzers of texts or statistics. These automatic techniques do not substitute ontology designers but assist them in the process of ontology design consisting in identifying concepts and relations. NLP techniques are of course relevant for building ontologies dedicated to IR. Meanwhile, we claim that part of these methods may be used while building ontologies dedicated to other tasks such as educational systems [6], decision making systems, or ontologies providing interoperability between systems [18].

References

1. N. Aussenac-Gilles, B. Biébow and S. Szulman. Revisiting ontology design : A method based on corpus analysis. In: Proceedings of Knowledge Engineering and   Knowledge Management. Methods, Models and Tools, Juan-les-Pins, France (2000) 172-188
2. T. Bench-Capon. Task Neutral Ontologies, Common Sense Ontologies and Legal Information Systems. In: Second International Workshop on Legal Ontologies, JURIX 2001, Amsterdam, Neederlands (2001)
3. D. Bourigault. Analyse distributionnelle étendue. In: Proceedings of Traitement Automatique des Langues, Nancy, France (2002)
4. D. Bourigault and G. Lame. Analyse distributionnelle et structuration de terminologie, application à la construction d'une ontologie documentaire du droit. Traitement automatique des langues, vol.43, n°1, Ed. Hermès, Paris, France (2002) 129-150
5. G. Braibant. La problématique de la codification. Savoir Innover en Droit. Concepts, Outils, Systèmes. Ed. La documentation française (1999) 55-65
6. J. Breukers and A. Muntjewerff. Ontological modelling for designing educational systems. In: Proceedings of Workshop on Ontologies for Intelligent Educational Systems, Le Mans, France (1999)
7. M. Fernandez, A. Gomez-Perez and N. Juristo. Methontology: From ontological art towards ontological engineering. In: Proceedings of AAAI Spring Symposium Series on Ontological Engineering, Stanford, USA (1997) 33-40
8. A. Gangemi, D. Pisanelli and G. Steve. An Overview of the ONIONS Project : Applying Ontologies to the Integration of Medical Terminologies. Data and Knowledge Engineering, vol. 31 (1999) 183-220
9. S. Gauch, J. Wank, S. Rachakonda. A Corpus Analysis Approach for Automatic Query Expansion and Its Extension to Multiple Databases. ACM Transactions on Information Systems, vol. 17, n°3 (1999) 250-269
10. M. Gruningen and M. Fox. Methodology for the design and evaluation of ontologies. In: Proceedings of IJCAI Workshop on Basic Ontological Issues in Knowledge Sharing, Montreal, Canada (1995)
11. C. Holsapple and K. Joshi. A collaborative Approach to Ontology design. Communications of the ACM, vol. 45, n°2 (2002) 42-47
12. D. Jones, T. Bench-Capon and P. Visser. Methodologies for ontology developement. In: Proceedings of IT-KNOWS Conference, XV IFIP World Computer Congress, Budapest, Hungaria (1998)
13. G. Lame. Constructing an IR-oriented legal ontology. In: Second International Workshop on Legal Ontologies, JURIX 2001, Amsterdam, Neederlands (2001)
14. G. Lame. Construction d'ontologie à partir de textes. Une ontologie de droit dédiée à la recherche d'information sur le Web. PhD dissertation, Ecole des mines de Paris, Paris, France, http://www.cri.ensmp.fr/ (2002)

15. M.-F. Moens, Automatic indexing and abstracting of document texts, Kluwer (2000)
16. L. Mommers. A Knowledge-based ontology of the legal domain. In: Second International Workshop on Legal Ontologies, JURIX 2001, Amsterdam, Neederlands (2001)
17. K. Spark-Jones, Index term weighting. Information storage and retrieval (1973) 619-633
18. H. Stuckenschmidt, E. Stubkjaer and C. Schleider. Modeling Land Transactions : Legal Ontologies in Context. In: Second International Workshop on Legal Ontologies, JURIX 2001, Amsterdam, Neederlands (2001)
19. M. Uschold. Building Ontologies: Towards a unified methodology. In: Proceedings of Expert System, Conference of the British Computer Society Specialist Group on Expert Systems, Cambridge, England (1996)

A Methodology to Create Legal Ontologies in a Logic Programming Information Retrieval System

José Saias and Paulo Quaresma

Departamento de Informática,
Universidade de Évora,
7000 Évora, Portugal
{jsaias, pq}@di.uevora.pt

Abstract. Legal web information retrieval systems need the capability to reason with the knowledge modeled by legal ontologies. Using this knowledge it is possible to represent and to make inferences about the semantic content of legal documents.

In this paper a methodology for applying NLP techniques to automatically create a legal ontology is proposed. The ontology is defined in the OWL semantic web language and it is used in a logic programming framework, EVOLP+ISCO, to allow users to query the semantic content of the documents. ISCO allows an easy and efficient integration of declarative, object-oriented and constraint-based programming techniques with the capability to create connections with external databases. EVOLP is a dynamic logic programming framework allowing the definition of rules for actions and events.

An application of the proposed methodology to the legal information retrieval system of the Portuguese Attorney General's Office is described.

1 Introduction

Modern legal information retrieval systems need the capability to represent and to reason with the knowledge modeled by legal ontologies. In fact, the creation of ontologies allow the definition of class hierarchies, object properties, and relation rules, such as, transitivity or functionality. Using this knowledge it is possible to represent semantic objects, to associate them with legal documents, and to make inferences about them.

OWL (Ontology Web Language) is a language proposed by the W3C consortium (http://www.w3.org) to be used in the "semantic-web" environment for the representation of ontologies. This language is based on the previous DAML+OIL (Darpa Agent Markup Language - [1]) language and it is defined using RDF (Resource Description Framework - [2]).

In this paper a methodology to automatically create an OWL ontology from a set of legal documents is proposed. The methodology is based on the following steps:

V.R. Benjamins et al. (Eds.): Law and the Semantic Web, LNCS 3369, pp. 185–200, 2005.

- Definition of an initial top-level ontology;
- Identification of concepts referred in the legal documents and extraction of its properties;
- Identification of relations between the identified concepts;
- Creation of an ontology using the identified concepts and relations;
- Merge of the created ontology with the initial ontology;

In the first step, an already existent top-level legal ontology was chosen. At present we are using the legal ontology from the Portuguese Attorney General's Office, consisting of around 6,000 classes and having around 10,000 relations [3]. However, other top-level ontologies could be used, such as, the DOLCE proposal [4] or the FOLaw and LRI-core proposal [5] used in the context of the IST programs E-POWER and E-COURT [6]. In the future, we expect to use the results of the e-Content project LOIS – Lexical Ontologies for legal Information Sharing, which aims to create an european-wide top-level legal ontology.

In the second step, identification of concepts and its properties, several natural language processing techniques are used, namely, a syntactical parser, and a semantic analyzer able to obtain a partial interpretation of the documents. As it will be described in detail, the semantic representation allows the identification of the set of concepts that are referred in the documents and the extraction of some of their properties.

In the third step, identification of relations between concepts, an unsupervised method for acquiring word classes and relations is used [7, 8]. This method, which has some similarities with the work of [9], allows the identification of related and more specific concepts (subclasses). Starting from parsed documents, a subcategorisation analysis is performed and, for each word, subcategorisation patterns are extracted. Finally, a statistical analysis is performed identifying clusters of words with similar subcategorisation patterns.

In the fourth step, the results of the previous two steps are integrated in an ontology: concepts with their properties are new classes; class hierarchies and relations are created accordingly with the statistical analysis of subcategorization patterns (several examples will be shown in the following sections).

Finally, in the fifth step, the initial top-level ontology is merged with the new one. The proposed strategy is to search for common concepts in the two ontologies and to merge the ontologies via these concepts. New classes are inserted into the top-level ontology using the information from the semantic analyser (animal, human, action, . . .).

At this stage it is important to point out that the proposed methodology is based on a bottom-up approach for the definition of the legal low-level concepts: it allows the identification of the concepts and some of the relations, but additional work will be necessary to fully integrate these concepts with the upper legal ontology. We do not intend to propose any kind of standard for legal ontologies; our aim is to define a methodology to automatically create a base ontology from a specific set of legal documents.

As referred, this work has some relations with the proposal of Lame aiming to identify components of legal ontologies from the analysis of legal texts [9].

However, we believe our proposal has a more ambitious goal: the identified components are used to create an ontology and the initial documents are enriched with instances of this ontology. This process allows the definition of semantic web agents able to query the semantic content of these documents.

As stated before, after the creation of legal ontologies expressed in OWL, documents are enriched with instances of legal classes.

Then, a logic programming based framework is used to support inferences over the ontology. The logic programming framework is based on ISCO [10] and EVOLP [11].ISCO is a new declarative language implemented over GNU Prolog with object-oriented predicates, constraints and allowing simple connections with external databases. EVOLP is a dynamic logic programming language that is able to describe actions and events, allowing the system to make inferences about events, user intentions and beliefs and to be able to have cooperative interactions.

This logic programming framework seems to be quite adequated to represent and to make inferences over OWL ontologies. In fact, recent advances in the semantic web technology support this claim: some partners in the RuleML workgroup (http://www.ruleml.org) are adopting logic programming as its inference engine and there already exists a translator from RDFS to Prolog [12]. Moreover, in the scope of this work, a translator of a subset of OWL to Prolog was also built (correct accordingly with the OWL formal semantic description).

However, other inference engines could be chosen and used to answer queries about the legal knowledge conveyed by the documents. One possible option might be to use the results of the Mandarax project (http://mandarax.sourceforge.net), which already supports RuleML.

Section 2 describes the proposed architecture. Section 3 describes the methodology for the creation of the ontology, namely, the natural language processing techniques used to process the documents. Section 4 describes the NLP techniques used to create the OWL instances associated with each document. Section 5 describes ISCO, the basic logic programming framework. Section 6 describes EVOLP, the dynamic logic programming framework defined over ISCO and Prolog. Section 7 describes the interaction manager and section 8 provides a simple example. Finally, in section 9 some conclusions and future work are pointed out.

2   Architecture

The system's architecture is based on several independent and modular processes. Figure 1 shows graphically these processes and their relations.

The architecture may be divided in three major modules:

- Inference of an adequate OWL ontology of classes;
- Inference of OWL instances and document enrichment;
- Inference engine.

The first module, inference of an adequate OWL ontology of classes, receives as input a top-level ontology and a set of legal documents. After a syntactical and semantical analysis, it obtains a partial semantic representation (a DRS –

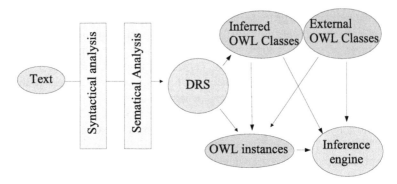

Fig. 1. System's architecture

Discourse Representation structure [13]) for each sentence. From the DRS of each sentence, noun expressions and verbs are extracted, and they are used to define legal classes. These classes will be clustered, classified, and merged with the initial top-level ontology (section 3 describes this step in detail).

The second module, inference of OWL instances, receives as input the DRS of each sentence and the inferred OWL ontology from the first module. With this information, and using an abductive inference mechanism, OWL instances are inferred. This step is usually called pragmatic interpretation of natural language sentences (section 4 describes these processes in more detail).

Finally, OWL classes and OWL instances are used by an inference engine, based in a logic programming framework, in order to answer queries about the semantic content of documents (sections 5, 6 and 7 describe the logic programming framework).

3   OWL Ontology Creation

In order to be able to deal with documents from different domains, a methodology to automatically create basic ontologies of concepts is proposed. This methodology allows the definition of a base ontology with the relevant concepts with some inferred relations. After having defined this ontology, it may be necessary to develop manual work by human experts in order to fully organize the set of extracted concepts.

The methodology is based on the following steps:

- Definition of an initial top-level ontology;
- Identification of concepts referred in the legal documents and extraction of its properties;
- Identification of relations between the identified concepts;
- Creation of an ontology using the identified concepts and relations;
- Merge of the created ontology with the initial ontology;

3.1   Top-Level Ontology

As referred in section 1, an already existent top-level legal ontology was chosen: the legal ontology from the Portuguese Attorney General's Office, consisting of around 6,000 classes and having around 10,000 relations [3]. As and example of some concepts in this ontology we have:

- Tribunal *Court*; properties: name, address, ...
- Tribunal Militar *Military Court* – subclass of Tribunal
- Supremo Tribunal *Supreme Court* – subclass of Tribunal

This legal ontology was merged with a general top-level ontology of concepts defined by Eckhard Bick in the VISL project [1] [14], which has around 150 top concepts: animal, human, place, vehicle, concrete object, abstract object, food, ...

3.2   Identification of Concepts and Properties

The methodology to automatically identify the concepts and the properties referred in the documents is based on the output of natural language processing tools:

- Text syntactical parsing. The documents are analyzed by the syntactical parser PALAVRAS developed by E. Bick. This parser is available for 21 different languages,including Portuguese.
- Partial semantic analysis.
- Entities extraction. From the semantic analysis output, entities and properties are extracted and represented by ontology classes.

Syntactical Analysis. The parser developed by E. Bick is based on the Constraint Grammars [15] formalism and covers a major portion of the Portuguese sentences. However, its output is in a non-standard format and it was necessary to transform it into a structured form, like XML and Prolog terms. A translation tool from the VISL output into XML and Prolog terms was developed and it is available to the VISL users (a detailed description of this tool was presented in [16]).

As an example, suppose the following sentence:

O bombeiro Manuel salvou a criança. *The fireman Manuel saved the child.*

This sentence has the VISL output:

```
STA:fcl
SUBJ:np
=>N:art('o' M S)        O
=H:n('bombeiro' M S)    bombeiro
```

---

[1] http://visl.hum.sdu.dk/visl

```
==N<:prop('Manuel' M S) Manuel
P:v-fin('salvar' PS 3S IND)     salvou
ACC:np
=>N:art('a' F S)        a
=H:n('criança' F S)     criança
```

As it can be seen, the subject, predicate and direct object were correctly parsed.

Semantic Analysis. Each syntactical structure is translated into a First-Order Logic expression. The technique used for this analysis is based on DRS's (Discourse Representation Structures [13]). The partial semantic representation of a sentence is a DRS built with two lists, one with the rewritten sentence and the other with the sentence discourse referents.

At present, we are only dealing with a restricted semantic analysis and we are not able to handle every aspect of the semantics: our focus is on the representation on concepts (nouns and verbs) and the correct extraction of its properties (modifiers, agents, objects).

From the XML structure, using XSL transformations, it is possible to obtain the semantic representation of each sentence.

The semantic representation of the example presented in the previous subsection is:

sentence(doc1, [fireman(A), name(A,'Manuel'), child(B), save(A,B)], [ref(A), ref(B)]).

This structure represents an instance of a fireman A, named 'Manuel', and an instance of a child B which are related by the action *to save*.

A general tool able to obtain similar semantic partial representations for every sentence was developed and it was applied to the full set of legal documents of the Portuguese Attorney General's Office (7000 documents).

Entities Extraction. From the sentence semantic representation, entities are extracted and they are the basis for the creation of an ontology of concepts. In fact, for each new concept, a new class, subclass of a top-class 'Entity', is created.

On the other hand, from the output of the semantic analyser it is possible to identify some potential class properties:

- Modifiers, such as adjectives, are candidates to be properties of nouns;
- Direct objects of transitive verbs are candidates to be properties of the associated verbs;

For instance, for the expression *the black cat* it is possible to identify *color* as a property of *cat*, because it is known that *black* is an instance of a color (from the correspondent semantic tag in the dictionary).

In the referred example it would be possible to extract the following entities:

– bombeiro *fireman*, with a property: 'name'
– salvar *to save*
– criança *child*

3.3   Identification of Relations Between Classes

As it was shown in the previous sub-section, the identification of concepts does not allow the creation of relations, hierarchical or others, between them.

Our approach is to use an an unsupervised method for acquiring word classes and relations [7, 8]. The goal is to learn, for each word, what kind of modifiers and what kind of heads it subcategorises. For instance, the word *republic* may appear as an head of a noun phrase, such as *republic of Ireland, republic of Portugal*, or as a modifier, like *president of the republic, government of the republic*. The obtained subcategorisation patterns are clustered into classes and relations are extracted.

Using this approach it is possible to identify hierarchical relations, such as the existent between *republic* and *republic of Portugal* and also to identify other semantic relations, such as the ones between *lei – law* and *norma – norm*. The strategy is to use statistical analysis to identify clusters of words with similar subcategorisation patterns (words which have similar modifiers and heads).

As methodology, we start from the parsed documents and, for each word, subcategorisation patterns are extracted and clusters and relations are identified. A detailed description of the methodology is described in [8].

Note that this approach has some limitations and it is not able to identify correctly what kind of relations exist between two concepts. For instance, two related concepts may be synonyms or the opposite. A more deep knowledge-aware approach is needed to handle these kind of problems.

The inferred relations are used to create an hierarchy of classes in the ontology and to link them via a *related* relation.

3.4   Creation of the Ontology

In the fourth step of the methodology, the results of the previous two sub-sections are integrated into a new ontology:

– Concepts with their properties are new classes;
– Class hierarchies and relations are created accordingly with the results of the previous sub-section;

For instance, using this approach to the previous example, *republic of Portugal* will be a sub-class of *republic*.

3.5   Merge of the Ontologies

Finally, in the fifth step, the initial top-level ontology is merged with the new one.

In this process new classes are inserted into the top-level ontology using their names and information from the semantic analyser:

- If a class exists with an equal name in the top-level ontology, then the two classes are merged;
- Otherwise, a search is made in the top-level ontology for a class with semantically compatible information and the new class is created as a sub-class of the existent one.

For instance, if a new class named *fireman* is classified to be a *human* concept by the NLP analysers, then the new class will be a sub-class of the *human* top-level concept.

The overall strategy is to search for common concepts in the two ontologies and to merge the ontologies via these concepts.

4   OWL Instances Creation

After having defined an ontology of classes, it is necessary to extract and to represent instances of those classes and to associate them with documents.

The proposed methodology tries to infer instances of those ontologies using the following three steps:

- Translation of the OWL ontologies into a logic programming form;
- Definition of logic programming rules allowing the inference of instances;
- Generation of OWL instances.

OWL Translation. The first step, translation of OWL ontologies into Prolog, was implemented in Java and it creates a Prolog term for each OWL class, sub-class, or property. The translation of this subset on OWL is correct accordingly with the OWL formal semantic description [17].

For instance, suppose there exists a definition in OWL for a class *citizen* and for a sub-class *military*. After the translation, we'll have:

```
class(citizen, 'external.owl#citizen').
class(military, 'external.owl#military').

subclass('external.owl#military', 'external.owl#citizen').
```

Moreover, suppose class *military* has a property of having a *rank*, which can have one of several possible values: general, colonel, ...

In this situation, we'll have the following Prolog terms:

```
property(rank, 'external.owl#rank',
            'external.owl#military').

hasPossibleValue('external.owl#rank', general).
hasPossibleValue('external.owl#rank', colonel).
```

Prolog Rules. In the second step of this methodology, logic programming rules are defined allowing the inference of instances from the DRS representation of each sentence and the Prolog representation of the ontology.

One of these rules allows the inference of class and properties from values:

```
infer(Value, Class, Property) :-
            hasPossibleValue(PropertyURI, Value),
            property(Property, PropertyURI, ClassURI),
            class(Class, ClassURI).
```

In this LP rule, *Value* is the name of an entity (input) and *Class* and *Property* are identifiers of classes and properties that may have this value (output).

For instance, the sentence

```
The colonel saved the child.
```

has the following DRS form:

```
sentence(d1, [colonel(X), child(Y), save(X,Y)],
        [ref(X),ref(Y)]).
```

From this DRS form and, using the Prolog rules, it is possible to infer the following new form (because *colonel* is a possible value for the *rank* property of the *military* class):

```
sentence(d1, [military(X), rank(X,colonel), child(Y),
        save(X,Y)], [ref(X),ref(Y)]).
```

This process is usually called, in the natural language processing field, pragmatic interpretation of sentences and it can be seen as an abductive process where properties (antecedents) are inferred from values (consequents) [18].

Similar approaches can be applied to capture different natural language sentences characteristics.

OWL Generation. In the third step, the results of the pragmatic interpretation of each sentence are transformed into correspondent OWL instances. For instance, for the last example of the previous sub-section, the following OWL instances would be created:

```
<pgr:Military rdf:ID="m11">
    <pgr:rank rdf:resource="external.owl#Colonel"/>
    <pgr:belong rdf:resource="external.owl#Army"/>
</pgr:Military>

<pgr:Child rdf:ID="c2">
</pgr:Child>

<pgr:ToSave rdf:ID="s5">
    <pgr:subject rdf:resource="#m11"/>
    <pgr:object rdf:resource="#c2"/>
</pgr:ToSave>
```

These instances define and relate a military (colonel and from the army), a child, through the instance of the action *to save*.

As a final result of this step, every document is enriched with the OWL instances obtained from the pragmatic interpretation of its sentences.

5   ISCO

In this section, the logic programming framework that is going to be used as the inference engine for answering queries about the semantic content of documents (OWL instances) is briefly described.

ISCO [10] is a logic based development language implemented in GNU Prolog that gives the developer several distinct possibilities:

- It supports Object-Oriented features: classes, hierarchies, inheritance.
- It supports Constraint Logic Programming. Specifically, it supports finite domain constraints in ISCO queries.
- it gives a simple access to external relational databases through ODBC. It has a back-end for PostgreSQL and Oracle.
- It allows the access to external relational databases as a part of a declarative/deductive object-oriented (with inheritance) database. Among other things, the system maps relational tables to classes – which may be used as Prolog predicates.
- It gives a simple database structure description language that can help in database schema analysis. Tools are available to create an ISCO database description from an existing relational database schema and also the opposite action.

Taking these ISCO features into account, a translator from OWL into ISCO class definitions was developed. This translator was applied to every OWL class described in the previous section and, as a consequence, correspondent SQL tables and ISCO classes definitions were obtained. Moreover, each OWL class instance was transformed into an SQL table row and an ISCO logic programming fact. As an example, the *toSave* presented previously is translated into the following fact:

```
toSave(ID=s5, subject='#m11', object='#c2').
```

For each defined class a set of Prolog predicates implementing the four basic operations are created: query, insert, update and delete.

Variables occurring in queries are mapped to SQL and may carry CLP(FD) constraints, which will be expressed in SQL, whenever possible. For example, suppose variable X is an FD variable whose domain is (1..1000), the query

$$\text{document(number = X, title = Y)} \tag{1}$$

will return all pairs (X, Y) where X is a document number and Y is the document's title. X is subject to the constraints that were valid upon execution of the query, ie. in the range 1 to 1000.

ISCO class declarations feature inheritance, simple domain integrity constraints and global integrity constraints.

6   EVOLP

As it was described in the previous section, ISCO allows a declarative representation of ontologies and object instances. However, there is also a need to represent actions and to model the evolution of the knowledge.

In [19] it was introduced a declarative, high-level language for knowledge updates called *LUPS* (Language of UPdateS) that describes transitions between consecutive knowledge states. Recently, a new language, EVOLP [11], was proposed having a simpler and more general formulation of logic program updates. In this section a brief description of the EVOLP language will be given. A detailed description of the language and of its formalization is presented at the cited article.

EVOLP allows the specification of a program's evolution, through the existence of rules which indicate assertions to the program. EVOLP programs are sets of generalized logic program rules defined over an extended propositional language L_{assert}, defined over any propositional language L in the following way [11]:

- All propositional atoms in L are propositional atoms in L_{assert}
- If each of $L_0, \ldots, L_n$ is a literal in L_{assert}, then $L_0 \leftarrow L_1, \ldots, L_n$ is a generalized logic program rule over L_{assert}.
- If R is a rule over L_{assert} then $assert(R)$ is a propositional atom of L_{assert}.
- Nothing else is a propositional atom in L_{assert}.

The formal definition of the semantics of EVOLP is presented at the referred article, but the general idea is the following: whenever the atom $assert(R)$ belongs to an interpretation, i.e. belongs to a model according to the stable model semantics of the current program, then R must belong to the program in the next state. For instance, the following rule form:

$$assert(b \leftarrow a) \leftarrow c \qquad (2)$$

means that if c is true in a state, then the next state must have rule $b \leftarrow a$.

EVOLP has also the notion of external events, i.e. assertions that do not persist by inertia. This notion is fundamental to model interaction between agents and to represent actions. For instance, it is important to be able to represent actions and its effects and pre-conditions:

$$assert(Effect) \leftarrow Action, PreConditions \qquad (3)$$

If, in a specific state, there is the event *Action* and if *PreConditions* hold, then the next state will have *Effect*.

7   Interaction Management

The interaction manager is built on the ISCO+EVOLP logic programming framework.

As final goal, we aim to handle the following kind of questions:

- Situations where action A is performed
- Situations where action A is performed having subject S
- Situations where S is the subject of an action

Note that the inference engine needs to be able to deal with the ontology relations. For instance, the question "situations where action A is performed having subject S" means "situations where action A (or any of its sub-classes) is performed having subject S (or any of its sub-classes)".

The interaction manager is composed by the following main tasks:

- Query management
- Interaction management

7.1   Query Management

The analysis of a natural language query is split in three subprocesses: Syntax, Semantics, and Pragmatics.

Syntax. As syntactic analyser we are using the analyzer developed by E. Bick and referred previously [14]. The VISL output is translated into Prolog facts by the same translator referred in section 3. This translation can be handled by the same translator because there is a direct relation between the XML structure and the Prolog term structure.

As an example, the following query:

```
Quem salvou crianças?
''Who saved children?''
```

Has the following syntactical structure:

```
sentence(syn(que(fcl,
          subj(pron_indp('quem','M/F','S','<interr>'),'Quem'),
          p(v_fin('salvar','PS','3S','IND'),'salvou'),
          acc(n('criança','F','P','<H>'),'crianças', '?')))).
```

Semantics. As referred in section 3, each syntactical structure is translated into a First-Order Logic expression (DRS). The semantic representation of a sentence is a DRS built with two lists, one with the rewritten sentence and the other with the sentence discourse referents. For instance, the semantic representation of the sentence above is the following expression:

```
child(B), toSave(A,B),
```

and the following discourse referents list:

```
A : [ref(A),ref(B)]
```

These structures represent instances of children B related with instances of the *toSave* action.

Note that, at present, we are not able to deal with general unrestricted queries and to translate them from a syntactical into a semantic structure. In fact this a quite complex NLP problem and we have decided to deal only with specific subsets of the Portuguese language, namely, with interrogatives about specific domains.

Pragmatic Interpretation. The pragmatic module receives the semantic query representation and tries to interpret it in the context of the database information, which was constructed from the translation of the OWL instances into ISCO facts (as described previously in section 5).

In order to achieve this behavior the system tries to find the best explanations for the sentence logic form to be true in the knowledge base. As already referred, this strategy for interpretation is known as "interpretation as abduction" [18].

From the description of the OWL (and ISCO) classes it is possible to obtain the correspondent ISCO query:

```
child(id=B),
toSave(id=C, subject=A, object=B),
```

The interpretation of the ISCO predicates is done by accessing the knowledge base in order to collect (and constraint) all entities identifiers:

```
- $A=_\#(104..109:156..157)$ -- A constrained to all
    entities with the desired properties
```

The above expression contains the possible interpretations of the query in the context of the knowledge base.

7.2   Interaction Management

The interaction manager has to represent the actions associated with the queries (*informs* or *request*), and to model the user attitudes (intentions and beliefs).

This task is also achieved through the use of the EVOLP language (see [20] for a more detailed description of these rules). For instance, the rules which describe the effect of an inform, and a request speech act are:

$$assert(bel(A, bel(B, P))) \leftarrow inform(B, A, P). \tag{4}$$

$$assert(bel(A, int(B, Action))) \leftarrow request(B, A, Action). \tag{5}$$

These rules mean that if an agent A is informed of a property P, then it will start to believe that the other agent believes in P; additionally, if B requests A to perform an action $Action$, then A starts to believe that B intends $Action$ to be performed.

In order to represent collaborative behavior it is also necessary to model the transference of information between the agents:

$$assert(bel(A, P)) \leftarrow bel(A, bel(B, P)). \tag{6}$$
$$assert(int(A, Action)) \leftarrow bel(A, int(B, Action)). \tag{7}$$

These two rules means that if an agent A believes another agent believes in P, then it will start to believe in P (it is a cooperative, credulous agent); moreover, it will also adopt the intentions of the other agents.

There is also the need for a rule linking the system intentions and the accesses to the databases:

$$assert(inf(A, B, P)) \leftarrow int(A, inf(A, B, P)), isco(P). \tag{8}$$
$$assert(not\ int(A, B, inf(A, B, P))) \leftarrow inf(A, B, P). \tag{9}$$

The first rule defines that, if the system intends to inform the user about some property, then it will access the ISCO database and it will perform an inform action. The second rule means that the inform action will end the intention to perform the inform action!

8   Example

Considering the already presented query:

> Quem salvou crianças?   ''Who saved children?''

The interaction manager receives the query pragmatic interpretation:

Q = [child(id=B), toSave(id=C, subject=A, object=B)].

After having the sentence rewritten into its semantic representation form, the speech act is recognized:

> request(user, system, inform(user, system, Q))

Using the *request* and the transference of intentions rules the following property is supported:

> int(system,inform(system, user, Q))

Now, using the rules presented in the previous section, the system accesses the ISCO databases and it is able to obtain the final constraints to the discourse referent variables:

- $A=_\#(104..109:156..157)$

Using the inferred constraints it is possible to obtain the set of solutions to the user query and to answer:

    m11: Military - rank: colonel; belong: army.

9   Conclusions and Future Work

A methodology to automatically create legal ontologies was proposed.

The methodology uses syntactical, semantical and pragmatical analysers to obtain sentence representations and to identify entities and entity relations. The obtained ontologies are merged with other externally defined top-level ontologies.

The obtained new ontology is used, with the semantic representation of sentences, to infer class instances and to enrich documents with this semantic information. The inference of the instances associated with each sentence is done via an abductive process – interpretation as abduction.

Ontologies and the inferred instances are represented in the OWL language.

On the other hand, translators from OWL into ISCO/Prolog were developed and a logic programming based interaction manager was developed. The interaction manager uses many important features from its base LP framework: objects, constraints, inheritance.

As future work we need to improve several areas:

- Ontology creation. The ontology was created automatically but it was not possible to identify many relations between the classes. In order to be able to define these relations we intend to extend the statistical analysis of word subcategorisation to take into account semantic information from the dictionary and existent Wordnets.
- OWL translation into ISCO/Prolog. A full translation of the OWL language needs to be implemented and its correction has to be proved.
- Evaluation. The system needs to be fully evaluated and to be tested by users. Moreover it should be applied to other legal documents, such as, legislation.

References

1. W3C: DAML+OIL – DARPA Agent Markup Language. www.daml.org. (2000)
2. Lassila, O., Swick, R.: Resource Description Framework (RDF) - Model and Syntax Specification. W3C. (1999)
3. Quaresma, P., Rodrigues, I.P.: PGR: Portuguese attorney general's office decisions on the web. In Bartenstein, Geske, Hannebauer, Yoshie, eds.: Web-Knowledge Management and Decision Support. Lecture Notes in Artificial Intelligence LNCS/LNAI, Springer-Verlag (2002)
4. Guangemi, A., Guarino, N., Masolo, C., Oltramari, A., Schneider, L.: Sweetening ontologies with dolce. In Gomez-Perez, A., Benjamins, V.R., eds.: Proceedings of the EKAW'2002, Springer-Verlag (2002) 166–181

5. Breuker, J., Winkels, R.: Use and reuse of legal ontologies in knowledge engineering and information management. Journal of Artificial Intelligence and Law (2003) In this issue.
6. Boer, A., Hoekstra, R., Winkels, R., van Engers, T., Willaert, F.: Proposal for a dutch legal xml standard. In: EGOV2002 – Proceedings of the First International Conference on Electronic Government. (2002)
7. Gamallo, P., Agustini, A., Quaresma, P., Lopes, G.: Using semantic word classes in text information retrieval systems. In Pinto, S., ed.: SBIE'2002 – XII Simpósio Brasileiro de Informática na Educação, Workshop de Ontologias, Porto Alegre, Brasil, Unisinos (2002) 593–597 ISBN 85-7431-133-2.
8. Gamallo, P., Agustini, A., Lopes, G.: Using co-composition for acquiring syntactic and semantic subcategorisation. In: ACL-SIGLEX'02, Philadelphy, USA (2002)
9. Lame, G.: Using text analysis techniques to identify legal ontologies' components. In: Workshop on Legal Ontologies of the International Conference on Artificial Intelligence and Law. (2003)
10. Abreu, S.: Isco: A practical language for heterogeneous information system construction. In: Proceedings of INAP'01, Tokyo, Japan, INAP (2001)
11. Alferes, J., Brogi, A., Leite, J., Pereira, L.: Evolving logic programs. In Flesca, S., Greco, S., Leone, N., Ianni, G., eds.: JELIA'02 – Proceedings of the 8th European Conference on Logics and Artificial Intelligence, Springer-Verlag LNCS 2424 (2002) 50–61
12. Damásio, C.: W4 – well-founded semantics for the world wide web. In Boley, H., Grosof, G., Tabet, S., Wagner, G., eds.: Rule Markup Techniques for the Semantic Web, Dagstuhl, Germany (2003)
13. Kamp, H., Reyle, U.: From Discourse to Logic. Kluwer, Dordrecht (1993)
14. Bick, E.: The Parsing System "Palavras". Automatic Grammatical Analysis of Portuguese in a Constraint Grammar Framework. Aarhus University Press (2000)
15. Karlsson, F.: Constraint grammar as a framework for parsing running text. In Karlgren, H., ed.: 13th International Conference on Computational Linguistics. Volume 3., Helsinki, Finland (1990) 168–173
16. Gasperin, C., Vieira, R., Goulart, R., Quaresma, P.: Extracting xml syntactic chunks from portuguese corpora. In: TALN'2003 - Workshop on Natural Language Processing of Minority Languages and Small Languages of the Conference on "Traitement Automatique des Langues Naturelles", Batz-sur-Mer, France (2003)
17. Saias, J.: Uma metodologia para a construção automática de ontologias e a sua aplicação em sistemas de recuperação de informação – a methodology for the automatic creation of ontologies and its application in information retrieval systems. Master's thesis, University of Évora, Portugal (2003) In Portuguese.
18. Hobbs, J., Stickel, M., Appelt, D., Martin, P.: Interpretation as abduction. Technical Report SRI Technical Note 499, 333 Ravenswood Ave., Menlo Park, CA 94025 (1990)
19. Alferes, J.J., Pereira, L.M., Przymusinska, H., Przymusinski, T.C., Quaresma, P.: Preliminary exploration on actions as updates. In Meo, M.C., Vilares-Ferro, M., eds.: Procs. of the 1999 Joint Conference on Declarative Programming (AGP'99), L'Aquila, Italy (1999) 259–271
20. Quaresma, P., Lopes, J.G.: Unified logic programming approach to the abduction of plans and intentions in information-seeking dialogues. Journal of Logic Programming **54** (1995)

Iuriservice: An Intelligent Frequently Asked Questions System to Assist Newly Appointed Judges

V.R. Benjamins[1], P. Casanovas[2], J. Contreras[1],
J.M. Lopez Cobo[1], and L. Lemus[1]

[1] Intelligent Software Components (iSOCO), Spain
www.isoco.com
rbenjamins@isoco.com
[2] Department of Political Science (GRES),
Autonomous University of Barcelona, Barcelona, Spain
pompeu.casanovas@uab.es

Abstract. In this paper, we describe the use of legal ontologies as a basis to improve IT support for professional judges. In the ontology, we emphasize the importance of professional knowledge and experience as an important pillar for constructing the ontology. We describe an intelligent FAQ system for junior judges that intensively uses the ontology.

1   Introduction

Building ontologies is hard. An ontology is a shared and agreed explicit representation of some domain [1], [2]. Many of the ontologies that exist today are private conceptualizations of domains. Although they are explicit representations, they are not shared and agreed by a professional group. Whereas this might be a workable situation in many domains, in the legal domain it is not. Any computer system that provides some kind of support to judges and lawyers should be based on a common, agreed upon model of the law. With "law" we do here not only mean as it is described in books, but we mean the set of knowledge that legal professionals use while performing their jobs. This includes normative, jurisprudential and experiential knowledge. Especially experiential knowledge is hard to get and represent, as it involves gathering knowledge in the field.

Once a shared ontology has been constructed, it can be used as the cornerstone for many applications, such as case retrieval, case forwarding, FAQs, knowledge management, etc. In this paper, we will describe one of such applications, namely an intelligent frequently asked questions (FAQ) system to support young judges in their first assignment.

In the Spanish system, if one wants to become a judge, and once obtained the corresponding university degree, one has to perform a public exam in which only the best are invited to be judge. Between obtaining the university degree and passing the public exam, many years of private study can pass. The consequence is that young judges have ample theoretical knowledge but encounter problems when having to take practical decisions. One particular problem newly appointed

V.R. Benjamins et al. (Eds.): Law and the Semantic Web, LNCS 3369, pp. 201–217, 2005.

judges face occurs when they are on duty. When they are confronted with situations in which they are not sure what to do (e.g. in a voluntary confession ("autodenuncia"), which process of questioning should be applied?), they can phone to another judge for resolving the issue. In case of a judge in his first year, the likelihood is considerable that he/she does not know the correct answer, and usually refers to a colleague or to a more experienced judge for more information. The system we describe in this paper is meant to relieve experienced judges from this effort by providing FAQs to judges in their first appointment. Only in the case that the questions are not in the system and cannot be reformulated in existing questions, an experienced judge may be contacted.

In order to build a scalable and useful FAQ system, the following requirements have been identified:

- Judges should not be bothered with a complex user interface. A simple natural language interface is probably appropriate.
- The decision as to whether a new question is similar to a stored question (with its corresponding answer) should be based on semantics rather than on simple word matching. An ontology can be used to perform this semantic matching of questions.
- The questions included in the system should be of high quality, i.e. be rather exhaustive and reflect the actual situation. An extensive survey with more than 250 Spanish judges forms the basis for the questions (see also paper on "Statistical Study of Judicial Practices" in this book).

An example of a question-answer pair is the following.

Question: What problems can we foresee with the analysis of small amounts of drugs, where the identification test destroys the drugs?

Answer: This is an unrepeatable piece of evidence at the trial. In these cases, the Spanish Criminal Procedure Act states that the adversarial principle should be respected. While the trial proceedings are prepared, the judge must explain to all parties that they may choose an expert to perform these tests.

It is the *semantic* matching of questions that requires Semantic Web Technology. In the Semantic Web, "meaning" is added to content. In our case the content is formed by the stored questions and the new question posed by a judge. The meaning is added automatically by parsing the content and classifying or "understanding" the questions in terms of the ontology. Once this is done, the systems understands -in legal terms- what the questions are about.

The rest of this paper is organized as follows. Section 2 describes the approach of how we collected more than 300 high-quality FAQs. In Section 3, we elaborate on the ontology we have built to support the FAQ system. Section 4 describes the intelligent FAQ application to help inexperienced judges. Finally, in Section 5 we present conclusions.

2   Frequently-Asked Questions by Judges

Based on the "Statistical Study of Judicial Practices" paper, also published in this book, several legal professionals were able to compile a long list (more than

Table 1. Some of the questions posed to the judges, related to their professional activity

---

Questions:

• What kind of judicial cases (civil or criminal cases) were more frequent in your first destination?
• What were the two most important doubts that you had in your first three months as a judge?
• What were the most complicated civil cases that you had to solve in your first year as a judge? Why?
• What were the most complicated criminal cases that you had to solve in your first year as a judge? Why?
• Could you define the civil case that has given you more work?
• Could you define the criminal case that has given you more work?
• Which are the most frequent problems that you have found in the hearings?

Table 2. Fragments of questionnaire answers of judges containing the word "on-duty"

• 1 ON-DUTY PROBLEMS
• 2 ON-DUTY SERVICE
• 3 BEHAVIORS DURING ON-DUTY PERIODS
• 4 TREATMENT OF URGENT FAMILY MATTERS DURING THE DUTY
• 5 ON-DUTY MATTERS, PERSONS INVOLVED IN SPECIFIC ACTIONS
• 6 CRIMINAL: ON-DUTY PERIODS
• 7 ON-DUTY PROBLEMS CONCERNING MINORS PROTECTION
• 8 SOLVING SPECIFIC ON-DUTY MATTERS
• 9 ON-DUTY MATTERS
• 10 ON-DUTY/ CALLS FROM THE POLICE CONCERNING CERTAIN ASPECTS WHICH DO NOT FIGURE IN THE BOOKS/ PRACTICAL ASPECTS DURING ON-DUTY PERIOD)
• 11 DOUBTS ARISING DURING ON-DUTY PERIODS
• 12 WHAT SHOULD BE UNDERSTOOD BY ON-DUTY ACTIONS
• 13 OF THE ON-DUTY COURT
• 14 WHEN THE LEGAL RESPONSIBILITY FILE COULD BE OPENED, ESPECIALLY IF IT COULD OCCUR DURING THE ON-DUTY PERIOD
• 15 AT THE BEGINNING, DURING THE FIRST THREE MONTHS, MY DOUBTS CONCERNED IMPORTANT DECISIONS TO BE TAKEN DURING THE ON-DUTY PERIOD
• 16 CANNOT CONCRETE, THE MOST IMPORTANT DOUBTS ARISEN DURING THE ON-DUTY PERIODS
• 17 IF THE DISTRICT JUDGES HAD TO DO ON DUTY PERIODS

Table 3. Examples of FAQs relative to problems that judges experience while on duty

---

Questions about data and facts

• What should be done when a detainee accused of a minor crime which does not imply jail is brought to a judge and the public defender who has been designed delays his arrival to the judicial premises?

• What should be done, given the case that a mother files a complain against her son whom she wants to exclude from home for ill treatment and cruelty?

• A corpse is produced at home, at 2 o'clock a.m. During the legal search, millions of pesetas appear in a drawer in the bedroom. What should the judge do in this case?

Questions related to legal culture

• In which cases is a judge on-duty allowed to send a detainee to jail, when he depends on another court?

• What must a judge on duty do when a detainee with several pending criminal offences in different courts, if they do not belong to the same jurisdiction?

---

400) of frequently asked questions with corresponding answers. Some example questions used in the study are shown in Table 1

Statistical methods were used to find the main problem areas of young judges. The topic *guardia* was recognized as an important source of problems. Table 2 illustrates some of those problems related to being "on-duty".

Finally, from these indicators, legal experts have formulated a collection of questions covering the problems arising in the on-duty period. Table 3 illustrates some examples.

3   An Ontology of Professional Legal Knowledge

3.1   Domain Considerations

The application of AI techniques to the law field has contributed to make explicit some of the implicit ontological assumptions that may be found in the work of legal theorists throughout the twentieth century. Legal entities (norms, rules, interests, privileges...) have been asserted, used, reused and discussed by Formal Positivists, Social Positivists, American and Scandinavian Realists or members of the Critical Legal Studies Movement.

However, when social and computer scientists use some of the hints of the legal theory they are not necessarily defending any particular theoretical position. To a great extent, the building of a legal ontology has more to do with legal models than with general theories about law. Any purpose or aim needs to be specified. There is no such thing as "task neutrality" in building ontologies [3].

[4] offered the following summary of legal ontologies and their basic knowledge categories (quoted several times in the current literature):

1. LLD [Language for Legal Discourse, L.T. McCarty, 1989]: Atomic formula, Rules and Modalities.
2. NOR [Norma, R.K. Stamper, 1991, 1996]: Agents Behavioral invariants, Realizations.
3. LFU [Functional Ontology for Law, A.Valente, 1995]: Normative Knowledge, World knowledge, Responsibility knowledge, Reactive knowledge, Creative knowledge, Legal metaknowledge.
4. FBO [Frame-Based Ontology of Law, R.W.van Kralingen, 1995; P.R.S. Visser, 1995]: Norms, Acts and Concepts Descriptions].

Some researchers have noticed that, compared to the former two ontologies, the later ones (by van Kralingen, Visser and Valente) tried to define building blocks of legal reasoning in a more comprehensive way than logical relationship among discrete entities [5].

According to the recent Reports of the Legal Ontologies Working Group (OntoWeb SIG1), we should have also these new trends in mind:

5. LRI-Core Legal Ontology [J. Breuker et al., 2002]: Objects, Processes, Physical entities, Mental entities, Agents, Communicative Acts.
6. IKF-IF-LEX Ontology for Norm Comparaison [A. Gangemi et al., 2001]: Agents, Institutive Norms, Instrumental provisions; Regulative norms; Opentextured legal notions, Norm dynamics.

These six legal ontologies are called "legal core ontologies" [6], capturing concepts like agent, role, intention, document, right, responsibility. A "legal core ontology" is intended to mediate between a foundational ontology (primitive general terms) and "legal domain ontologies" (ontologies for specific regulations in sub-domains such as criminal law, banking, e-commerce, copyright, etc.).

The "legal core" is intended to bridge the particular statutory level and top-level ontologies. This latter upper-level is needed: (i) to index and represent schemes for libraries, "scaling the ontologies on ontology features" [7] ; (ii) to provide the basis for argumentation, legal aid and legal decision support systems [8].

Legal aid ontologies structure legal knowledge for practical aims (support systems) by several means (developing techniques for extracting domain knowledge, inferencing techniques or providing explanations for the decisions reached) [8].

The shared and reusable legal knowledge to build up legal core or domain ontologies is commonly acquired from sources that range from statutes, treatises and legal texts to precedents and judiciary rulings.

But it may be noticed that even support systems are usually set forth representing legal knowledge and legal reasoning similarly to van Kralingen's (1995) and Visser's (1995) frame-based description approach or to Valente's (1995) functional approach (normative, world, responsibility, reactive, creative knowledge and legal metaknowledge).

3.2   Ontologies of Professional Legal-Knowledge (OPLK)

In our case, legal knowledge stems from a different source. As said before, we started with an extended survey about the most frequent problems that judges face in their first appointment. The first results allowed us to identify three main areas in which newly appointed judges have problems: (i) the organization of daily relationships within "the legal office" (Oficina Judicial: clerks, civil servants...); (ii) the interpretation and implementation of a new procedural Spanish Statute (Ley de Enjuiciamiento Civil, January 2002); and (iii) the on-duty time (guardia: the week in which the entire Court is on duty tackling the preliminary investigation and procedures of the criminal cases that keep entering to the Courts). Then, we were provided with a rich material containing problems of practical procedural criminal law (adjacency pairs of questions and answers) by the Judicial School. We selected the restricted area of on duty time problems. The question is which kind of legal knowledge were we working out to build up the ontology.

We realized that this knowledge is by no means doctrinaire. Judges are experts: they take for granted the acquaintance with legal texts, textbooks and former legal decisions. What it is at stake here is a different kind of legal knowledge, a *professional* legal knowledge (PLK).

We define PLK as the type of knowledge shared by the members of a legal profession and conveyed through professional training and organizational means. PLK is: (i) corporate knowledge (other legal professionals are especially excluded); (ii) non-equally distributed along the members of the corporate group; (iii) experience-based; (iv) context-sensitive (depending on the places, cases and personal history); (v) institutionally conveyed through training in specific places (law faculty, law practice schools, law schools, the Judicial School, courts, lawyer offices, state agencies...).

The boundaries of PLK are loose. Provided that law and the law practice are indeed very different in any country, it is assumed that there is common shared knowledge among the legal professions (judges, magistrates, prosecutors, lawyers, . . .). However, at the same time, due to the way they behave on a daily basis, there is a particular set of beliefs, attitudes and experiences that belong only to a single profession. This kind of distributed group-centered knowledge is what we are referring to here.

It is our contention that interpretations of legal texts (statutes, regulations, decrees, etc.) that legal domain ontologies try to capture are also "anchored" -as Breuker would say- within this professional knowledge. Through PLK, legal domain ontologies overlap with legal core ontologies. This is an intermediate domain in which legal contexts and shared legal knowledge are linked up to particular statutes and specific regulations. From this point of view, PLK is the swivel of the legal chain.

3.3   An Ontology for Spanish Judges in Their First Appointment

In order to design the ontology, we started from the rich information and the FAQs provided by the study of Newly Appointed Judges (class-49/50 of the Judicial School) (see Section 2). We used the 'competency approach' [9] to identify relevant aspects and the coverage of the ontology. Below we show two typical questions that illustrate the importance of *processes* in our domain. It may be noticed that for several legal Spanish notions (e.g. diligencias indeterminadas) there are no equivalent expressions in English nor in the common law. In Spanish criminal proceedings, the process is commonly split up in two different kinds of procedures and hearings, conducted by different judges. The first proceedings constitute the instrucción (preliminary hearings), while the later ones are the juicio ordinario or the trial properly called.

(1) Question
- While on duty, an investigating magistrate receives a call from a hospital, reporting a sexual assault. The victim has still not made an official report of the incident. Procedures to be followed. Which rules apply?
(2) Rewriting
- In a case where a medical center telephones to report a sexual assault, what must be done by the investigating magistrate who receives the call, and if the victim has not officially reported the incident, which procedure must be followed?
- If an investigating magistrate is informed by a hospital that there has been a sexual assault, what procedures must he or she follow in order to ascertain the facts of the case, and which of the established official procedures must be followed if the victim has not officially reported the assault?
(3) Reply:
As for the procedures to be followed, a forensic scientist should be sent to the hospital in order to examine the victim and to take samples. If the crime has not yet been officially reported, the judge except in very exceptional circumstances may begin no procedures. Provided that it is clear from the telephone call alone that this is a case of sexual assault and that no other crime has been committed, then criminal proceedings must be initiated by the victim.

Fig. 1. Example FAQ

Under the Spanish law, there is a judge (juez instructor) who must conduct the investigation of the police officers. When the judge in on duty (semana de guardia) he has to take a lot of quick decisions about the facts and the cases that have been reported to the police or to the court. Therefore, the most usual set of questions take for him the following form, "what I should do in such and such situation?"

Judicial experience tries to offer a reply. Judicial PLK contains a repository of know-how solutions, next steps to take, ready made procedural and practical

(1) Question
- While on duty, an investigating magistrate receives a call from a hospital, reporting a sexual assault. The victim has still not made an official report of the incident. Procedures to be followed. Which rules apply?
(2) Rewriting
- In a case where a medical center telephones to report a sexual assault, what must be done by the investigating magistrate who receives the call, and if the victim has not officially reported the incident, which procedure must be followed?
- If an investigating magistrate is informed by a hospital that there has been a sexual assault, what procedures must he or she follow in order to ascertain the facts of the case, and which of the established official procedures must be followed if the victim has not officially reported the assault?
(3) Reply:
As for the procedures to be followed, a forensic scientist should be sent to the hospital in order to examine the victim and to take samples. If the crime has not yet been officially reported, the judge except in very exceptional circumstances may begin no procedures. Provided that it is clear from the telephone call alone that this is a case of sexual assault and that no other crime has been committed, then criminal proceedings must be initiated by the victim.

Fig. 2. Example FAQ

knowledge, for a huge amount of similar cases which are not covered by statutory provisions.

Our ontology for this professional legal knowledge (OPLK) is based on the common ground of knowledge that any inexperienced judge shares with the more experienced ones. That is to say, we inferred some matching concepts from the bulk of materials that we had before us (hard cases, rare cases, legal interpretations, legal analogies, professional attitudes, and common standards).

Next, we will explain the different sources that we considered in constructing the current version of the ontology.

The most general concept we found in the judicial criminal field is *proceso* (process, trial, procedures), the Spanish procedural notion that stands for all kinds of proceedings under the Spanish law. This notion constitutes the kernel of a wide network of related concepts that shape the backbone of the judicial culture. A possible representation offered below:

1. Ordinary Trial: [(i) beginning + (ii) agents].
2. Preliminary Investigation: 2a . [Building of the Records: (i) findings (ordering) + (ii) personal area (ordering, rights) + (iii) liability + (iv) secondary liability.] 2b. [End of the Records: (no criminal case OR opening of the proceedings)].
3. Criminal Hearing [(summary trial OR instruction)].
4. Misdemeanor (Petty Offences)Trial
5. Preliminary Investigation (Committal) + Jury Trial.

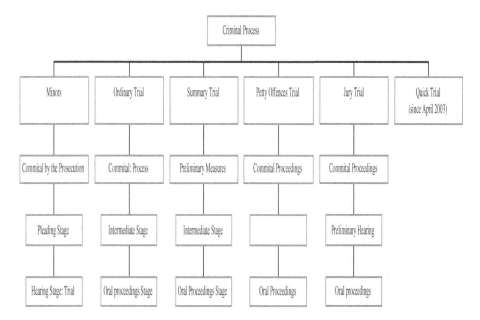

Fig. 3. Different types of professional knowledge relevant for young judges

Figure 3 represents this professional knowledge graphically. It is a mixture of taxonomic (first level), part-of (second and third levels) and decision and procedural knowledge (fourth level). The most important decision to be taken after the preliminary investigation (instrucción) is going ahead with the proceedings (apertura de juicio oral) or finishing them up and state that there is no criminal case to be ruled (sobreseimiento).

Judges use this knowledge as a kind of cognitive tool for a quick understanding of the facts that are submitted to them, and through which they can select the appropriate legal procedure. It serves as a kind of guideline as to what to do first. In this sense it resembles cognitive schemas and scripts or prototypes. A schema is an organized framework of objects and relations which has yet to be filled in. A script is a set of expectations about what will happen next in a well-understood situation [10]. A prototype is created through the filling in of the slots of a schema with an individual's standard default values [11].

We assume that our preliminary ontology for professional legal knowledge, even if still lightweight and only formulated in a semiformal language, captures the templates that judges must fill in almost automatically by the bulk of cases and situations that they encounter while being on duty. Therefore, the structure of our ontology will allow the system to reply through the same set of basically related concepts that users (young judges) will have in mind in their consultations. The current version of the ontology (implemented in Protégé 2000 [12]) for professional legal knowledge is illustrated in Figure 4, and includes the following terms:

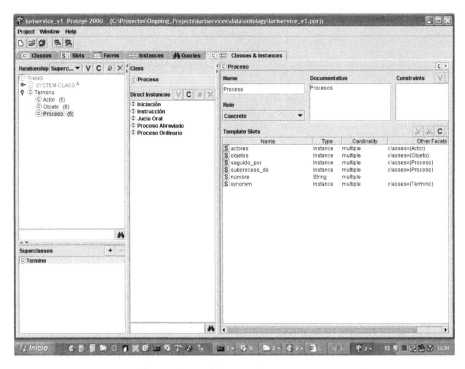

Fig. 4. Screenshot of the legal ontology in Protégé

- Process and its instances: different trial processes or their parts.
- Object and its instances: physical or abstract inanimate objects representing documents, information, physical items used by a process or an actor, as an input or result of a process.
- Actor and its instances: Persons or organizations able to execute changes within the model. This concept is similar to *Agent* as in [13].

These concepts are linked through the following attributes, which represent relations:

- Generalization: the *is-a* relation that allows representing that one concept is more general than another, e.g. an actor *is a* person. Can be applied to any concept.
- Equivalence: allows relating two concepts that are synonyms in this domain. Can be applied to any concept.
- Actor: process instances are associated with actors that participate in that process. The link is made through this (actor) attribute.
- Follows: attribute for processes to determine the logical or temporal order for processes or their parts.
- Part of: applied to processes or objects to represent when one concept is a part of another, e.g. instruction is *part of* the trial process

As one can see, the ontology is not the typical taxonomy we often see in ontologies. This is not to say that the taxonomic relation is not important. Indeed, the relation is included in the ontology, besides other relevant relations. The Protege editor allows us to view the ontology according to any relation available.

Another observation we make is that the ontology is an eclectic selection of ideas and approaches from the literature based on our purpose. In its current state it is difficult to state what the exact relation is between our ontology and the existing approaches as mentioned in this section. The ontology is still under development.

4   Iuriservice: Application

Iuriservice is a web based application that retrieves answers to questions in the legal domain. It provides judges access to frequently asked questions through a natural language interface. The system responds with an ordered list of similar question-answer pairs that might solve the problem of the judge. The application can also be used as a traditional FAQ, by selecting questions from a list.

Fig. 5. User interface: getting a query

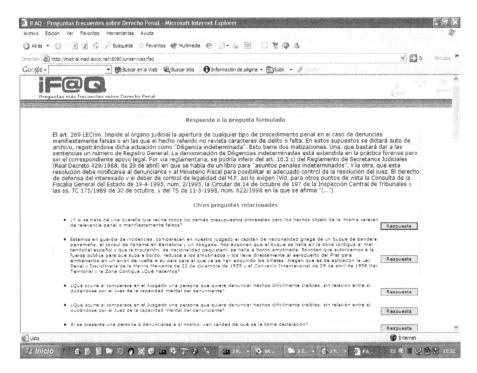

Fig. 6. User interface: an answer to a query

The technical objective of the iuriservice application is to match the user input (a question in natural language) *semantically* to the stored questions. The following three processes are involved:

- Analyze input sentence using NLP techniques and link terms in the sentence to the ontology.
- Calculate the semantic distance between the set of terms of the input sentence and the set of terms of the stored questions. This process is ontology-based.
- Prefer questions with maximum term coverage with respect to the input sentence.

4.1   Matching Algorithm

We designed a matching algorithm that considers the three factors mentioned above in order to calculate a measure for sorting questions and answers by semantic similarity.

NLP: Term Identification and Ontology Linking. The step first of the algorithm is to break down the input sentence into lemmas and POS (part of

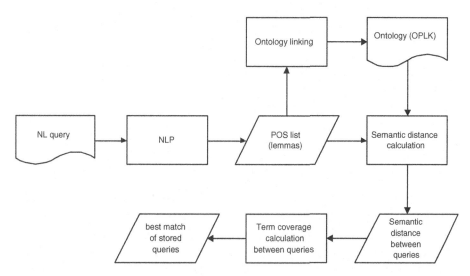

Fig. 7. Main steps of algorithm, indicating the processes and information involved. Rectangles indicate processes, diamonds denote information or data, and rectangles with one curly side represent inputs to the algorithm

speech) using NLP techniques. For Iuriservice, we have used the CLIC system [14] and the natural language software from Bitext (www.bitext.com). A lexical tokenizer breaks the user input into a list of words. Each word is recognized using a morphological analyzer based on tabular paradigm where all possible word forms are stored in a directly accessible table. The CLIC system for the Spanish language covers more than 1.100.000 words.

After the morphological analysis each word has associated a list of its possible part-of-speech categories together with lemmas. Only nouns, verbs, adjectives and adverbs are considered as meaningful and pass to the next step, in which we link the recognized lemmas to the domain ontology. Each instance of the ontology is associated with a list of lemmas indicative for that instance. This way of linking lemmas to the ontology is straightforward and effective when concepts are retrieved (as opposite to relations). In future versions we plan to use external general semantic lexicons such as WordNet [13] and EuroWordNet [15]. Another improvement concerns considering multi-word units or phrases, qualia structures [16], speech acts, etc.

Ontology-Based Semantic Distance Calculation. Once the input sentence has been reduced to a set of meaningful terms and each of them is linked to the ontology, the semantic distance is calculated between this set of terms and the corresponding sets of terms of the stored questions. The ontology plays an essential role in this process. The semantic distance is based on the weighted navigation distance between terms in the ontology. Navigation through the ontology means that one moves from one concept to another concept, via one of its

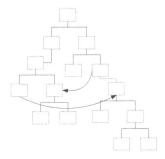

Fig. 8. Semantic distances in an ontology

relations or attributes. Traversing a relation or attribute has a related distance. For example, if one moves up the taxonomy (navigating the *is a* relationship, the more general term has a certain distance to the original term. Likewise, navigating from a concept representing a phase in a legal process, via the attribute, *follows* is associated with some distance cost. The semantic distance between two terms related through the attribute *synonym* is obviously 0. The distance between two actors that both are related to the same legal process would be lesser than the distance between actors of different processes. The task of associating distance costs to relation/attribute navigation, is a domain specific one, and thus needs to be performed by legal experts. Note that we can only navigate through attributes whose allowed value is a concept of the ontology.

In this way, we can determine the semantic distance between each pair of terms of the input sentence and the stored questions. The algorithm determines all possible paths from each input term to terms of the stored question. These path are list of concepts and attributes (relations) in the ontology. The semantic distance between two texts, then, is determined by the minimal distance between the terms they are composed of. Figure 8 illustrates an example of semantic distances in the ontology. This approach works well for small size ontologies, as is the case in this application. For larger ones there is a need for heuristics limiting the computational cost.

In [17], an analysis is presented related to semantic distance in Wordnet. First of all, they distinguish between semantic "relatedness" (hot-cold, wheel-car) and semantic "similarity" (home-house, plane-train). Obviously, we are interested in semantic *relatedness*. Budanitsky and Hirst analyze various algorithms for calculating semantic distances in Wordnet, using combinations of "path length", "link direction" (changing link type increases distance), "relative depth in taxonomy", "density", and "most-specific common subsumer". Links considered include "is-a", "part-of" and other Wordnet-specific relations. As described above, in our approach, we use a similar notion to path length whereby the steps of a path may have different costs depending on the domain ontology.

Term Coverage. Apart from considering semantic distance in the matching algorithm, also *term coverage* is considered. So far the algorithm achieves the following: terms of the input question are filtered by their part-of-speech category; only nouns, verbs, adjectives and adverbs are further considered. Each term is linked to the ontology if possible, and the algorithm constructs a semantic path from each input term to terms of the stored query. Based on this, we can calculated the semantic distance between any two fragments of text. Two situations need further elaboration.

- Terms which are linked to the ontology are domain-meaning carriers, and thus are important for calculating the semantic distance. When terms can be linked to the ontology, but no corresponding term (through ontological navigation) can be found in the stored questions, the semantic distance is considered infinitely large.
- When terms cannot be linked to the ontology, there are two possibilities. The terms of the input sentence have a corresponding term in the stored questions (e.g. with the same lemma), and thus the distance is zero. Or the input term cannot be covered (i.e. no corresponding lemma in the stored questions) and the distance is infinite.

Not covered terms introduce penalties in the overall matching algorithm. The penalty for a not covered term is more severe when the terms of the input sentence can be linked to the ontology, because those terms carry *legal* meaning. In other words, an infinite semantic distance is considered worse than two terms not being related lexically.

4.2   Implementation

The system's back-office allows the application administrator to perform two main functionalities. The first one is to manage the FAQ with updates (modify/add/remove) of existing questions and answers. The user has the possibility to evaluate the response after each interaction, confirming or rejecting the given answer. In this way, the system can provide suggestions as to make changes in the FAQ database.

The second functionality is related to the underlying ontology that describes the legal domain. We use Protégé 2000 as ontology tool [12]. Protégé is used to manage the ontology of professional legal knowledge legal practice ontology. Administrators are split into two groups:

- Ontology schema managers: in charge of defining new concepts, relations or attributes in the ontology. These are considered major changes.
- Instance Managers: responsible for updates (add/modify/remove) of instances according the defined schema.

We use a standard three-tier web architecture, consisting of a presentation layer (front end web pages), a persistence layer storing all FAQs, NLP resources and user information, and a business logic layer that contains navigation support, the matching algorithm and basic website functionalities.

5   Conclusions

In this paper, we have presented a FAQ system for judges in their first appointment. We have especially focused on the problems faced by newly appointed judges during their on duty period ("guardia"). To obtain the FAQs, a survey followed by extended fieldwork has been conducted. The system uses ontologies for calculating the semantic distance between user queries and stored FAQs. The ontology is based on professional legal knowledge, which we define as the knowledge shared by the members of a legal profession and conveyed through professional training and organizational means. The ontology considers knowledge about kernel procedural concepts such as "proceso" (process, procedures, proceedings). The ontology has been built with help from experienced magistrates of the Spanish Judicial School. The ontology is based on the description of a cognitive structure that all judges share to understand and manage the legal and practical problems that they usually have to face while they are on duty. However, this first description has still to be improved in order to refine the ontology.

Iuriservice is a multi-year, multi-organization effort aimed at providing intelligent IT support to professional judges. This paper reports on the first year. In future publications, we plan to report on (i) a national survey with recent judges in order to get more high-quality FAQs, (ii) experience of judges with the tool and (iii) integration of the tool with a new meta search engine for legal resources.

Acknowledgements

Part of this research has been carried out in the context of the projects "Observatorio de Cultura Judicial", SEC-2001-2581-C02-01/02 funded by the Spanish Ministry of Science and Technology, "Iuriservice: red telemática de soporte a los jueces en su primer destino, dependiente del Consejo General del Poder Judicial", PROFIT project nr. FIT-150500-2002-562, also funded by the Spanish Ministry of Science and Technology, and SEKT, project nr. IST-2003-506826, funded by the European Commission. We would like to thank the legal professionals that provided us with the required domain information, and in particular the "Consejo General del Poder Judicial" (Spanish General Council for Juridical Power).

References

1. Gruber, T.R.: A translation approach to portable ontology specifications. Knowledge Acquisition Journal **5** (1993) 199–220
2. Benjamins, V.R., Fensel, D., Decker, S., Gomez-Perez, A.: (KA)^2: Building ontologies for the internet: a mid term report. International Journal of Human-Computer Studies **51** (1999) 687–712

3. Bench-Capon, T.J.M.: Task neutral-ontologies, common sense ontologies and legal information systems. In: Proceedings of the Second International Workshop on Legal Ontologies, 13 December, University of Amsterdam. (2001) 15–19

4. Visser, P.R.S., Bench-Capon, T.J.M.: A comparaison of four ontologies for the design of legal knowledge sustems. In: Artificial Intelligence ad Law 6. (1998) 27–57

5. Stuckenschmidt, S., E, S., Schlieder, C.: Modeling land transactions: Legal ontologies in context. In: Proceedings of the Second International Workshop on Legal Ontologies, 13 December, University of Amsterdam. (2001) 58–66

6. Gangemi A., B.J.: Harmonizing legal ontologies. In: Gangemi A., Guarino N., Doerr M. (Ed.) Deliverable 3.4 IST-Project-2000-29243. Ontoweb. (2002)

7. Visser, P.R.S., T. J. M, B.C.: Ontologies in the design of legal knowledge systems; towards a library of legal domain ontologies. In: Applied Ontology. Proceedings of the Marvin Farber Conference on Law and Institutions in Society. Department of Philisiphy, SUNY, Buffalo, 24 April. (1998)

8. Zeleznikow, J., Stranieri, A.: An ontology for the construction of legal decision support systems. In: Proceedings of the Second International Workshop on Legal Ontologies, 13 December, University of Amsterdam. (2001) 67–76

9. Grüninger, M., Fox, M.: Methodology for the design and evaluation of ontologies. In: Proceedings of the Workshop on Basic Ontological Issues in Knowledge Sharing held in conjunction with IJCAI-95, Montreal, Canada (1995)

10. Schank, R.: Tell me a story. narrative and intelligence. In: Evanston I11: Northwestern Univ. Press. (1990)

11. D'Andrade, R.: The development of cognitive anthropology. In: Cambridge University Press. (1995)

12. (http://protege.stanford.edu/)

13. Miller, G.: Wordnet: A lexical database for english. In: Communications of the ACM 38(11). (1995) 39–41

14. (http://clic.fil.ub.es/)

15. Vossen, P., ed.: EuroWordNet A Multilingual Database with Lexical Semantic Networks. Kluwer Academic publishers (1998)

16. Pustejovsky, J.: The generative lexicon. In: MIT Press. (1995)

17. Budanitsky, A., Hirst, G.: Semantic distance in wordnet: An experimental, application-oriented evaluation of five measures. In: Workshop on WordNet and Other Lexical Resources, Second meeting of the North American Chapter of the Association for Computational Linguistics, Pittsburgh (2001)

NetCase: An Intelligent System to Assist Legal Services Providers in Transnational Legal Networks

Jesús Contreras[1] and Marta Poblet[2]

[1] Intelligent Software Components, S.A. (iSOCO),
Pedro de Valdivia 10, Bajos, 28006 Madrid
jcontreras@isoco.com
[2] Dep. de Ciencia Política i Pret Públic, Universitat Autònoma de Barcelona,
Facultat de Dret, Campus UAB, 08193 Bellaterra (Barcelona)
marta.poblet@uab.es

Abstract. Globalization and international trade have transformed the delivery of transnational legal services worldwide. Law firms face market competition through a variety of strategies, ranging from expansion in size, specialization of services, international alliances or creation of networks. Transnational legal networks (TLN) have emerged as one of those alternatives, but they face a number of organizational challenges: cross-referral of cases, knowledge management strategies, exchange of information, etc. The Netcase project aims at addressing those major challenges by proposing an intelligent system of automatic case forwarding within TLN. Netcase is able to analyze incoming cases and assign them to the most appropriate law firms and lawyers. The selection is based on law firm specialties, availability of resources, and lawyers' skills. The model results in a central market where lawyers and law firms are skill producers, law firms are also skill containers, and legal cases are goods that need skills to be solved.

1 Introduction

Recent years have witnessed profound changes in the structure of domestic and international legal markets, both in quantitative and qualitative terms. The economic processes of globalization have fuelled both the restructuring of law firms and a massive diversification of traditional legal services. In the USA as well as in Europe, the legal market is transforming law firms from small collections of general practitioners to large business-like entities operating not only in their own local or national jurisdictions, but also expanding beyond those boundaries.

In Europe, the speed and magnitude of the changes are without historical precedent and they need to be framed within a context of growing economic integration and development of EU law. Despite segmentation of legal markets and the difficulties of harmonizing legal professions throughout Europe, cross-border legal practice has become routine. Furthermore, foreign auditing and mega law firms have entered massively the European market and compete successfully as legal service providers

V.R. Benjamins et al. (Eds.): Law and the Semantic Web, LNCS 3369, pp. 218–232, 2005.

with domestic law firms. To face formidable competitors such as the American and London-based megafirms, or the Big Five accounting firms—the Final Four,[1] after the disintegration of Andersen in the wake of the Enron scandal in 2001—local firms have developed new forms of organization, work methods, and strategies to market legal services. Partnerships, mergers, and, especially, networking of small and middle firms are in their heyday.

Our purpose in this chapter is threefold. First, we will take stock of recent global trends and strategies to deliver legal services in an international context, with a closer attention to the European market. Second, we will provide a more detailed analysis of what we refer as transnational legal networks (TLN). Finally, we will use the description of TLN to present NetCase, an intelligent system facilitating automatic cross-referral and case-forwarding within TLN.

2 Legal Markets and Global Trends

Despite the slowdown of global economy in 2001, the growth of international trading for most of the past decade has inevitably led to an increasing demand of transnational legal services. Compared to other services, the legal profession has been affected to a lesser extent by the slowdown in corporate activity [1]. The main areas of legal work include corporate and commercial law (mergers and acquisitions, company law, corporate restructuring, etc.), tax law, capital markets, banking, insurance law, ICT law, private international law, and so forth. From 1997 to 2002, the head count of the top 50 law firms grew by 51 percent, while revenue increased by 62 percent [1]. In general, legal markets are forecast to grow in different world areas, as Table 1 shows.

Table 1. Legal Services Market Forecast (2002-2007)

	Expected Percent Growth	Expected Value in 2007 (US $)
China	65,3	2066 million
Japan	67	1,6 billion
Australia	38	8,5 billion
UK	14	16,5 billion
France	37	20,2 billion
US	21	200 billion

Source: [2]

As the trend towards delivering legal services in a cross-national scale continues, some tendencies have been identified at the global level:

---

[1] These are PriceWaterhouseCoopers, Ernst & Young, KPMG and Deloitte Touche Tohmatsu.

a) Creation of a new lex mercatoria "constructed from below, bottom-up from the legal work done to solve problems for individual clients, as well as top-down through standard-setting bodies [3].

b) Expansion of law firm sizes. In the last decades corporate law firms have exploded in size ([4], [5], [6]) both at the national and supranational levels, easily employing more than 1,000 lawyers. The drive to expand has been explained in terms of internal organizational structure ([4], [5], [7]) and internal growth, merger movements, and external increased demand for larger legal projects [6].

c) Consolidation of law firms as professionally managed business organizations in a competitive environment. Growing competition for legal markets has provoked a shift in paradigm [8] by turning traditional law firms into "hybrid entities by necessity" that are forced to combine a profession and a business component [9]. The partnership model of traditional law firms tends to be replaced by Limited Liability Partnerships (LLP) "employing managers and marketing directors, and creating business plans and financial strategies to maximize efficiency in profit making" [9]. Careful cost accounting and a drive to maximize profitability are often viewed as the key to measure success.

d) Leading position of internationalized American and UK law firms. Whether accounting-based or law-based, the overwhelming dominance of those firms, especially in international financial transactions, is out of discussion. As a result, US-UK megafirms are not only "international standard-setters in terms of size, specialization, (…), foreign expansion, administration, and aggressive marketing of their services" [10] but American and English laws prevail in an increasing number of areas:

> Law is domestic by definition, which has meant that truly global law firms have been very difficult to assemble. At the present time, however, U.S. law (and to a lesser extent English law) and legal approaches are essential materials for international business transactions. American concepts are the basis for drafting contracts and for contract enforcement mechanisms, including arbitration and alternative dispute resolution, as well as the approaches to the regulation of securities, the environment, trade, and antitrust. Even international human rights law, also with a major U.S. component, has become a central concern for both states and international businesses. It is now difficult to be a successful corporate lawyer anywhere without a facility in U.S. law and legal approaches. This new landscape provides huge opportunities for global U.S. law firms and their counterparts based in the U.K. It is hard to see any imminent threat to the global power of these firms and their methods of doing business [8].

Table 2 confirms this point. Both in terms of gross revenues and numbers of lawyers, the ranking of major law firms in the word is exclusively topped by US-UK based firms:

The global trend toward consolidation of law firms across borders is particularly pronounced in Europe, where "Big Four" law affiliates are major providers of both legal and accounting services in several countries. By 2001, four of the six largest law

Table 2. Top Law Firms in the World

2003 Rank	2002 Rank	Firm Name	Headquarters	Gross Revenue (million $)	Number of Lawyers
1	1	Clifford Chance	UK-International	1,467	1294
2	2	Skadden, Arps, Slate, Meagher & Flom	US- New York	1,310	1827
3	3	Freshfields Bruckhaus Deringer	UK-International	1,200	1135
4	5	Linklaters	UK-International	1,080	1145
5	4	Baker & McKenzie	US-International	1,060	3214
6	6	Allen & Overy	UK-International	970.5	1205
7	7	Jones Day	US-National	908	2136
8	8	Latham & Watkins	US-National	906	1624
9	9	Sidley Austin Brown & Wood	US-National	831	1559
10	14	Mayer, Brown, Rowe & Maw	US-National	705	1376
11	10	Shearman & Sterling	US-New York	700	1089
12	12	Weil, Gotshal & Manges	US-New York	688	1125
13	11	White & Case	US-International	675	1681
14	17	McDermott, Will & Emery	US-National	628	1002
15	16	Sullivan & Cromwell	US-New York	624	745
16	20	Kirkland & Ellis	US-Chicago	611	958
17	18	Akin Gump Strauss Hauer & Feld	US-National	575	977
18	15	Davis Polk & Wardwell	US-New York	570	689
19	19	Gibson, Dunn & Crutcher	US-Los Angeles	569	784
20	23	O'Melveny & Myers	US-Los Angeles	565	974
21	26	Lovells	UK-International	562.5	787
22	13	Morgan, Lewis & Bockius	US-National	557.5	1196
23	21	Simpson Thacher & Bartlett	US-New York	543.5	744
24	22	Cleary, Gottlieb, Steen & Hamilton	US-New York	531	831
25	25	Holland & Knight	US-National	514.5	1164

Sources: [11], [12]

firms in France were affiliated with Big Five firms [13]. By 2003, after the demise of Andersen, three of the seven Spanish largest firms remain affiliated to the Big Four. But these leading positions are generally shared with London and American-based firms. Freshfields ranked first in Germany and Italy (2003) and six in France (2002); Clifford Chance ranked three in Germany (2003) five in France (2002) and six in Spain and Italy (2003). The Spanish ranking of law firms clearly reflects this European pattern:

Table 3. Top Law Firms in Spain (2003)

Law Firm	Gross revenue (mill. €)	% benefits (2002-2003)	Number of lawyers
Garrigues*	164.00	2.5	1,258
Cuatrecasas	121.70	7.04	551
Uría & Menéndez	92.98	11.15	288
Landwell-PwC	68.60	1.33	595
Ernst & Young	52.10	0.77	359
Clifford Chance	43.60	13.36	140
KPMG	39.50	3.27	294
Gómez-Acebo & Pombo	37.00	10.12	170
Baker & McKenzie	36.20	8.38	153
P&A	35.73	18.35	237

*Garrigues had been merged with Andersen from 1997 to 2002
Source: [14]

e) As the practice of law is increasingly transactional, arbitration, mediation, and negotiation become prominent methods of delivering legal services. Although arbitral justice and non-adjudicative mechanisms of resolving disputes enjoy a venerable reputation among international trade agents [15], law firms have developed sophisticated ADR techniques as a cost-effective and flexible way of dealing with transnational cases [16] and leaving aside traditional litigation. London, one of the neuralgic centers of international dispute resolution, holds up to 5,000 international arbitrations and mediations per year [1]. Ultimately, the emergence of online dispute resolution (ODR) providers (governments, international bodies, consumer organizations, business organizations, law firms, etc.) is likely to expand the avenues of ADR services [17].

f) Advances in information technologies. Law firms and legal services organizations in general are knowledge-intensive organizations which produce huge amounts of information and data. In 1988, Klein predicted in the *American Lawyer* that:

> Eventually, through artificial intelligence, computers will be able to economically and efficiently scan documents, accurately convert them into digital data, and then analyze those documents for the appropriate legal issue. Computers will also extract the key points of a document, write a summary, classify the document, and file it" [18].

For the last decades, ICT applied to law firms was primarily inward looking, with the focus on creating, storing, and retrieving standardized documents and developing internal case management systems (CMS). But the increasing need to move data across organizations to provide transnational legal services in a rapid, cost-effective manner has made time ripe for implementing advanced ICT solutions.[2] As in many other areas, therefore, "system developers are moving their core technologies away from desktop/LAN environments and toward Internet database environments" [20]. Large firms such as Clifford Chance or Linklaters have already implemented integrated web-based systems for their lawyers and their clients to access documents and share information anywhere in the world—i.e. virtual filing, FAQs to lawyers, syndicated loans, etc. [1].

3 Alternative Ways of Delivering Legal Services

The trends highlighted above result in different ways for law firms to tackle the competitive market of legal services. Although different theoretical models have been applied [21], there are fewer attempts to set an empirical typology of law firms' strategies. In this line, Maney [22] has referred to five alternative ways of delivering legal services in an international context:

1. The "London model". Following the strategy of the leading London-based firms, law firms under this model get into cross-border mergers but keep operating as a single brand. They offer a blend of both civil and common law lawyers able to provide home country legal expertise as well as international law advise. The "London model" law firms may charge the highest rates of the current legal market: approximately £500 (or about $725) an hour.
2. The "niche model". This model is adopted by small firms that prefer to complement large firms in a particular practice area (i.e. doing litigation in local or national courts) rather that compete with them. They may also specialize as small boutiques in areas such as planning, zoning, immigration law, etc. "Niche model" firms usually bill their clients at a lower rates and may have billing practices that are tailored to the client specific needs and the home country legal culture [23].
3. The "targeted focus model". This model includes firms focusing on particular areas of practice and developing capabilities in just some limited areas. Instead of mergers, firms look for individual lawyers with outstanding expertise to train them in the law firm culture, bring them into the firm and then offer them an international partnership.
4. The "best friends/good friends model": Under this model firms remain independent and establish "preferred relationships" with other independent firms from other jurisdictions on a non-exclusive basis (they may establish preferred relations with more than one firm in a given jurisdiction to expand the choice of referrals).

---

[2] But one has to remain cautious at this point. In a research on Norwegian law firms, the hypothesis according to which "the greater the importance of knowledge to a law firm, the greater the extent of information technology use to support knowledge management" was not supported, perhaps because the direct link suggested between importance of knowledge and IT use for KM requires a different formulation [19].

5. The "association model". Association of independent firms may consist of networks between large law firms, middle size firms, or specialized boutiques. Membership is usually established through formal criteria, either on exclusive or non exclusive bases. In this regard, this model seems to be compatible with each of the former strategies [24]. While keeping their independence, networked firms normally operate under a common brand. At present, the Martindale on-line directory lists 114 law associations operating around the world.

Table 4. Transnational Legal Networks by Size (2004)

TLN	Firms	Lawyers	Countries	Offices
Lex Mundi	161	15000	99	560
Terralex	145	12000	93	N.A.
World Law Group	49	10000	37	N.A.
Eurojuris	650	5000	17	650
Interlaw	121	5000	50	120
Techlaw	15	5000	24	118
TagLaw	125	4600	70	245
Multilaw	62	4500	47	120
Globalaw	70	2600	65	102
Legal Network International	34	2300	25	50

Source: [25], [26]

We consider Translational Legal Networks (TLN) as falling within the association model.[3] In this regard, TLN may be described as organizations consisting of multiple locally-based law firms specializing in their own national, regional, and local law systems (one or more per jurisdiction) which create formal systems of cross-referral work.

The configuration of TLN exemplifies the new challenges of law practice in a number of relevant ways. TLN emerge as an organizational alternative to the global law firm: while preserving the autonomy of local firms, they target broader markets to cover the needs of their clients. As Garth & Silver (2002: 935) put it:

---

[3] In 2000-2001, the Sociolegal Studies Group of the Autonomous University of Barcelona (GRES-UAB) carried out a preliminary survey on law associations. We interviewed eleven representatives of law firms associated to different European and global networks, focusing on both quantitative and qualitative questions (access to membership, size of the association, organization of the network, number of referrals, average value of cases, etc.). These preliminary results revealed that law firm associations had many different sizes, membership requirements, and inner structures. Most associations, for instance, were non-exclusive, that is, allowed their members to belong to other associations, while few of them required exclusive membership. Some of them targeted large firms in different jurisdictions, while others preferred mid-size firms as members. Some associations had permanent professional staff, while others were run out of the office of the president or chair of the moment. The "association model", in sum, happened to be split in different "association models."

Globalization challenges law firms to be more open and international, and at the same time less imperialistic. In the global competition to provide professional services, which includes such tasks as setting up a business and making initial introductions, handling human relations issues, and meeting environmental requirements, the truly international firm, whether accounting- based or law-based, may have tremendous advantages. Such a firm presents a very strong challenge to U.S.-based law firms and the U.S. legal profession. That does not mean that all law firms must go global in this sense in order to succeed, but it means once again that the competitive pressures of globalization—all other things being equal—favor the firms that can operate successfully from many local bases.

This is consistent with the advantages of the association model indicated by Anduri (2002): (i) getting global support without giving up local control; (ii) attracting new clients without having to open or maintain additional offices abroad; (iii) gaining flexibility to access firms and offices that are best for a particular case or assignment. In sum, TLN allow associated law firms to expand contacts and market penetration. In contrast, Anduri also remarks the potential pitfalls of the model: (i) risk of being little more than a directory listing, and (ii) limited utility of membership dues (as payment for a directory listing) which may lead to disengagement.

Apart from articulate flexible rules and organizational strategies to govern themselves—access to membership, fees, referral systems, assurance of quality standards, marketing strategies, liability issues, etc.—TLN need to apply and develop new information technologies to share and manage both their local know-how and their segmented expertise. Most TLN already have a full range of communication devices at work: web sites, newsletters, databases and directories, e-mail addresses, etc. that make it easy to make referrals. All of these devices facilitate enormously the delivery of international legal services under a "global brand". Among the most important challenges that TLN have to face, nevertheless, are how to establish intelligent case forwarding systems that further increase referral potential and provide cost-effective strategies of communication between members of the network. Another important aspect is how to identify interdisciplinary teams of lawyers to deal with complex transnational cases in a very short amount of time.

The NetCase project brings together experts in Artificial Intelligence and networks, information technologies, decision-making, and legal organizations. The main objectives of the project are:

- Establishing a standardized system of cross-referral and exchange of information for TLN
- Providing quick answers to any client in any node of the network
- Achieving competitive advantages, since the system can be run without a large investment in professional staff (the outside support is minimal)
- Contributing to the development of the "global brand" of TLN

4   NetCase: Intelligent System for Cross-Referral and Case-Forwarding

The case life in any legal organization (and TLN are not an exception) contains administrative, content, and knowledge cycles. The administrative (including contractual, billing, commercial, etc.) cycle is currently fully supported by commercial tools. The content management cycle is similarly covered by well proven systems that allow for efficient case retrieval and storage. The knowledge management part, in contrast, is the less covered part in the everyday work of legal firms. In everyday practice, this task relies on experimental workers, lawyers who use their experience to manage incoming cases according to their content and features.

The Netcase tool allows for automating the assignment process according the legal features of both the case and law firms. The assignment process includes tasks of analysis of the incoming case and selection of the most appropriate law firm or lawyers' team. The selection is made according to both law firm specialties and availability of resources for the concrete case resolution. To perform the selection in an automatic and objective way an underlying model of the case and law firms is therefore required.

The Netcase project includes the following functionalities:

- An automatic legal case analysis
- A management tool for cases and node description in terms of their features and skills
- An automatic case forwarding to net nodes according to the case features and node skills

4.1   Domain Modeling

The essential part of the Netcase application is the underlying model that allows for automatic case assignment. There are three basic concepts in the model:

- The legal case
- The law firm
- The lawyer

All of the concepts are characterized by capabilities or skills. We use the consumer and producer metaphor for the assignment procedure. The assignment occurs in a so called central market. Lawyers are skill producers: they are able to offer their skills to the central market. They are organized in law firms that become skill containers. In this way each law firm becomes also a skill producer. In the opposite site of the central market there are the legal cases that need of skills to be solved.

4.1.1   The Skills – The Goods
A skill reflects the knowledge and/or capacity a person has to perform a certain task. Skills can refer to law-specific knowledge, such as 'Maritime Law' or 'Criminal Law'. Skills can be organized in a skill hierarchy, where higher-level skills are more general than lower-level skills. Higher-level skills are used to categorize the lower-level skills. It is not the case that a parent skill is defined by its children skills; rather

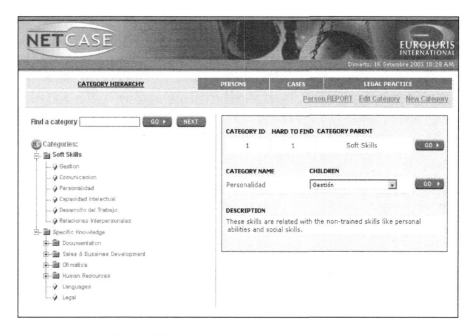

Fig. 1. Skill hierarchy with description of skill levels

it is the other way around: the children are defined through their parent. Fig. 1 illustrates a skill hierarchy for a non-existing company.

As can be seen in the left part of Fig 1, there is defined a taxonomy of existing and interesting skills for Netcase purposes. The right part illustrates an explanation of what the different levels of a skill mean in terms of capacities. 'Scarceness of skill' reflects how difficult it is to find the skill on the labour market. Such skill hierarchies can be obtained from various locations, for free or paid, or developed in-house.

4.1.2 The Lawyers – The Producers

Skills are owned by people. In the knowledge economy, knowledge workers apply their skills to perform tasks that are part of projects of assignments. In this sense, lawyers can be considered as knowledge producers, whereas the cases are knowledge consumers. The values of the skills are expressed in levels, reflecting their rate of mastering. On a five-point scale, the levels could mean: 1: beginner, 2: can work with significant support, 3: can work independently, 4: advanced, 5: expert. Other scales are possible (e.g. 3-point, 7-point, 10-point) depending on the granularity needed. It is important that the persons who associate skill levels to people (the lawyers themselves, their peers, managers, etc.) apply the same criteria, otherwise the results will reflect more personal opinions rather than intellectual capital. Apart from levels, people usually have a degree of interest in a skill expressing their attitude towards elaborating the skill. Fig. 2 illustrates the skills of a particular lawyer acquired through self-evaluation.

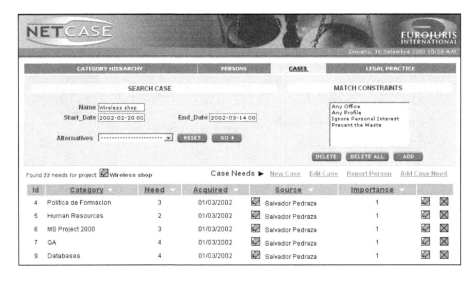

Fig. 2. Skill needs belonging to a case with their corresponding level, acquisition date, source and interest level

4.1.3   The Cases - The Consumers

On the opposite side of the central market, there are the cases that play the role of skills consumers. They need a set of skills with some degree and importance to be solved. The vocabulary used to express those requirements is defined through the skill hierarchy.Thus for example, a case could need a specific skill like 'adoption law' with level 3 and with importance: 5 (on a five-point scale). This would mean that for the particular case, intermediate knowledge of adoption law is required, and the importance that this skill be present in the case team is very high (i.e. its non-presence may lead to severe problems in case resolution).

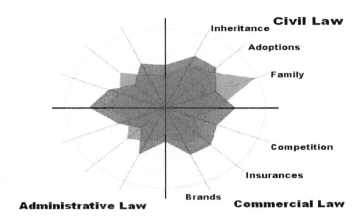

Fig. 3. Graphical visualization of knowledge coverage. The two areas represent the coverage of the required knowledge with the available knowledge. For example: the family law skills are not covered by the assignment

4.2 The Market Mechanism – Matchmaking

Since we have implemented the approach in a software program, we have created an electronic online marketplace of knowledge. Producers and consumers can now be brought together through a matchmaking algorithm. We have designed an algorithm able to deal with approximate matches when no perfect matches exist. The algorithm considers the following factors:

- The skills needed versus offered
- The skill level needed versus offered
- The importance of the skill required
- The agents who introduced the skill level

If there are several agents who evaluated a skill of a lawyer, a weighted average is taken based on a hierarchy of permissions: the higher in the hierarchy, the more weight the evaluation of that agent has. The algorithm can be parameterised on the following points:

- The availability of the producers (e.g. lawyers not assigned to other cases)
- Ignore, prevent or penalize higher skill levels than required
- Consider or ignore the interest of the persons in the skill
- Consider or ignore other relevant factors as location, opportunity cost, etc.

Any user with the required permissions can perform this parameterisation through the web-based interface. The factors mentioned above are considered in the current application. However, one could add any constraint useful for a particular organization as long as the needed knowledge is stored somewhere in a corporate database.

The essence of the algorithm can be described as follows. For each skill-level required (to consume), we find all lawyers having that skill (whatever its level). A person having (to produce) all the skills with the required level will obtain a high ranking. Persons covering fewer skills or inferior levels, have lower ranking. The ranking is based on the contribution of the producer to the consumer's need.

4.3 Usage of Netcase and Ongoing Work

Netcase application implements several use cases that allows users managing skills and capacities. The most common one helps the user assigning a case to a law office.

4.4 The Software Program

The tool is based on Java technologies, using Java servlets, JSP, J2EE, JDBC and Javascript. It is a web-based architecture consisting of the following components, and illustrated in Fig. 4. We have used open source software such as the Resin application server (http://www.caucho.com/), the Postgress Object-Relational database management system (http://www.postgresql.org/). However, the tool also works with other application servers and DBMS. The visualization software is based on Java Webstart (http://java.sun.com/products/javawebstart/).

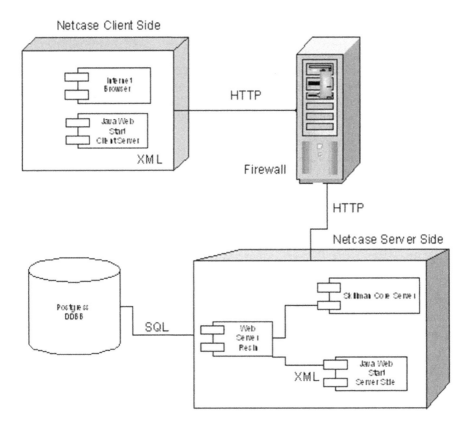

Fig. 4. Architecture of Netcase

One of the principles we have applied in developing the tool is *non-intrusiveness*. We believe firms are tired of the significant implications software acquisition can have on their existing information structure and business processes. Those implications carry with them a large risk; both technological and social (change management). With this principle in mind, Netcase is designed to run on Windows and Linux platforms, and with MS Internet Explorer and Netscape. It integrates with existing corporate information systems in order to use already available data in the organization.

Acknowledgements

Part of this research has been carried out in the context of the project ``NETCASE: diseño de un sistema de software para la gestión de servicios jurídicos en redes transnacionales (PROFIT, FIT-150500-2003-152) funded by the Spanish Ministry of Science and Technology.

References

1. International Financial Services: Legal Services (2003) [available at http://www.ifsl.org.uk]
2. Euromonitor International: Major Market Profiles (2004) [available at http://www.euromonitor.com]
3. McBarnet, D.: Transnational Transactions: Legal Work, Cross-border Commerce and Global Regulation. In: Likosky, M. (ed.) Transnational Legal Processes, Butterworths Lexis-Nexis, London (2002) 98-113
4. Galanter, M., Palay, T.: Why the Big Get Bigger: The Promotion-to-Partner Tournament and the Growth of Large Law Firms, Virginia Law Review 76 (1990) 747-811
5. Galanter, M., Palay, T.: The Many Futures of the Big Law Firm, South Carolina Law Review 45 (1994) 905-928
6. Thomas, R. S., Schwab, S. J., Hansen, R. H.: Megafirms, North Carolina Law Review 80 (2001) 115-198
7. Galanter, M., Palay, T.: A Little Jousting about the Big Law Firm Tournament, Virginia Law Review 84 (1998) 1683-1693
8. Garth, B., Silver, C.: The MDP Challenge in the Context of Globalization, Case Western Reserve Law Review 52 (2002) 903-942
9. Adams, E. S.; Albert, S.: Law Redesigns Law: Legal Principles as Principles of Law Firm Organization", Rutgers Law Review 51 (1999) 1133-1206
10. Silver, C.: Globalization and the U.S. Market in Legal Services: Shifting Identities, Law & Policy International Business 31 (2000) 1093-1150
11. American Lawyer Media: The 2003 Global 100 (2003)
12. Legal500.com: The Legal 500 Series (2003) [available at http://www.legal500.com/index.php]
13. Daly, M.: Monopolist, Aristocrat, Or Entrepreneur?: A Comparative Perspective on the Future of Multidisciplinary Partnerships in the United States, France, Germany, and the United Kingdom after the Disintegration of Andersen Legal," Washington University Law Quarterly 80 (2002) 589-648
14. Expansión: Ránking Anual de Despachos de Abogados (2004) 47
15. Dezalay, I., Garth, B.: Dealing in Virtue: International Commercial Arbitration and the Construction of a Transnational Legal Order, The University of Chicago Press, Chicago (1996)
16. Pfeifer, M., Drolshammer, J.: Introduction: On the Way to a Globalized Practice of Law?!, European Journal of Law Reform 2 (2000) 391-403
17. Rabinovich-Einy, O.: The Ford-Firestones of the Future: Resolving Offline Disputes in an Online Society. In A. R. Lodder et al. (eds.): Essays on Legal and Technical Aspects of Online Dispute Resolution, Papers from the ICAIL 2003 ODR Workshop, June 28, 2003, Edinburgh, Scotland, UK, Amsterdam: CEDIRE: 37-50
18. Klein, L.: Applying Artificial Intelligence to Litigation, American Lawyer (1988) 12
19. Gottschalk, P.: Knowledge Management in the Professions: The Case of IT Support in Law Firms, Proceedings of the 33rd Hawaii International Conference on System Sciences, IEEE (2000) 1-10
20. Holmes, J.: The Technological Revolution for Legal Services Organizations May Change your Practice, Texas Bar Journal 65 (2002) 496-498
21. Silver, C.: Regulatory Mismatch in the International Market for Legal Services, Northwestern Journal of International Law and Business 23 (2003) 487-550

22. Maney, M., *et al.*: How Lawyers and Firms Are Positioning Themselves to Serve International Clients in Today's Environment. In: Delivery of International Legal Services in the Coming Decade, Annual Meeting of the International Law and Practice Section of the NYSBA, International Law Practicum 15 (2002) 67-100

23. Zulack, J. F.: The Niche Model. In: Maney, M., et al., How Lawyers and Firms Are PositioningThemselves to Serve International Clients in Today's Environment. In : Delivery of International Legal Services in the Coming Decade, Annual Meeting of the International Law and Practice Section of the NYSBA, International Law Practicum 15 (2002) 67-100

24. Anduri, C.: The Association Model. In: Maney, M., *et al.*: How Lawyers and Firms Are Positioning Themselves to Serve International Clients in Today's Environment. In: Delivery of International Legal Services in the Coming Decade, Annual Meeting of the International Law and Practice Section of the NYSBA, International Law Practicum 15 (2002) 67-100

25. Martindale-Hubbell: International Law Directory, Lexis-Nexis (2003)

26. GRES-UAB unpublished research on transnational legal networks (2001)

No Model Behaviour: Ontologies for Fraud Detection

John Kingston, Burkhard Schafer, and Wim Vandenberghe

Joseph Bell Centre for Forensic Statistics & Legal Reasoning, School of Law,
University of Edinburgh, Edinburgh EH8 9YL
www.josephbell.org

Abstract. This document discusses the status of research on detection and prevention of financial fraud undertaken as part of the IST European Commission funded FF POIROT (**F**inancial **F**raud **P**revention **O**riented **I**nformation **R**esources using **O**ntology **T**echnology) project, and in particular the interplay of, and tension between, modelling factual and legal aspects of a case.

1 Introduction

It is estimated that the EU loses hundreds of millions euro per year due to financial fraud. Therefore it should not come as a surprise that prevention and early detection of fraudulent activity is an increasingly important goal for the EU and its Member States. To this end, the FF POIROT (**F**inancial **F**raud **P**revention **O**riented **I**nformation **R**esources using **O**ntology **T**echnology) project follows in the footsteps of the fictional detective Hercule Poirot to provide law enforcement agencies with a novel approach to solve the financial fraud problem.[1] The goal of the project is to build a detailed ontology in the financial fraud domain of European Law, preventive practices and knowledge of the processes of financial fraud within the European Union. This paper discusses the fraud problem in general terms and outlines the approaches being taken by the FF POIROT project to developing relevant and useful solutions. In the final part, we compare the performance of a selection of existing core ontologies against the specifications developed in the first part.

Global markets and the ubiquitous interconnectivity of systems and information processes in cyberspace that they bring with them have dramatically increased our awareness of the problems created by conceptual mismatches and failing system interoperability. For the question of crime investigation and prevention, this poses both a challenge and an opportunity. Global markets provide new opportunities for criminals. VAT fraud, one of the applications investigated in the project, is essentially a cross-border crime, because it takes advantage of EU regulations regarding intra-community trade. Internet based investment fraud, the other application, is a remote crime, allowing criminals to hide behind jurisdictional boundaries. Efficient investigation of these crimes requires interoperability of police databases across state

---

[1] This work was supported under the IST project FF POIROT (Financial Fraud Prevention Oriented Information Resources using Ontology Technology), which is sponsored by the European Union's Information and Systems Technology Directorate (5th framework) under grant number IST-2001-38248.

V.R. Benjamins et al. (Eds.): Law and the Semantic Web, LNCS 3369, pp. 233–247, 2005.

boundaries [14]. At the same time, both private and public sector initiatives have dramatically increased the amount of commercial information available (in principle) online, information that can play a vital role in crime investigation and prevention. When in the past, fraudulent companies claimed to be registered and regulated in exotic and far away places, they counted on the prohibitively high transaction costs for their victims to verify these claims. These days, the necessary information is often only a mouse click away. A British investor or police investigator could for instance ascertain if a suspicions company is really registered in Germany by searching a website like the one provided by the Swiss-German Chamber of Commerce - provided s/he speaks sufficient German, and has a basic grasp of German law and business culture. A German investor conversely will soon be able to check online if business premises in Edinburgh which are offered as security are really owned by the prospective business partner. However, to make appropriate use of this facility, he needs to have a rather profound understanding of the "'ontology' or conceptualization of Scots property law, many aspects of which only match imperfectly his own legal categories. He would need to understand e.g. the difference between Sasine and Land register, how to combine information from both of them, or the different approaches to the concept of 'publicity' of the register in Germany and Scotland. Ontology driven skills management systems like the one envisaged here are developed as part of the semantic web initiative to develop machines that can interpret and appropriately combine this information [16, 1].

2   User Requirements for Fraud Ontologies

2.1   Features of Fraud

Fraud cases are notorious for their complexity. While the law is quite often comparatively simple, the facts and evidence surrounding a fraud can be highly complex, not the least because complexity is a way of concealment for fraudsters. Therefore, the ontology has to be able to manage and control the masses of data that can be gathered during financial fraud investigations. This can aid the investigator in focusing on relevant areas of law, on the relevant facts in issue and on the links and associations inherent in the evidence. Some associations between hypotheses, law and facts in a fraud model may be obvious, but others may be less obvious, so simply modeling these relations is an important part of investigative methodology.

As financial fraud is a very broad field, the FF POIROT project has selected two specific sub-domains that exist in the fraud area: cross-border Value Added Tax fraud within the EU and unauthorized online investment solicitation. This paper will focus on the latter; the user partner for this work is CONSOB,[2] the public authority responsible for regulating the Italian securities market (a similar body to the UK's Financial Service Authority The purpose of securities regulatory authorities is to protect investors from unfair, abusive or fraudulent practices, and fostering fair, efficient and competitive capital markets that will provide investment opportunities and access to capital. To this end CONSOB is analyzing investment scams on the World Wide Web and developing appropriate software.

---

[2] Commissione Nazionale per le Societa' e la Borsa (http://www.CONSOB.it).

2.2 Present Approach

What key features and requirements of the financial fraud ontology are important from the user's point of view? This section will set out a systematic requirements analysis by identifying and documenting the main needs of fraud investigators.

The main objective for CONSOB is a systematic and scalable "web crawler" procedure that enables the user to detect more fraud with fewer false positives. We can distinguish here two related tasks for CONSOB: first, there is the *identification* of fraud. After a fraudulent website has been identified, there is the possibility for legal *sanctions*, which requires developing a case that can withstand legal scrutiny. For the first activity, the user requires in principle (only) *intelligence* (in the sense of information). For the second task, he requires *evidence* that is intelligence that was obtained in legally permissible ways, observes other procedural rules and is convincing enough to fulfil the respective burdens of proof. The first task is necessary for the second, but it is not sufficient for it. Consequently, the requirements for the first task are less demanding that that for the second, although they should already take some it into account; there is little sense for CONSOB to identify fraudulent websites on the sole basis of legally inadmissible information. For the first activity, the user requires as a tool an unassisted agent that crawls the net and flags up warnings if it hits a suspicious website. For the second task, the information that the agent reports back is but one input into a knowledge management system that supports the investigator in preparing a legally sound case, e.g. by directing him to other sources that need to be consulted to confirm the suspicion or to other types of evidence that are required by law.

CONSOB's current procedure is fundamentally based on keyword-search using different Internet search engines (such as Altavista, Google, Yahoo, etc). The search result is a list of web sites whose content is investigated by CONSOB's inspection officers in order to analyse and identify market abuse phenomena, abusive provisions of investment services and unauthorised investment solicitation. The keywords are selected and combined to manually create complex queries based on the experience acquired during the ordinary supervision activity of the CONSOB's operative units. The use of the FF POIROT ontology in CONSOB's business case is related to the use of tools able to automate the query launching and to optimise the web information retrieval results. The web crawler should find sites on the web that are selling securities without relevant authorisation and ideally filter found pages to help prioritise likely fraudulent websites. The notion of 'relevance' and the task of prioritising hits require a rich semantic understanding of the website. Obvious 'spoofs', e.g. websites simulating frauds that are developed for entertainment purpose, should be eliminated, as should websites that offer fraudulent services, but are not within the jurisdiction of CONSOB because they don't target the Italian market. An automated tool therefore must be able to examine possible fraudulent websites, and the links included on that website.

Based on a literature review of financial fraud, we conducted a number of structured interviews with representatives from relevant user institutions. From these, we determined a set of user requirements. Fraud investigations are complex activities where a user infers from certain indicators (evidence) that certain actions have taken place (offence elements) which may or may not be labeled as specific crimes in a specific legal system. As an analytical tool, we used the epistemic framework of Wigmore to break down these complex activities into several levels of detail; broadly speaking, legal rules were decomposed into postulates, facts, and evidence that might match those facts [17, 23]. On the level of postulates or laws, the system needs to represent national and supranational law regarding online investment solicitation. This requirement amounts to a representation of how substantive law constructs the crime of fraud. In addition, we need to model procedural aspects of the investigation. This includes laws regarding enforcement authority and capabilities or laws relating to seizure of evidence. At its most basic, these procedural aspects are separate from the substantive aspects of fraud and enable the user e.g. to identify the correct agency in another country when asking for assistance. In the fraud domain however, procedural and substantive aspects can often interact. US law for instance recognizes a specific (substantive) crime of "lying to a federal agent" if this agent is in the process of investigating a crime (a question of procedural law). Below the level of legal conceptualizations are the actions that constitute the "offence elements" of fraud and their constituent parts. This involves firstly representing objects like services and products or commodities including highly complex financial products. Secondly, it requires representing commercial transactions in terms of a sale, lease, security etc. Thirdly, it requires the representation of actors and their roles, e.g. a vendor and a purchaser. Some of these actors are in turn complex entities and require modeling of their internal structure and parts, some of which are again going to be (possibly complex) actors e.g. companies which may or may not have other companies as shareholders. Finally, we have to represent indicators or evidence for the offence elements just described. This includes representation of fraud plans and consequent indicators of fraud, representations of websites, and certain relations between individuals (e.g. suspicious money transfers between husband and wife acting as separate one-person enterprises).

2.3 Structuring Fraud Cases with Wigmore Charts

The next part of this paper concentrates on the method used for breaking down two of the above requirements into sub-requirements. The requirements in question are the representation of laws regarding online investment solicitation and the representation of fraud plans and consequent indicators. The method used is that of "inference networks of law", in the tradition of Wigmore and Twining [17]. Inference networks of law are directed acyclic graphs for complex probabilistic reasoning tasks that are often based on masses of evidence [13]. This is highly useful because online investment fraud cases are notorious for huge data files to be investigated. Using a logical model to untangle complex scams and solve the complicated puzzles of crime can mean the difference between dead reckoning that can steer an investigator in the right direction and random guessing that can make things hopelessly confused. As importantly for our purpose however is that it helps to clarify how the different layers that we identified above interact in a concrete legal argument, and to develop appropriate systems of classification. Argumentation systems used this way become a heuristic tool for ontology development. It is only when looking at legal arguments in context that we can decide if a certain concept is a legal or factual i.e. if it raises questions of law or fact. In a multi-jurisdictional environment, this distinction is particularly important as facts are jurisdiction invariant while laws are not.[3] Wigmore is chosen here over the more familiar (for the AI community) Toulmin. Wigmore is primarily known as an evidence lawyer, and his "Treatise on Evidence", first published as early as 1904, is still highly influential especially in the US. It is at the same time a lawyer's manual of practice and an incisive and highly critical survey of the law of evidence. Despite his background in US evidence law, Wigmore has a strong interest in comparative law, as can be seen in his *Panorama of the World's Legal Systems* [22]; the way in which he incorporated ideas from different jurisdictions in his analysis of evidentiary reasoning make him an ideal starting point for our investigation. The diagrammatic representation of argumentation that he developed is intimately linked to the vocabulary and concepts of evidence law, and while it is possible that all the relevant relations could be expressed as well in a Toulmin system, the renewed interest in using Wigmore charts in legal education creates a familiarity with his approach that might help with the acceptance of the technology by evidence lawyers.

The main idea of the model is that fraud cases can be broken down into three distinct layers of information: a proposition (hypothesis) layer, a law layer and an evidence layer. Any case will therefore have a layer of information about the hypothesis or case theory, for example, (X Defrauded Y), a layer of information about specific elements of law that need to be satisfied if a case of fraud is to be proven and, thirdly, an evidence layer comprising all the material facts and evidence that go to make up the facts of the case. In the domain that we are considering, the ultimate intended aim is usually to make money by fraudulent means, and the laws that may be breached will normally be those CONSOB regulations relating to authorization of investment solicitation services. The actions that need to be undertaken to implement the fraud will be the steps in the fraud plan (which, in our domain, will always include "setting up a website" and "offering investment services"), and the actions that are actually seen (the carrying out of the fraud plan) must be demonstrated by evidence -- facts, testimonies, and other known indicators of fraud.

Based on his experience as an evidence lawyer, Wigmore emphasized the contextual and holistic nature of individual items of evidence. Evidence is not a collection of pure sense data, but tools used for a specific purpose in a specific context, and malleable to the interests of the user. Facts are evidence only insofar as they play a role in a teleologically directed argument (e.g. the argument *by the prosecutor* that a person should be punished). Evidence is hence inseparably linked with procedural and substantive legal provisions. Wigmore's method can therefore be understood as an analysis of the interaction between law and facts in complex cases through a process of "decomposition".

We tested this methodology on an actual case file of unauthorized online solicitation that occurred within the jurisdiction of the Italian financial market

---

[3] To complicate matters further, different legal system might draw the distinction between facts and laws differently. It has been argued that facts are therefore not jurisdiction-invariant; rather, for the purpose of legal ontologies, all facts should be seen as constructed by the respective legal systems (see [19] w.f.r.). In this paper, however, we will assume that there is a clear distinction between facts and laws.

regulated by CONSOB.[4] The company (whom we will call SX) with headquarters in the British Virgin Islands, has stated its aim to become an unofficial 24-hour stock exchange on which any company in the world can be listed at no charge. In return the investors are asked to purchase shares in SX, in exchange for a stake in the venture. Shares are then to be traded between partners in this unofficial stock exchange. Investors were solicited by a WWW Page advertising financial investment services (specifically, a public offering of participation certificates).

In order to establish the need to prevent this apparent fraud, it is necessary to consider whether CONSOB has appropriate jurisdiction. CONSOB considered that its jurisdiction was asserted as SX targeted the national investment market of Italy, even though the company's registered address and its director's addresses were all outside Italy.[5] Further investigation determined that the soliciting agent was not licensed to trade as required under Directive 93/22/EEC (and its implementation in Italy: CONSOB Legislative Decree 58) and false statements were made on the web page. Wigmore charts proved efficient at representing the legal and evidentiary reasoning underlying this assessment [9].

3 Ontology Building

In this part, we analyze how existing ontologies could be reused to fulfill the requirements that we identified analyzing fraud cases based on Wigmore charts.
A legal ontology is a kind of a proto-theory which indicates concepts that exist within the legal domain and how these concepts are related to one another. Legal core ontologies consist of concepts that are general for all legal domains. Concepts being captured by such legal core ontologies include agent, role, intention, document, norm, right, and responsibility. Thus, a legal core ontology mediates between a foundational (reference or upper-level) ontology and specific legal domain ontologies.

3.1 Legal Core Ontologies

A small number of legal core ontologies are available, and we will review three of them here. Valente's *functional ontology of law* (FOLaw), adopts a *functional* perspective of law [18]. The main function of a legal system is to regulate social behaviour (law as a social control system). By using this functional view of law, categories of legal knowledge are distinguished which are represented in the ontology. Another legal core epistemology is the ontology developed by Van Kralingen [20, 21]. This *frame-based ontology of law* (FBO) is decomposed into the generic legal ontology (norms, acts, concept descriptions) and the statute-specific ontology. Finally, the *LRI core ontology* (LRI-Core) [3,4] is being developed in the context of the E-court and E-power projects.[6] It includes Valente's FOLaw functional ontology, but differs from it by being a more generic ontology with reference to legal roles, procedures, documentation, communication and legal sources. In doing so, it

---

[4] See CONSOB delibera 12410 and 13305 (decisions are available – in Italian - at http://www.CONSOB.it).
[5] For an analysis of the jurisdictional aspects of the case, see [6].
[6] E-court (IST-2000-28199), http://www.intrasoft-intl.com/e-court. E-power (IST-2000-281250), http://www.lri.jur.uva.nl/research/epower.html

not only encompasses substantive law (as FOLaw already did), but also procedural law.

LRI-Core considers objects and processes to be the primary entities of the physical world, so that objects participate in processes, while processes transfer or transform energy. Mental entities are considered to behave in a manner which is largely analogous to physical objects. So facts (mental objects) exist and are stored in memory, and these facts may or may not be believed (mental process). The mental and physical world overlap in agents, and in time and space. Social organization and processes are composed of roles that are performed by agents; the law associates norms with these roles.

The next section will consider the applicability of the proposed ontologies (FOLaw, FBO, and LRI Core) to the knowledge categories of importance for the financial fraud ontology (captured by the user requirements analysis). In doing so, it will pay attention in particular to the re-usability of the above discussed ontological layers.

Van Kralingen & Visser's top level distinction between norms, acts and concepts seems to map well to the distinctions identified in our domain between laws, fraudsters' plans & actions, and supporting facts/evidence. The proposed properties of 'norms' layer in the FBO ontology are also useful for the legal fraud domain and its abundance of legal statutes and regulations, as are the properties of concepts, which allow determination of necessary and sufficient conditions – which maps well to the Wigmorean method used in the FF POIROT project. However, the two norm types (norm of conduct or norm of competence) are not sufficient to distinguish the wide array of EU law and its implementation by Member States in the fraud domain; for these laws differ in hierarchy (primary EU law, secondary EU law, national legislation, etc), applicability and in character (statutes, guidelines, etc) as well as in content.

Fraud cases typically involving multiple agents, often with multiple roles. There is the organizer, the co-organizer, 'strawmen', etc. Not all of them will be held accountable to the same extent. Valente's FOLaw ontology is capable of representing this diversity through its emphasis on agents; it is able to represent agents' responsibility, causation by agents, sanctions to be applied to agents who breach laws, and the creation of new agents. The last point is critical to a domain where agents may be discovered in the course of an investigation, or even hypothesised without ever being fully instantiated. Unfortunately, agents' actions and intentions can only be represented in a rather roundabout manner: actions must be represented as causal knowledge, and intentions by identifying that the agent is legally responsible as well as causally responsible. It may be that Valente considered that actions were already sufficiently well covered by existing ontologies of AI planning, but it would have been helpful if actions and intentions had been made more explicit in the FOLaw ontology. FF POIROT not only needs to represent fraudulent acts by fraudulent agents, but also to act through legal enforcement agents combating these fraudulent acts. The ontology is very capable of representing legal rules, however, with its helpful subdivision of norms into commanding norms, empowering norms and derogating/permitting norms.

The LRI-Core ontology is still under development, and is more general that the other ontologies studied here. However, the distinctions between mental objects and mental processes, with agents as physical and mental objects who have roles, and law as norms applied to roles, allows the FF POIROT project to represent fraud plans and intentions, actions to implement these plans, fraudsters as performers of these plans, and laws that apply to them. Even the motive of a fraudster can be represented via the energetic process category. Despite the fact that LRI-Core's notion of a legal role (judge, defence counsellor, clerk-of-court, etc) differs somewhat from the roles considered by FF POIROT (perpetrator, accomplice, actors unknowingly part of fraud, victim and investigators), it seems that LRI-Core is strong in the areas where FOLaw is weak.

In FBO, the concepts of 'aim of an action', 'cause for an action' and 'intentionality' would allow us to represent correspondingly fraud goals, fraud motives and the intention of the actor to commit fraud. Another strength of FBO is that it is able to represent the results and consequences of an action ('final state').

LRI-Core's central category of procedural law (conceptualized by the LRI developers as 'formal law') is useful to conceptualize the criminal procedural law in investigating financial fraud. It knows about 'hierarchy of authority' which is important if one has to represent for example who gives the authority to obtain information and access to premises and records in fraud cases. LRI is also capable of representing the structure of an organization, e.g. a fraud department (so-called 'has-as-part social roles'). However, as noted above, the distinction between procedural and substantive law might well be specific to individual legal systems, and LRI's category therefore placed at too high a level of abstraction.

Products or commodities consist of physical objects (goods) or conceptual objects (such as many financial products) that may be offered for sale. Since products are primarily financial rather than legal concepts (though they may be involved in legal concepts, if their ownership changes or is disputed, or if they are discovered to be not fit for purpose), they are not directly addressed by any of the legal ontologies investigated here. However, the concept descriptions suggested by FBO include categories for the "range of application" of a concept description and for the "conditions under which a concept is applicable", which is useful in identifying if a particular product is only useful or only available in a particular geographical area (e.g. Italy) or temporal span (e.g. financial futures). The other ontologies only consider products as peripheral concepts: in FOLaw, they may constitute the circumstances of a case (a sub-sub-category of world knowledge), while in LRI-Core, they are objects that participate in processes. This shortcoming is the main motivation behind the analysis of a financial ontology below.

The representation of companies and their structure is important because fraud often involves newly-created (or newly-vanished) companies, "buffer" companies, and chains of suppliers. These relationships can be captured by a small variation on LRI-Core's emphasis on agents and communication between them. LRI-core's ability to represent companies as a legal entity or person is also useful. For FOLaw, companies fall under the category of "world knowledge"; in FBO, companies must be represented as concepts, and structure as relationships between concepts or (possibly) as scoping restrictions on concepts. Individual's relationships are even more complicated to capture than company links, because individuals may be linked to others through family relationships, friendships, membership of the same organization, or regular working relations. The ontological requirements are therefore similar to those required to represent companies and their structure, but with an additional need to represent relationships and associations among agents of different types. LRI-Core's emphasis on agents and de-emphasis of static relationships should allow representation of relationships between different types of agents relatively smoothly; the division between dynamic and static relationships in FOLaw may also be useful.

Financial fraud investigation involves a wide range of measures in several sub-domains. This involves international finance, accountancy, tax law, police procedure and evidence handling, general legal and law enforcement knowledge, comparative law knowledge, and knowledge of databases and linguistic descriptions. As a result, the FF POIROT ontology is not exclusively confined to the legal domain: it needs to draw from ontologies of laws, of evidence, of finance, and even of computer science. This should explain some of the shortcomings of the existing legal ontologies for supporting FF POIROT. Considering the ontologies that were examined in this study, it seems that laws or legal rules can be represented adequately in any of them. It is in the associated areas that the most differences appear: FOLaw's functional perspective is useful for dynamic situations where new agents or concepts are being created (such as investigations), FBO is particularly useful for representing static items that have many finely detailed features (such as company prospectuses), and LRI-Core is particularly useful when considering agents and communication between them (e.g. representing individuals and their relationships).

3.2 Financial Core Ontologies

As we saw in 3.1, existing legal ontologies are not detailed enough to model the factual substratum of fraud law - the evidence layer in Wigmore's terms. We therefore include in our evaluation two examples of financial ontologies. They will need to complement, if not replace, legal ontologies. The ontologies that will be considered are SUMO's financial ontology and ontology of services [15] and McCarthy's REA ontology [11, 12].

McCarthy's ontology of REA (economic Resources, economic Events, and economic Agents) was originally designed for accounting [10]. The REA business model is still largely used for reasoning about accounting concepts [11]. However, at a foundational level, the REA ontology is a robust domain ontology for enterprise business phenomena (backed by well-accepted economic theory). The REA template contains four object primitives: economic resource, economic event, external agent, internal agent; and five relationship primitives: stock-flow, control for external-agent, control for internal agent, duality, and responsibility [7]. With only these ontological primitives it is possible to model the economic activities of a company (or organization). REA is a minimal ontology, but its semantic model is nevertheless broad (covering the whole supply chain) and deep (covering all relevant business activities). REA can therefore link economic events together across different companies, industries, and nations. Core economic phenomena included in the REA ontology are exchanges, resource-agent dependencies, resource dependencies, agent dependencies and commitments [11]. This non-proprietary ontology is generally recognized and used.[7]

The Teknowledge ontology suite[8] holds two interesting financial related domain ontologies which extend SUMO (the Standard Upper & Middle Ontology[9]). First of

---

[7] REA is used in the ebXML and UN/CEFACT catalog of common business processes. Further, REA has been adopted by ECIMF, the European E-Commerce Integration Meta-Framework.

[8] See, http://www.teknowledge.com

[9] See, http://ontology.teknowledge.com/

all, there is a financial ontology (sumoF) which inherits content from SUMO. This ontology is focusing mainly on banking finance and investment finance. Secondly, there is an ontology of services (sumoS) which inherits content from SUMO and from the financial ontology. This ontology is capable of representing e-commerce services, and has potential added value to the online investment fraud side of FF POIROT.

Products and commodities in financial services are somewhat more complex than in other domains. This arises because most purchases involve a transaction in which goods or services are exchanged for money, but in the financial world, the goods themselves consist of money – or a promise thereof – in some form. For this reason, financial products have developed to include an interest in someone else's financial success (equities, bonds, etc), a promise of money if certain unlikely circumstances occur (insurance policies, lottery tickets or other gambling), money which is provided now and repaid later at a premium (credit, loans or savings accounts), and combinations of these (e.g. financial options and futures). The investment products are quite varied since the products that are of most concern to FF POIROT are ones that are involved in investment schemes that try to evade the usual restrictions of the authorized investment market. And FF POIROT is also concerned with financial services – for much of the regulation that affects financial products does not address the (often bewildering) variety of financial products that are available, but rather the way in which these products are sold.

Looking at our two ontologies, we see that SumoF is capable of representing 'financial assets'. It defines this concept as "a predicate that relates any item of economic value to the Agent that owns the item". Examples given by SUMO's financial ontology include cash, securities, accounts receivable, inventory, office equipment, a house, a car, and other property.

Secondly, SumoF provides the specific category of 'financial instrument'. This subclass of Certificate is defined as "A document having monetary value or recording a monetary transaction". Financial instrument has many subclasses relevant to FF POIROT's investment domain. For example: Bond; Stock (with many types of stock represented); and Security. SumoF is therefore capable of representing all three categories of financial product defined above: equities, insurance policies and credit agreements can all be considered to be financial instruments of one kind or another. It is also capable of representing the ownership of these financial products by an agent, and is therefore able to represent the transfer of ownership from one agent to another.

In REA, products or services can be represented as 'economic resources'. A resource is the concept that is transferred or transformed in an event (e.g. transaction). Examples of types of resources are money (in a Payment event), labor (in a labor consumption event) and items (in a Sale event). Each event in REA usually has one resource, which is a value that can be modeled as a simple value (e.g. money) or composite value (e.g. collection of items).

REA is therefore also capable of modeling what is required, but its built-in primitives – money as a subclass of a resource – are too general to be used directly by FF POIROT. SumoF, too, requires more detail in order to represent FF POIROT's domain fully – specifically, it requires a breakdown of financial instruments into subcategories. Some levels of breakdown area available but are of questionable accuracy – for example, BOND and SHARE are not considered to be subclasses of SECURITY. A category of financial services – investment, insurance, credit, etc. – would also be a useful feature to represent FF POIROT's domain.

Essentially, a commercial transaction is a legal process that is carried out by (normally) two agents. SumoF contains a 'financial contract' category (which is a sub attribute of Contract), able to represent the materialization (legal documentation) of such a process. 'Financial contract' is defined in SumoF as a "financial agreement between two or more parties". SumoF also has a specific category to represent agents who are participants to such a contract (instances of 'agreement Member'). Also highly relevant is SumoF's subclass of 'authorization of transaction'. This subclass of financial service and regulatory process is very interesting for the compliance (authorization) side in FF POIROT.

Several subclasses of financial transactions are conceptualized in SumoF. However, they seem to be situated mainly in the banking domain. Examples are the opening of bank accounts or using bank accounts. More useful for the investment side of FF POIROT is SumoF's category of investing (a subclass of Financial Transaction), defined as "an activity of committing money or capital in order to gain a financial return." SumoF does provide some transactions specific to the investment domain, such as 'StockMarketTransaction' and 'Financial order'.

SumoF is capable of representing payment of a financial transaction. Payment is defined as "the partial or complete discharge of an obligation by its settlement in the form of the transfer of funds, assets, or services equal to the monetary value of part or all of the debtor's obligation". Payment methods consist of one or more financial instruments. Also, SumoF can represent the transaction amount, which is defined as an instance of CurrencyMeasure. It's therefore necessary to be precise in definitions within SumoF, since a transaction may involve payment for a Financial Instrument using another Financial Instrument of an amount which is an instance of CurrencyMeasure.

A weakness with SumoF's concept of transaction is that it requires a change of possession. The concept of transaction would probably better be conceptualized as one or more actions that affect some or all rights to a resource. It may also be helpful to insist that a Financial Contract accompanies some classes of transaction.

A business process in the REA ontology is typically a multiparty collaboration. *Agents* are a primary component in REA and are defined as those who participate in the (economic) events. An agent is a person, organizational unit, or organization that performs a role in an event. Each agent is a subclass of an Entity, which may perform different roles in different transactions. For each event, two agents must be identified: one within the business unit who was responsible for the event (e.g. clerk, salesperson, supervisor), and the second, outside the business unit, with whom the event was performed (e.g. customer, vendor, investor). Thus *Agent* has two subclasses: *InsideAgent* (or internal) and *OutsideAgent* (or external).

Whereas SumoF offers a wide range of types of economic agents in the financial/investment domain (e.g. stock holder, broker, etc), REA offers a detailed range of more *common* economic agents. Examples are: manufacturer, customer, product supplier, logistics vendor, etc. All these agent types can be very helpful in representing various business agents and their roles.

An 'agreement' in REA is represented as an exchange of promises. Agreements are considered "*to execute an economic event in a well-defined future that will result in either an increase of resources or a decrease of resources*" [12]. An Economic Contract is a *type* of Economic Agreement that is legally enforceable [11]. Therefore, economic transactions in REA always affect resources, may have associated contracts, and always result in a *commitment*[10].

An activity such a financial order (a concept derived from SumoF) does not result in a physical resource flow but in a commitment. The company (broker) commits to buy (buy order) or sell (sell order) a specified amount of a particular security or commodity and the customer (client) commits to pay a price. The concept of a commitment therefore provides a more flexible definition of transactions than that provided by SumoF, although it still does not explicitly allow for agreements that transfer rights to resources, rather than the resources themselves; it merely allows for time-delayed agreements. However, the comparison of commitments against actual events – particularly in "duality" relationships where a two-way exchange is promised but only one of the two- sub-transactions takes place -- provides a good way to represent typical activities of fraudsters.

SumoF, relying on the SUMO upper ontology, defines *Corporation* as a subclass of Organization, which in turn is a subclass of a group of agents. However, a corporation can also be considered to be a single agent. SumoF's ability to represent banks as a subclass of financial organization is useful. Its ability to represent (financial) intermediaries and stock markets (defined as "general term for organizations where stocks are traded, either in formal exchanges or over-the-counter) is also practical for the online investment fraud domain.

Information about a company's bank accounts is often essential in financial fraud investigation. SumoF can represent various details of bank accounts. Especially in fraud investigation, bank details are important as be able to follow the money trail. SumoF can represent various bank accounts and also its relationships with financial organization, bank, etc. It is also able to represent the account holder.

Another essential investigative point is the profit of a company (e.g. a sudden high rise in profit in a fraud sensitive sector may indicate a fraud). Profit in SumoF is well defined as: "the positive gain from an investment or business operation after subtracting for all expenses." As a concept it is found in the domain of financial transaction, and also in the domain of currency measure.

In REA, companies are represented as organizations to which agents belong, but may also be considered to be agents themselves. There are three types of possible associations between agents. A *responsibility* association is the hierarchical relationship between agents inside a corporation. Secondly, an *assignment* association is the relationship between specific inside and outside agents, such as a salesman working exclusively with a specific client. Lastly, a *cooperation* relationship describes existing dependencies between external agents such as a customer being a subsidiary of a vendor or a joint venture existing between two vendors.

As a semantic Web, REA can link economic events together across different companies, industries, and nations. The links associations can be activity-to-activity, agent-to-agent or person-to-person, not just company-to-company. This means each individual in a REA supply chain can be linked directly to each other individual. REA is therefore capable of representing information about a company's structure well, while SumoF is stronger on representing a company's financial details.

---

[10] *Contra* is D.A. Gertzenstein [8] who argues that not all agreements have commitment events.

4 Analysis and Conclusion

Maybe unsurprisingly, given their different methodological starting points, the analyzed legal and financial ontologies seem to complement each other, with each having strength in different fields and addressing different aspects of the user requirements identified in 2. However, the Wigmore-inspired analysis also indicates that simply enriching a legal core ontology with the relevant conceptual distinctions of a financial ontology, while possibly a good pragmatic solution for a "light" application ontology, raises several interesting theoretical questions that need to be kept in mind if a "reference" or "foundational" ontology is envisaged [5]. Financial fraud is a prime example for a "legally constructed" crime, something that becomes particularly obvious in a multi-jurisdiction environment. FOLaw, with its commitment to a functional approach to law, seems *prima facie* a good candidate to model comparative legal knowledge. Mirroring the traditional functionalist approach to comparative law [24], legal provisions receive their meaning through the social reality they regulate. Different national legal conceptualizations are comparable/translatable because they are grounded in the same extra-legal reality. FOLaw's distinction between institutional (legal) and physical acts therefore ought to be particularly useful in the representation of cross-border crime. Since there is no single fraud offence in Europe, the physical act of defrauding someone may then be classified as any of the following institutional acts: theft; conspiracy; cheating; etc. For many crimes, and some examples of financial fraud, this seems unproblematic. The physical act say of "shooting another person" remains constant across jurisdiction. Nation-specific legal conceptualizations are then linked to this act, allowing for differences in the key distinctions (the distinction between "murder" and "manslaughter" in the UK for instance doesn't correspond precisely to the similar distinction between "Mord" and "Totschlag" in Germany). However, laws on financial fraud quite often create the very objects they regulate. If there isn't a law that establishes a financial service authority, and a law that creates an obligation to register with that authority, there can't be a "physical act" in this jurisdiction of "avoiding registration" or "fraudulently claiming to be registered". Wigmore's holistic approach is more sensitive to this element of legal constructivism of social reality. For him, laws do not decompose into discrete bits of extra-legal reality, but into elements of "evidence", that is social reality structured by law. Law is thus self-contained, a closed system in the sense of Luhman and Teubner. This makes comparative legal analysis more difficult, but is truer to its subject matter and better capable of modeling some of the very real legal problems of cross-border prosecution of fraud.

Another consequences of the different use of financial concepts in legal reasoning in fraud cases is the reason for the main shortcoming of the analyzed financial ontologies: They describe business events that are correct from the perspective of the business community. In dealing with financial fraud though, we will encounter typically objects that are similar to, but not identical with the objects postulated by a "correct" ontology of finance. In many instances, it is an arbitrary decision *internal* to the criminal law of a country whether it regards acts committed abroad and not conceptualized as crimes according to the *lex fori* as crimes for its internal purposes, though the international dimension introduced by EU law reduces these conceptual conflicts to some extend. For the purpose of POIROT, this raises the question of how to best integrate financial (extra-legal) ontologies and legal ontologies. In FOLaw and related approaches, the distinctions made in financial ontologies would apply across national boundaries. The resulting ontology is therefore more abstract (on a higher level) than the legal ontologies and ultimately give legal ontologies their meaning. In the Wigmorean approach, this relation reverses. Core legal distinctions limit what can and what cannot exist in the financial realm. The combination of transnational (EU) regulation and issues reserved to the nation state and its legislators in the POIROT environment makes the choice between these two approaches a problematic one and requires further analysis.

Acknowledgements

This work was supported under IST project IST-2001-38248, FF POIROT. The FF POIROT consortium comprises STARLab at the Vrije Universiteit in Brussels; the Joseph Bell Centre for Forensic Statistics and Legal Reasoning, based at the University of Edinburgh; Erasmus Hogeschool, Brussels; KnowledgeStones S.p.A.; Commissione Nazionale per le Società e la Borsa, Italy; Language & Computing N.V.; VAT Applications N.V.; and the Romanian Academy Research Centre on Artificial Intelligence. The IST and the universities and companies comprising the FF POIROT consortium are authorised to reproduce and distribute reprints for their purposes notwithstanding any copyright annotation hereon. The views and conclusions contained herein are those of the authors and should not be interpreted as necessarily representing official policies or endorsements, either express or implied, of the IST or any other member of the FF POIROT consortium.

References

1. Alonso J.L., Carranza C., Castells P., Foncillas B., Lara R., R., Rico, M.: Semantic Web Technologies for Economic and Financial Information Management http://nets.ii.uam.es/%7Eaniceto/publications/iswc03-poster.pdf *(2003)*
2. Breuker, J.A. & Winkels, R.: Use and Reuse of Legal Ontologies in Knowledge Engineering and Information Management. In Proceedings of The ICAIL Workshop on Legal Ontologies, ICAIL-03, Edinburgh (2003)
3. Breuker, J.A. & Boer, A.: Developing Ontologies for Legal Information Serving and Management. In Proceedings of the EKAW Workshop on Knowledge Management through Corporate Semantics Webs, EKAW-02, Siguenza, Spain (2002)
4. Breuker, J., Elhag, L., Petkov, E., & Winkels, R.: Ontologies for legal information serving and knowledge management. In T. Bench-Capon, A. Daskalopulu & R. Winkels (eds.), Legal Knowledge and Information Systems. IOS Press, Amsterdam (2002)
5. Guarino, N.: Formal Ontology in Information Systems. In Formal Ontology in Information Systems, ed. N. Guarino. Amsterdam: IOS (1998) 3-15
6. Graham, J.A.: The Cybersecurities' Notion of Targeting in General Private International Law. Cyberbanking & Law (2003)
7. Geerts, G.: The Timeless Way of Building Accounting Information Systems. OOPSLA Workshop on Business Object Design and Implementation, Atlanta, Georgia (1997)
8. Gertzenstein, D.A.: An Object Oriented Framework for Business Systems Based on the REA Pattern, http://mysite.verizon.net/agertzen/REAFramework.pdf (2003)

9. Leary, R., Vandenberghe, W. & Zeleznikow, J.: Towards a Financial Fraud Ontology; A Legal Modeling Approach. ICAIL Workshop on Legal Ontologies, ICAIL-03, Edinburgh (2003)
10. McCarthy, W.E.: The REA accounting model: a generalized framework for accounting systems in a shared data environment", The Accounting Review 57 (1982) 554-578
11. McCarthy, W.E. & Geerts, G.: The Ontological Foundation of REA Enterprise Information Systems, http://www.msu.edu/user/mccarth4/rea-ontology/index.htm (2000)
12. McCarthy, W.E. & Geerts, G.: An Ontological Analysis of the Economic Primitives of the Extended-REA Enterprise Information Architecture, The International Journal of Accounting Information Systems Vol. 3, 1-16 (2002)
13. Schum, D.A.: Evidential Foundations of Probabilistic Reasoning, Wylie (1994)
14. Sheptycki, J.: Policing the Virtual Launderette. Money Laundering, New Technology and Global Governance. In Sheptycki J. (ed) Issues in Transnational Policing. London, Routledge (2000)
15. SUMO: "Financial Ontology" available at http://ontology.teknowledge.com/ (2004)
16. Sure, Y., & Lau, TH.: Introducing Ontology-based Skills Management at a large Insurance Company. In: Modellierung 2002, Modellierung in der Praxis - Modellierung für die Praxis, Tutzing, (2002) 123-134
17. Twining, W.: Rethinking Evidence. Oxford (1990)
18. Valente, A., Breuker, J.A. & Brouwer, P.W.: Legal Modeling and Automated Reasoning with ON-LINE. International Journal of Human Computer Studies, 51, (1999) 1079–1126
19. Vandenberghe W., Schafer B., and Kingston J.: "Light Ontologies for Heavy Criminals? Ontological Modelling and Fraud Investigation in the EU" *IFOMIS Report*, Vol. 4, (2003) 23-33
20. Van Kralingen, R.W.: A Conceptual Frame-based Ontology for Law. In Proceedings of The First International Workshop on Legal Ontologies. University of Melbourne (1997)
21. Visser, P.R.S., R.W. van Kralingen and T.J.M. Bench-Capon.: A Method for the Development of Legal Knowledge Systems. In Proceedings of ICAIL'97, Melbourne (1997)
22. Wigmore, J.H.: A Panorama of the World's Legal Systems. Washington Law Book Company: Washington (1928)
23. Wigmore, J.H.: The Science of Judicial Proof: as Given by Logic, Psychology, and General Experience and Illustrated in Judicial Trials. Little, Brown: Boston (1937)
24. Zweigert, K., Koetz, H.: An Introduction to Comparative Law (transl. Weir). Oxford: Clarendon (1987)

Author Index

Lecture Notes in Artificial Intelligence (LNAI)

Vol. 3191: M. Klusch, S. Ossowski, V. Kashyap, R. Unland (Eds.), Cooperative Information Agents VIII. XI, 303 pages. 2004.

Vol. 3187: G. Lindemann, J. Denzinger, I.J. Timm, R. Unland (Eds.), Multiagent System Technologies. XIII, 341 pages. 2004.

Vol. 3176: O. Bousquet, U. von Luxburg, G. Rätsch (Eds.), Advanced Lectures on Machine Learning. IX, 241 pages. 2004.

Vol. 3171: A.L.C. Bazzan, S. Labidi (Eds.), Advances in Artificial Intelligence – SBIA 2004. XVII, 548 pages. 2004.

Vol. 3159: U. Visser, Intelligent Information Integration for the Semantic Web. XIV, 150 pages. 2004.

Vol. 3157: C. Zhang, H. W. Guesgen, W.K. Yeap (Eds.), PRICAI 2004: Trends in Artificial Intelligence. XX, 1023 pages. 2004.

Vol. 3155: P. Funk, P.A. González Calero (Eds.), Advances in Case-Based Reasoning. XIII, 822 pages. 2004.

Vol. 3139: F. Iida, R. Pfeifer, L. Steels, Y. Kuniyoshi (Eds.), Embodied Artificial Intelligence. IX, 331 pages. 2004.

Vol. 3131: V. Torra, Y. Narukawa (Eds.), Modeling Decisions for Artificial Intelligence. XI, 327 pages. 2004.

Vol. 3127: K.E. Wolff, H.D. Pfeiffer, H.S. Delugach (Eds.), Conceptual Structures at Work. XI, 403 pages. 2004.

Vol. 3123: A. Belz, R. Evans, P. Piwek (Eds.), Natural Language Generation. X, 219 pages. 2004.

Vol. 3120: J. Shawe-Taylor, Y. Singer (Eds.), Learning Theory. X, 648 pages. 2004.

Vol. 3097: D. Basin, M. Rusinowitch (Eds.), Automated Reasoning. XII, 493 pages. 2004.

Vol. 3071: A. Omicini, P. Petta, J. Pitt (Eds.), Engineering Societies in the Agents World. XIII, 409 pages. 2004.

Vol. 3070: L. Rutkowski, J. Siekmann, R. Tadeusiewicz, L.A. Zadeh (Eds.), Artificial Intelligence and Soft Computing - ICAISC 2004. XXV, 1208 pages. 2004.

Vol. 3068: E. André, L. Dybkjær, W. Minker, P. Heisterkamp (Eds.), Affective Dialogue Systems. XII, 324 pages. 2004.

Vol. 3067: M. Dastani, J. Dix, A. El Fallah-Seghrouchni (Eds.), Programming Multi-Agent Systems. X, 221 pages. 2004.

Vol. 3066: S. Tsumoto, R. Słowiński, J. Komorowski, J.W. Grzymała-Busse (Eds.), Rough Sets and Current Trends in Computing. XX, 853 pages. 2004.

Vol. 3065: A. Lomuscio, D. Nute (Eds.), Deontic Logic in Computer Science. X, 275 pages. 2004.

Vol. 3060: A.Y. Tawfik, S.D. Goodwin (Eds.), Advances in Artificial Intelligence. XIII, 582 pages. 2004.

Vol. 3056: H. Dai, R. Srikant, C. Zhang (Eds.), Advances in Knowledge Discovery and Data Mining. XIX, 713 pages. 2004.

Vol. 3055: H. Christiansen, M.-S. Hacid, T. Andreasen, H.L. Larsen (Eds.), Flexible Query Answering Systems. X, 500 pages. 2004.

Vol. 3048: P. Faratin, D.C. Parkes, J.A. Rodríguez-Aguilar, W.E. Walsh (Eds.), Agent-Mediated Electronic Commerce V. XI, 155 pages. 2004.

Vol. 3040: R. Conejo, M. Urretavizcaya, J.-L. Pérez-de-la-Cruz (Eds.), Current Topics in Artificial Intelligence. XIV, 689 pages. 2004.

Vol. 3035: M.A. Wimmer (Ed.), Knowledge Management in Electronic Government. XII, 326 pages. 2004.

Vol. 3034: J. Favela, E. Menasalvas, E. Chávez (Eds.), Advances in Web Intelligence. XIII, 227 pages. 2004.

Vol. 3030: P. Giorgini, B. Henderson-Sellers, M. Winikoff (Eds.), Agent-Oriented Information Systems. XIV, 207 pages. 2004.

Vol. 3029: B. Orchard, C. Yang, M. Ali (Eds.), Innovations in Applied Artificial Intelligence. XXI, 1272 pages. 2004.

Vol. 3025: G.A. Vouros, T. Panayiotopoulos (Eds.), Methods and Applications of Artificial Intelligence. XV, 546 pages. 2004.

Vol. 3020: D. Polani, B. Browning, A. Bonarini, K. Yoshida (Eds.), RoboCup 2003: Robot Soccer World Cup VII. XVI, 767 pages. 2004.

Vol. 3012: K. Kurumatani, S.-H. Chen, A. Ohuchi (Eds.), Multi-Agents for Mass User Support. X, 217 pages. 2004.

Vol. 3010: K.R. Apt, F. Fages, F. Rossi, P. Szeredi, J. Váncza (Eds.), Recent Advances in Constraints. VIII, 285 pages. 2004.

Vol. 2990: J. Leite, A. Omicini, L. Sterling, P. Torroni (Eds.), Declarative Agent Languages and Technologies. XII, 281 pages. 2004.

Vol. 2980: A. Blackwell, K. Marriott, A. Shimojima (Eds.), Diagrammatic Representation and Inference. XV, 448 pages. 2004.

Vol. 2977: G. Di Marzo Serugendo, A. Karageorgos, O.F. Rana, F. Zambonelli (Eds.), Engineering Self-Organising Systems. X, 299 pages. 2004.

Vol. 2972: R. Monroy, G. Arroyo-Figueroa, L.E. Sucar, H. Sossa (Eds.), MICAI 2004: Advances in Artificial Intelligence. XVII, 923 pages. 2004.

Vol. 2969: M. Nickles, M. Rovatsos, G. Weiss (Eds.), Agents and Computational Autonomy. X, 275 pages. 2004.

Vol. 2961: P. Eklund (Ed.), Concept Lattices. IX, 411 pages. 2004.

Vol. 2953: K. Konrad, Model Generation for Natural Language Interpretation and Analysis. XIII, 166 pages. 2004.

Vol. 2934: G. Lindemann, D. Moldt, M. Paolucci (Eds.), Regulated Agent-Based Social Systems. X, 301 pages. 2004.

Vol. 2930: F. Winkler (Ed.), Automated Deduction in Geometry. VII, 231 pages. 2004.

Vol. 2926: L. van Elst, V. Dignum, A. Abecker (Eds.), Agent-Mediated Knowledge Management. XI, 428 pages. 2004.

Vol. 2923: V. Lifschitz, I. Niemelä (Eds.), Logic Programming and Nonmonotonic Reasoning. IX, 365 pages. 2003.

Vol. 2915: A. Camurri, G. Volpe (Eds.), Gesture-Based Communication in Human-Computer Interaction. XIII, 558 pages. 2004.

Vol. 2913: T.M. Pinkston, V.K. Prasanna (Eds.), High Performance Computing - HiPC 2003. XX, 512 pages. 2003.

Vol. 2903: T.D. Gedeon, L.C.C. Fung (Eds.), AI 2003: Advances in Artificial Intelligence. XVI, 1075 pages. 2003.